MW01681610

THE AFFORDABLE CARE ACT

A NATIONAL HEALTHCARE CRISIS: MONOPOLY, POWER, AND THE ABANDONMENT OF PUBLIC STEWARDSHIP

ERIC LAWRENCE FRAZIER MBA

The Affordable Care Act

Digital: 978-1949722253

Paperback: 978-1949722260

Disclaimer

The information in "The Affordable Care Act" is for general informational and educational purposes only. The content in this book is based on his personal experiences, research, and general knowledge and should not be considered professional financial advice.

Readers are encouraged to consult with a certified financial advisor, HUD-approved housing and credit counselor, or other qualified professionals before taking any action regarding their credit or financial situation. The author and publisher are not liable for any actions taken from reading this book.

Additionally, this book contains links to third-party websites for additional resources and information. These links are provided for convenience and informational purposes only. The author and publisher do not endorse or take responsibility for the content, accuracy, or reliability of any information on these external sites. The use of any third-party websites is at the reader's own risk.

By reading this book, you acknowledge and agree that the author and publisher shall not be held liable for any loss or damage, including but not limited to direct, indirect, or consequential losses, arising from the use or reliance on the information contained within this book or any third-party links referenced herein.

Dedication

This book is dedicated first and foremost to my family.

My wife and I raised four daughters, and today we are the proud grandparents of four grandchildren. For us, healthcare is not a theoretical debate or an abstract policy discussion. It is personal. It is foundational. Health is wealth. Without health, every other aspiration, education, work, financial security, and opportunity, becomes fragile.

What was once understood as a basic necessity has increasingly become a privilege reserved for those with high income or substantial wealth. As a family, we have had to plan carefully, sacrifice deliberately, and remain vigilant simply to maintain access to care. No family should have to live with that uncertainty.

This book is also dedicated to the future—specifically, to the hope that future generations will be represented by leaders worthy of public trust. Leaders whose promises are not performative, but binding. Leaders who understand that public office is a fiduciary responsibility, not a private asset. Trustees of the public interest, not agents of corporate power.

It is dedicated to my grandchildren, who may inherit a country in which access to healthcare is no longer assured, where government is weakened by conflicts of interest, and where elected officials increasingly serve corporate interests and billionaire donors rather than the people who elected them. A country where the erosion of healthcare today becomes the absence of healthcare tomorrow. A country that struggles even to protect foundational programs like Social Security, despite generations of contribution and reliance.

Finally, this book is dedicated to those willing to speak truth to power. To those who use whatever platforms they have, books, writing, campaigns, podcasts, or public discourse, to hold elected officials accountable. To those unafraid to confront misrepresentation, expose conflicts of interest, and remind those in power that authority flows upward from the people, not downward from donors.

This book is dedicated to the power of the vote, and to the responsibility that accompanies it. May we never forget it, may we never surrender it, and may we never allow it to be rendered meaningless through silence or resignation.

PREFACE

I did not set out to write this book as a political exercise, nor as an ideological argument aligned with any party. I am writing it because the gap between what Americans are told and what is actually happening has become too wide to ignore.

I am tired of the gamesmanship that now defines American politics. I am tired of facts being selectively presented, distorted, or omitted altogether to serve short-term political objectives. I am tired of policies being debated as slogans rather than examined as systems, and of serious national issues being reduced to talking points designed for soundbites rather than understanding.

I am also tired of politicians exploiting the realities of modern life. They know that most Americans are busy—working, raising families, managing obligations—and do not have the time to sit through hours of floor speeches delivered to nearly empty chambers. They know that few people read legislation, committee reports, or agency findings in full. This environment has allowed misrepresentation to flourish, not because the truth is unavailable, but because it is inconvenient.

Promises are made publicly and broken quietly. Positions shift without acknowledgment. Failures are reframed as inevitabilities. Accountability is deferred, diluted, or redirected. And all the while, elected officials continue to claim they are acting on behalf of the public.

My central contention is simple: too many of our representatives no longer function as trustees of the public interest. They function instead as intermediaries—absorbing the language of representation while advancing outcomes that consistently favor dominant corporate actors. This is not an accusation made lightly, nor is it based on ideology. It is an observation grounded in outcomes, patterns of inaction, and the persistent alignment between concentrated economic power and political decision-making.

Healthcare is the lens through which this book examines that failure, but it is not the only example. Healthcare simply reveals the problem most clearly because it affects nearly every American and involves vast sums of public and private money. The disconnect between rhetoric and results, between stated concern and actual policy, is difficult to explain without confronting the structural incentives that shape political behavior.

This book is an attempt to do what our public discourse too often avoids: to slow the conversation down, to trace how we arrived at our current system, to separate fiscal reality from political narrative, and to examine who benefits from the status quo and why it persists. It is written for readers who want more than reassurance and more than outrage—readers who want clarity.

I am not asking the reader to accept my conclusions without scrutiny. On the contrary, this work invites scrutiny. It relies on documented history, economic evidence, and institutional analysis. If the case it presents is uncomfortable, that discomfort arises not from exaggeration, but from proximity to the facts.

Ultimately, this book is about trust—how it has been eroded, why it matters, and what happens to a democracy when those entrusted to govern no longer behave as stewards of the people they serve. If that trust is to be restored, it will not come from slogans or promises. It will come from transparency, accountability, and a willingness to confront truths that are long overdue for examination.

THEY ARE NOT LIKE US

BY ERIC LAWRENCE FRAZIER, MBA

A People's Indictment of a Congress That No Longer Represents Us

A country rich in genius still betrays its fragile poor,
Where promises of health dissolve before a clinic's door.
Leaders sworn to guard us left the sick outside to rust,
And every wound grows deeper where they broke the people's trust.

Premiums rise like tempests while wages cannot climb,
And Congress turns the numbers into narratives of crime.
Thresholds bent for optics, every fact a polished spin,
As millions lose their lifelines to a vote they'll never win.

Where is the Congress that represents us?
They are not our trustees but guards for corporate trust.
They are not like us.
They are not like us.
Our faith in them has turned to dust.
Congress is a bust.

A nation minting billions still claims poverty for care,
Yet signs blank checks for warfare without question anywhere.
Scarcity is weaponized to break the people's trust,
But fades the moment citizens demand their rightful trust.

They speak of freedom loudly, as if truth were in their breath,
Yet bind our public purse to corporations fat with wealth.
They promise they protect us—every hardship, every cost—
While signing off tomorrow, just to keep the donor boss.

Where is the Congress that represents us?
They are not our trustees but guards for corporate trust.
They are not like us.
They are not like us.
Our faith in them has turned to dust.
Congress is a bust.

They boast that the market answers every burden we endure,
Yet markets stitched by mergers make the rich men more secure.
They name it competition while the doors slam year by year,
And preach that we be grateful as they monetize our fear.

They laud the VA in speeches meant to stir a passing cheer,
Then let the corporate whispers choose the funding year by year.
They spotlight every failure, hide the millions served with grace,
And claim its imperfection means the private side must take its place.

Where is the Congress that represents us?
They are not our trustees but guards for corporate trust.
They are not like us.
They are not like us.
Our faith in them has turned to dust.

Congress is a bust.

They claim that public systems crush the spark that makes us rise,
Yet every major breakthrough stands on government supplies.
No genius works in isolation; every dream needs a funded ground,
And every private triumph rests on public labor all around.

They chant of "skin in game," a myth they wield to shift the blame,
For those who walk with empty hands, already play the game in pain.
They claim that free assistance makes the struggling weak or flawed,
While Congress guards the wealthy like a priesthood serving gods.

Where is the Congress that represents us?
They are not our trustees but guards for corporate trust.
They are not like us.
They are not like us.
Our faith in them has turned to dust.
Congress is a bust.

They shout "socialism!" loudly when the public asks for care,
Pretending moral failure lies in lifting those who bear.
They claim that helping citizens betrays the nation's creed,
Though every thriving country meets its people in their need.

Justice keeps its vigil; it returns to balance scales,
And nations shaped by courage must not tremble when it calls.
For people are the power, they are history's living trust,
And when they rise as one, every empire turns to dust.

Where is the Congress that represents us?

They are not our trustees but guards for corporate trust.
They are not like us.
They are not like us.
Our faith in them has turned to dust.
Congress is a bust.

Ballots speak truth to power no hand can bend.
Voices rise in judgment when silence reaches end.
If Congress cannot remember we have placed them in our trust,
Then the people must replace the ones who turned that trust to dust.

When the final tally rises for the ones they cast aside,
The Congress that ignored them will confront the rising tide.
For power is a privilege, not a crown they call their own,
And those who broke the covenant will find their seats dethroned.

Justice keeps its vigil; it returns to balance scales,
And nations shaped by courage must not tremble when it calls.
For people are the power, they are history's living trust,
And when they rise as one, every empire turns to dust.
Where is the Congress that represents us?
They are not our trustees but guards for corporate trust.
They are not like us.
They are not like us.
Our faith in them has turned to dust.
Time to replace and gain new trust."

BUSINESS BOOKS

Available on Amazon

POETRY COLLECTION

ERIC LAWRENCE FRAZIER, MBA POETRY BOOKS

Available on Amazon

INTRODUCTION

The United States is the wealthiest nation in human history, yet its healthcare system bankrupts families, shuts hospitals, suppresses wages, shortens life expectancy, and blocks economic mobility. This crisis does not exist because of limited resources, weak medical innovation, or lack of institutional capacity. It exists because Congress has repeatedly chosen not to regulate monopolies, modernize care delivery, or build a national framework that aligns economic incentives with public health.

This paper traces the political and legislative decisions that shifted healthcare costs onto households while protecting private-sector profits. It documents the human consequences of those decisions and shows that the federal government already possesses both the legal authority and the economic capacity to build a functioning national healthcare system. The conclusion is not theoretical. It is practical, lawful, and achievable.

Public debate remains fixated on ACA subsidies and coverage mechanics. That focus misses the core problem. The private-market model Congress continues to defend cannot deliver affordable healthcare at scale. Rising premiums, soaring deductibles, narrow provider networks, and widespread underinsurance are not the result of individual behavior. They are structural failures.

Over the past three decades, Congress allowed insurance consolidation, pharmaceutical monopolization, hospital chain mergers, private equity capture of emergency and rural care, and opaque pricing regimes controlled by pharmacy benefit managers. Competition collapsed. Prices rose independently of wages, outcomes, or value.

The damage is measurable and ongoing. More than 100 million Americans carry medical debt. Rural hospitals continue to close. Life expectancy declines. Workers remain locked into employer-based insurance. Underinsurance persists even among those technically covered. These outcomes did not emerge organically. Congress produced them.

Claims that federal action is constrained by law do not survive scrutiny. The Constitution grants Congress clear authority through the Commerce Clause, the General Welfare Clause, and the Necessary and Proper Clause. That authority has already been exercised through Medicare, Medicaid, the Children's Health Insurance Program, and the Veterans Health Administration. No new legal theory is required.

Arguments about affordability are equally hollow. The United States spends more on defense than the next nine nations combined, finances major initiatives through deficit spending, and issues the world's reserve currency. Assertions of national poverty appear only when healthcare enters the conversation. Fiscal capacity exists. Political willingness does not.

This is not an abstract proposal. The United States already operates a national healthcare system for a defined population. The Veterans Health Administration demonstrates that direct public delivery works. It provides nationwide staffing, integrated mental and physical care, and efficiency without profit extraction. This model can expand without eliminating private insurance or private hospitals.

Public understanding has been distorted by strategic language. Terms such as "choice," "personal responsibility," "dependency," "skin in the game," "government takeover," and "socialism" function as political shields. They redirect blame away from policymakers and prevent accountability for legislative outcomes.

A workable national framework is straightforward. It includes expanding the VA model into underserved regions, integrating Medicare and Medicaid into a unified national system, negotiating medical and pharmaceutical prices nationally, placing failing rural hospitals under public ownership or lease, creating federal employment pathways for healthcare workers, allowing coexistence with private-sector insurers and providers, permanently eliminating medical debt, and guaranteeing universal preventive and chronic care.

None of this is radical. It mirrors how every other wealthy nation organizes healthcare.

America's healthcare crisis is not rooted in economics, innovation, or constitutional limits. It is rooted in congressional choices. Congress designed this system. Congress sustains it. Congress can change it.

The authority exists.

The capacity exists.

The need is undeniable.

What remains absent is political will.

CHAPTER 1
THE REAL CRISIS IS REPRESENTATION, NOT POLICY

CONGRESS IS NOT YOUR REPRESENTATIVE. CONGRESS WORKS FOR SOMEONE ELSE.

In 2024, the healthcare industry spent $743.9 million buying access to your elected officials (OpenSecrets, 2025)[1]. Pharmaceutical companies spent $374 million of that total. Insurance companies spent $186 million. Hospital systems and medical device manufacturers divided the rest. This money did not go to public education campaigns or policy research. This money went directly to lobbying firms whose sole job is to influence the members of Congress who write healthcare law.

Since 1999, pharmaceutical companies alone have spent $6.1 billion on federal lobbying (OpenSecrets, 2025)[2]. That number does not include campaign contributions. That number does not include dark money funneled through PACs. That number represents only the disclosed, legal payments made to gain access to the people who are supposed to represent you.

The health sector now outspends defense contractors, Wall Street banks, technology companies, and energy corporations combined

(OpenSecrets, 2025)[1]. Healthcare is the most powerful corporate lobby in Washington. And the return on investment is extraordinary.

For every dollar spent on lobbying, pharmaceutical companies see a return of $77 in protected revenue (Wouters et al., 2020)[3]. A 2020 study analyzed lobbying expenditures against policy outcomes and found that drug companies earned back seventy-seven times what they spent preventing price controls, blocking importation, and maintaining patent protections. The study covered the period from 1999 to 2018. The researchers calculated that pharma companies spent $4.7 billion on lobbying and political contributions during that time. In exchange, they preserved $357 billion in revenue that would have been lost under pricing reforms.

That is not lobbying. That is purchasing legislation.

THE NAMES AND THE NUMBERS

Some members of Congress take more money than others. The amounts matter. The pattern matters. Here is what the transaction looks like.

Senator Bob Menendez of New Jersey received $568,700 from pharmaceutical and health product companies between 2017 and 2022 (OpenSecrets, 2023)[4]. Menendez sits on the Senate Finance Committee, which has jurisdiction over Medicare and Medicaid. In 2021, he opposed allowing Medicare to negotiate drug prices. He called the proposal "detrimental to future innovation." Pfizer is headquartered in New York, but it operates major facilities in New Jersey. Johnson & Johnson is headquartered in New Brunswick, New Jersey. Merck is headquartered in Rahway, New Jersey. Menendez represents the state where three of the largest pharmaceutical companies in the world are based. His opposition to drug price negotiation protected his donors.

Senator Kyrsten Sinema of Arizona received $750,000 from pharmaceutical and health insurance PACs during her time in the Senate (OpenSecrets, 2023)[5]. She was a Democrat who left the party in 2022 to become an independent. In 2021, she opposed drug pricing provisions in the Build Back Better Act. Her opposition killed the most aggressive pricing reforms in the bill. After announcing she would not seek reelection in 2024, Sinema joined a lobbying and consulting firm. She now advises clients on healthcare policy.

Representative Scott Peters, a Democrat from California, received $282,000 from pharmaceutical companies between 2019 and 2022 (OpenSecrets, 2023)[6]. Peters sits on the House Energy and Commerce Committee, which oversees drug pricing policy. In 2021, he voted against H.R. 3, the Elijah Cummings Lower Drug Costs Now Act, which would have allowed Medicare to negotiate prices for up to 250 drugs. Peters was one of only three Democrats on the committee to vote no. He said the bill would "stifle innovation." His top donors that cycle included Amgen, Pfizer, and the Pharmaceutical Research and Manufacturers of America.

Representative Kurt Schrader, a Democrat from Oregon, received $256,000 from health professionals and pharmaceutical companies between 2019 and 2022 (OpenSecrets, 2023)[7]. He also sat on Energy and Commerce. He also voted against H.R. 3. He said the bill was "not the right policy." He lost his primary in 2022 after progressive groups targeted him for his healthcare votes.

Senator Richard Burr, a Republican from North Carolina, received $424,000 from pharmaceutical and health product PACs during his final term (OpenSecrets, 2023)[8]. Burr retired in 2023. He joined a lobbying firm where he now represents healthcare clients. The timeline is clean: vote to protect pharma, retire from Congress, get hired by pharma.

Representative Billy Tauzin, a Republican from Louisiana, chaired the House Energy and Commerce Committee from 2001 to 2004 (Public Citizen, 2019)[9]. In 2003, he shepherded the Medicare Prescription Drug, Improvement, and Modernization Act through Congress. That law created Medicare Part D. It also included a provision that prohibited Medicare from negotiating drug prices directly with manufacturers. That prohibition is the reason Americans pay the highest prescription drug prices in the world. Tauzin retired from Congress in 2004. He immediately became president and CEO of the Pharmaceutical Research and Manufacturers of America, the industry's lobbying group. His salary was $2.5 million per year. He had earned $174,000 per year as a member of Congress.

The gap between those two numbers is the price of betrayal.

THE VOTE THEY WILL NOT TAKE

The clearest proof of congressional betrayal is what Congress refuses to do.

In 2019, the House passed H.R. 3, the Elijah Cummings Lower Drug Costs Now Act (Congressional Budget Office, 2019)[10]. The bill allowed Medicare to negotiate prices for up to 250 prescription drugs. The Congressional Budget Office estimated it would save $456 billion over 10 years. It passed the House 230 to 192. Every Republican voted no. Five Democrats joined them.

The bill went to the Senate. Mitch McConnell, then Senate Majority Leader, refused to bring it to a vote (OpenSecrets, 2021)[11]. He called it "socialist price controls." The bill died. McConnell received $365,000 from health professionals and pharmaceutical PACs between 2013 and 2020.

In 2022, Congress passed a significantly weaker version (Congressional Budget Office, 2022)[12]. The Inflation Reduction Act allowed Medicare to negotiate prices for only 10 drugs in 2026, expanding to 20 drugs by 2029. The CBO estimated this version would save $98.5 billion over 10 years. That is $357.5 billion less than the original bill would have saved.

The difference between those two numbers represents the cost of lobbying. Pharmaceutical companies spent hundreds of millions of dollars to weaken the bill. They succeeded. Americans will pay $357.5 billion more for prescription drugs because Congress protected pharma profits.

The vote on the Inflation Reduction Act was 220 to 207 in the House. Every Republican voted no. In the Senate, the vote was 51 to 50, with Vice President Kamala Harris breaking the tie. Every Republican voted no.

Republicans say they oppose government interference in markets. That is the ideological explanation. Here is the financial explanation: In the 2022 election cycle, pharmaceutical companies gave Republican candidates $18.4 million (OpenSecrets, 2022)[13]. They gave Democratic candidates $14.7 million. Both parties take the money. Republicans kill the bills. Democrats weaken them.

This is bipartisan betrayal.

WHAT THEY SAY VS. WHAT THEY PROTECT

Congress claims the Affordable Care Act is too expensive. Congress claims the enhanced subsidies are unaffordable. Congress claims fiscal responsibility requires cuts.

Here are the numbers Congress does not mention.

The Congressional Budget Office estimates that making the enhanced ACA subsidies permanent would cost $335 billion over 10 years (Congressional Budget Office, 2024)[14]. That breaks down to $33.5 billion per year. The federal government spent $6.75 trillion in fiscal year 2024. The ACA subsidies represent 0.5 percent of annual federal spending.

In 2017, Congress passed the Tax Cuts and Jobs Act (Committee for a Responsible Federal Budget, 2017)[15]. That law reduced federal revenue by $1.9 trillion over 10 years. The law primarily benefited corporations and wealthy individuals. Congress did not pay for those tax cuts. Congress did not demand offsets. Congress did not claim fiscal crisis.

In 2024, Congress approved $886 billion for national defense (U.S. Department of Defense, 2024)[16]. That number does not include supplemental funding for wars, foreign military aid, or veterans' benefits. Total defense-related spending exceeded $1.1 trillion. Congress did not debate whether America could afford it. Congress did not demand cuts. Congress funded it without question.

The ACA subsidies cost $33.5 billion per year. Defense spending costs $1.1 trillion per year. Congress says it cannot afford the ACA. Congress is lying.

The subsidies cover 24 million Americans enrolled in ACA Marketplace plans (Centers for Medicare & Medicaid Services, 2025)[17]. That breaks down to $1,396 per person per year in federal support. For $1,396 per year, working Americans who do not receive employer-sponsored insurance get access to healthcare. Congress claims this is unaffordable.

The same Congress approved $160 billion in corporate tax breaks in 2017. The same Congress approved $80 billion in agricultural subsidies over five years. The same Congress approved $52.7 billion for semiconductor manufacturing under the CHIPS Act.

Congress funds what it values. Congress values corporations. Congress does not value you.

THE CRISIS CONGRESS WILL NOT ADDRESS

While Congress fights over the ACA, the real healthcare crisis grows unchecked.

Three companies control 80 percent of prescription drug pricing in America (American Medical Association, 2024)[18]. CVS Caremark, Express Scripts, and Optum Rx are pharmacy benefit managers. They negotiate prices between drug manufacturers, insurance companies, and pharmacies. They operate in the middle. They extract profit at every step. They are not regulated as monopolies. Congress has the authority to break them up under antitrust law. Congress does nothing.

In 15 states, a single insurance company controls more than 80 percent of the individual market (American Medical Association, 2024)[18]. In Alabama, Blue Cross Blue Shield holds 96 percent of the market. In Wyoming, Blue Cross Blue Shield holds 95 percent. In Delaware, Highmark holds 90 percent. These are monopoly conditions by any standard. Congress has the authority to enforce antitrust law. Congress does nothing.

Between 2010 and 2020, more than 1,500 hospitals merged into larger health systems (Beaulieu et al., 2020)[19]. These mergers reduced competition and raised prices. A 2020 study published in the Journal of the American Medical Association found that hospital mergers increased prices by 6 to 18 percent without improving patient outcomes. The Federal Trade Commission has the authority to block anticompetitive mergers. The FTC blocked only a handful. Most mergers were approved. Prices rose. Congress did nothing.

Pharmaceutical companies hold patents for decades beyond the original term by making minor modifications to existing drugs. This practice is called "evergreening." It keeps generic competitors off the market. It keeps prices high. Congress has the authority to reform patent law. Congress does nothing.

Insulin costs $10 per vial to manufacture (Medbelle, 2021)[20]. In the United States, insulin costs $300 per vial. In Canada, insulin costs $30 per vial. Americans die because they ration insulin. Congress has the authority to cap prices. Congress does nothing.

The reason Congress does nothing is simple. The companies profiting from these monopolies are the same companies funding congressional campaigns.

THE REVOLVING DOOR: WHERE MEMBERS GO AFTER THEY BETRAY YOU

The most obvious proof of corruption is what happens when members leave Congress.

Former Senator Max Baucus, a Democrat from Montana, chaired the Senate Finance Committee from 2001 to 2014 (Public Citizen, 2019)[9]. He played a central role in drafting the Affordable Care Act. He excluded the public option from the bill after receiving $3.97 million from health insurance and pharmaceutical interests during his career. After leaving the Senate, Baucus became a senior policy advisor at a law firm that represents healthcare companies.

Former Representative Pat Tiberi, a Republican from Ohio, served on the House Ways and Means Committee (Public Citizen, 2019)[9]. He voted repeatedly to repeal the ACA. He received $1.2 million from insurance companies during his time in Congress. He resigned in 2018. He became president and CEO of the Ohio Business Roundtable, which lobbies on behalf of insurance companies and healthcare corporations.

Former Senator Trent Lott, a Republican from Mississippi, served in Congress from 1973 to 2007 (Public Citizen, 2019)[9]. He left and joined a lobbying firm. His clients included pharmaceutical companies, insurance companies, and hospital systems. He earned millions representing the same industries he regulated while in office.

Former Representative Billy Tauzin is the clearest case (Public Citizen, 2019)[9]. He wrote the law that prohibited Medicare from negotiating drug prices. He left Congress. He became CEO of PhRMA. He earned $2.5 million per year. The same industry he protected in Congress paid him 14 times his congressional salary.

This is not coincidence. This is the business model. Members of Congress serve the industries that will employ them after they leave office. The corruption is not hidden. The corruption is the system.

WHAT THE ACA ACTUALLY DID

The Affordable Care Act was not perfect. The ACA was compromised before it became law. The public option was removed. The Medicaid expansion was made optional. Pharmaceutical pricing was not addressed. Insurance companies were left in control.

But the ACA still accomplished something Congress now wants to destroy.

In 2010, the uninsured rate in America was 16 percent (Centers for Disease Control and Prevention, 2024)[21]. That number represented 49.9 million people without health coverage. By 2016, after the ACA's major provisions took effect, the uninsured rate fell to 8.6 percent. That represented 27.3 million people. The ACA reduced the number of uninsured Americans by 22.6 million.

In 2024, the uninsured rate stood at 7.6 percent (Centers for Disease Control and Prevention, 2024)[21]. That number represents 25 million people. The number increased slightly after pandemic-era Medicaid protections expired. But the uninsured rate remains lower than at any point before the ACA.

Nearly 24 million Americans are enrolled in ACA Marketplace plans (Centers for Medicare & Medicaid Services, 2025)[17]. Another 21 million gained coverage through Medicaid expansion. Total coverage through ACA-related programs exceeds 45 million people.

This is what Congress calls unaffordable. This is what Congress calls unsustainable. This is what Congress refuses to fund.

The cost of the ACA is 1.8 percent of the federal budget (Congressional Budget Office, 2024)[14]. The uninsured rate has been cut by more than half. Forty-five million people have coverage they did not have before. And Congress says America cannot afford it.

Congress can afford $1.9 trillion in tax cuts for corporations. Congress can afford $886 billion for defense. Congress can afford $80 billion in farm subsidies. Congress cannot afford $33.5 billion per year to keep 24 million Americans insured.

The reason is not fiscal. The reason is ideological and financial. Republicans oppose the ACA because it represents federal responsibility for healthcare. Democrats fail to defend it because their donors profit from its failure.

Both parties betray you. One party does it openly. The other does it quietly. The result is the same.

THIS IS WHAT BETRAYAL LOOKS LIKE

Congress is supposed to represent the people. The Constitution grants Congress the authority to tax, spend, and regulate commerce for the general welfare. The general welfare means the health, safety, and prosperity of the American people.

Congress does not act for the general welfare. Congress acts for the welfare of its donors.

Healthcare corporations spent $743.9 million in 2024 to ensure Congress does nothing (OpenSecrets, 2025)[1]. They spent $6.1 billion over 25 years to protect their profits (OpenSecrets, 2025)[2]. They succeeded. Americans pay the highest healthcare costs in the world. Americans go bankrupt from medical bills. Americans die because they cannot afford insulin. And Congress does nothing.

This is not a failure of policy. This is a failure of representation. Your elected officials have been purchased. They serve someone else. The system is not broken. The system is working exactly as designed. It is designed to transfer wealth from working people to corporations. It is designed to protect the profits of pharmaceutical companies, insurance companies, and hospital systems. It is designed to keep you paying.

The crisis is not the Affordable Care Act. The crisis is Congress.

CHAPTER 2

THE ACA—PURPOSE, STRUCTURE, AND IMPACT

The Affordable Care Act is not a single program. It is not a government health system. The ACA is a set of federal rules designed to do one specific thing: ensure that people without employer-sponsored insurance can access affordable healthcare through private insurance.

To understand the ACA, you must understand who it serves, how it works, and what it has accomplished. You must also understand its limitations. The ACA is not perfect. But it works. And millions of Americans depend on it.

WHO THE ACA SERVES

The ACA serves a specific population: people who do not have access to affordable health insurance through an employer and do not qualify for Medicaid or Medicare.

This population is larger and more diverse than most people realize.

In 2025, approximately 24 million people were enrolled in ACA Marketplace plans (Centers for Medicare & Medicaid Services, 2025)[17].

An additional 21 million people had coverage through Medicaid expansion under the ACA (Kaiser Family Foundation, 2024)[22]. Together, over 45 million Americans depend on ACA coverage.

These people fall into distinct groups.

First are workers without employer-sponsored insurance. Approximately 48 percent of adult ACA Marketplace enrollees are self-employed, work at a small business with fewer than 25 employees, or are employed by a company that does not offer health insurance (Kaiser Family Foundation, 2025)[23]. These workers did not stop working. Their employers simply do not offer health insurance. Before the ACA, these workers had no affordable options. They paid full price for individual insurance on the private market, which was often three to five times the cost of employer-subsidized coverage.

Second are early retirees. People ages 50 to 64 without employer-sponsored insurance often choose ACA Marketplace coverage. Among enrollees with incomes above 400 percent of the federal poverty level, 51 percent are ages 50 to 64 (Kaiser Family Foundation, 2025)[24]. Many of these are people who retired early and are not yet eligible for Medicare. Before the ACA, these early retirees faced a healthcare nightmare: insurance companies charged them three times as much as younger people for the same coverage. If they had any health condition, they were often denied coverage entirely.

Third are gig workers and people with volatile income. Workers in the sharing economy, shift workers, and people whose income fluctuates seasonally depend on ACA Marketplace coverage because their employment does not offer stable health benefits (Kaiser Family Foundation, 2025)[25]. These are Uber drivers, Lyft drivers, independent contractors, and freelancers. Before the ACA, if a gig worker got sick or injured, they faced bankruptcy or untreated illness.

Fourth are workers whose employers do not offer coverage or offer coverage that is unaffordable. This includes many people working in restaurants, retail, agriculture, and small businesses that cannot afford to provide health insurance to their workforce. In retail and food service, many employers deliberately keep workers below full-time status to avoid having to offer health insurance. These workers have steady jobs but no benefits.

Fifth are people with incomes below the Medicaid expansion threshold but above the federal poverty level. In states that have not expanded Medicaid, people with incomes slightly above poverty have no access to Medicaid. The ACA Marketplace is their only option for coverage with financial assistance.

What ties all these groups together is one fundamental fact: they lack access to affordable employer-sponsored insurance. The ACA was designed to serve them.

UNDERSTANDING THE FEDERAL POVERTY LEVEL AND THE 400% THRESHOLD

To understand the ACA's structure, you must understand the federal poverty level and the 400 percent threshold. This is not complicated. But it is precise.

The federal poverty level is an income amount set by the federal government each year. It varies by family size and is adjusted annually for inflation. The poverty level represents the minimum income the government considers necessary to meet basic living expenses for food, housing, utilities, and transportation.

For 2025, the poverty level is: Single person: $15,650. Married couple: $21,150. Family of three: $26,650. Family of four: $32,150 (ASPE, 2025)[26]. These numbers increase by approximately $5,500 per additional family member.

The original ACA, passed in 2010, made people with incomes between 100 percent and 400 percent of the federal poverty level eligible for premium tax credits on the ACA Marketplace. For a single person in 2025, 400 percent of poverty is approximately $62,600. For a family of four, it is $128,600.

This 400 percent threshold was supposed to ensure that people with moderate incomes had access to affordable coverage. But in practice, it created a problem: people earning just slightly more than 400 percent of poverty faced a sharp cliff. They became ineligible for any financial assistance, even though their premium might still consume a large share of their income.

In 2021, Congress addressed this problem. The American Rescue

Plan eliminated the 400 percent income cap entirely. It also increased the subsidy amounts. Together, these changes made ACA coverage dramatically more affordable for everyone.

Under the enhanced subsidies, the share of income that people are required to contribute toward their health insurance premium declined significantly. For example: A person earning $28,000 per year (approximately 179 percent of the 2025 poverty level) now pays only about 1 percent of their income toward a benchmark plan, or approximately $280 per year, instead of the 6 percent ($1,680) they would pay under the original ACA formula (Kaiser Family Foundation, 2025)[27].

For people earning above 400 percent of poverty, the enhancement eliminated the subsidy cliff. These people, approximately 1.6 million marketplace enrollees, now receive subsidies if their premium would otherwise cost more than 8.5 percent of their income (Kaiser Family Foundation, 2024)[28].

This means a 60-year-old earning $85,000 now receives subsidies to keep their premium at no more than 8.5 percent of income. Without the enhanced subsidy, this person would be completely ineligible for any financial help.

THE ACA MARKETPLACE: HOW IT ACTUALLY WORKS

The ACA Marketplace is a platform where people who do not have employer-sponsored insurance can compare and purchase health plans. It is not a single insurance company. It is a shopping tool that allows people to see all available plans in their area and choose the one that works best for them.

The federal government operates HealthCare.gov, which serves 31 states. Nineteen states and Washington, D.C. operate their own state-based marketplaces (Centers for Medicare & Medicaid Services, 2025)[29].

Here is how it works.

When a person visits the Marketplace during open enrollment, they provide information about their household size, income, and current health coverage. The Marketplace uses this information to determine whether the person qualifies for subsidies, Medicaid, or the Children's Health Insurance Program.

If the person qualifies for subsidies, the Marketplace calculates how much financial help they can receive based on their projected income and family size. This financial help comes in the form of premium tax credits.

The process is straightforward. But the mechanics are important to understand.

THE PREMIUM TAX CREDIT: HOW SUBSIDIES ACTUALLY WORK

The premium tax credit is a subsidy designed to make health insurance premiums affordable. It is calculated using a specific formula that has been enhanced since 2021.

Here is how it works, step by step.

Step 1: Identify the benchmark plan. The Marketplace identifies the second-lowest-cost Silver plan in the person's area. This plan is called the "benchmark plan." The Marketplace looks up the total annual premium for this plan. Let's use a real example. For a single person in California, the benchmark Silver plan might cost $4,800 per year.

Step 2: Determine how much income the person should contribute. The Marketplace determines what share of their income the person is expected to contribute toward their health insurance. This share is based on a sliding scale. People with lower incomes contribute a smaller percentage. People with higher incomes contribute a larger percentage.

With the enhanced subsidies in place (through 2025), the sliding scale looks like this: Income at 100-150% of FPL: 0-2% of income. Income at 150-200% of FPL: 2-4% of income. Income at 200-250% of FPL: 4-6% of income. Income at 250-300% of FPL: 6-8.5% of income. Income at 300% of FPL and above: 8.5% of income (capped) (Internal Revenue Service, 2024)[30].

Step 3: Calculate the subsidy. So if a person earns $24,000 per year (approximately 153 percent of the 2025 poverty level for a single person) and the benchmark plan costs $4,800 per year, the Marketplace calculates that this person should contribute no more than 3 percent of their income.

Three percent of $24,000 is $720 per year, or $60 per month.

The federal government then pays the rest. The subsidy is $4,800 minus $720, which equals $4,080 per year, or approximately $340 per month.

The person pays $60 per month. The government pays $340 per month directly to their insurance company. The total premium is paid. The person's contribution is affordable relative to their income.

Step 4: Apply the credit to any plan the person chooses. This is crucial to understand: the premium tax credit works regardless of which plan the person chooses. If they choose the benchmark plan (the second-lowest-cost Silver), they pay $60 per month. If they choose a more expensive plan, they pay more out of pocket. If they choose a cheaper plan (perhaps a Bronze plan with lower premiums), they pay less out of pocket.

The credit also comes in the form of advance payments. Instead of waiting until tax time to receive the credit, the government sends the money directly to the insurance company each month. This is why people can afford their monthly premiums. They are not paying the full premium themselves and waiting for a refund later. The subsidy is delivered upfront.

This is the mechanism that makes the ACA work.

WHO RECEIVES SUBSIDIES AND HOW MUCH THEY SAVE

In 2025, approximately 22 million people received premium tax credits to help pay for their ACA Marketplace coverage (Centers for Medicare & Medicaid Services, 2025)[17]. This represents 92 percent of all ACA Marketplace enrollees.

The average subsidy saves enrollees $536 per month, or approximately $6,432 per year, on their premiums (Commonwealth Fund, 2025)[31].

But subsidies vary dramatically by income.

For people with the lowest incomes, subsidies are substantial. In 2023 and 2024, the enhanced subsidies provided millions of people with an average of nearly $700 in monthly premium savings (Commonwealth Fund, 2025)[32]. More specifically: In 2023 and 2024, 80 percent of Marketplace enrollees could find a plan for $10 or less per month on HealthCare.gov (Commonwealth Fund, 2025)[33].

This is historic. Before the subsidies were enhanced, only 36 percent of people eligible for subsidies could find a plan for $10 per month or less (Commonwealth Fund, 2025)[34].

For people with middle and upper-middle incomes, subsidies still provide substantial relief.

A family of four earning $85,000 (264 percent of the 2025 federal poverty level) enrolled in a benchmark Silver plan in 2025 with the following costs: Total annual premium: $19,068. With enhanced premium tax credits: $4,148 per year, or $346 per month. Required contribution: 4.88% of household income (Center on Budget and Policy Priorities, 2024)[35].

Without the enhanced subsidies, this family would have paid significantly more. Under the original ACA formula, they would have been required to contribute 9.5 percent of their income, or approximately $8,075 per year. The enhanced subsidy saves this family roughly $3,900 per year.

For people earning above 400 percent of poverty, the enhanced subsidies provided crucial access. These people, approximately 1.6 million Marketplace enrollees, were previously ineligible for any subsidies. Now they receive financial help if their premium exceeds 8.5 percent of their income.

THE FOUR METAL PLANS: HOW COVERAGE ACTUALLY WORKS

All ACA plans cover the same essential health benefits. They all cover the same services. The difference is in cost-sharing. Cost-sharing is the money you pay out of your own pocket when you actually use healthcare. Cost-sharing includes deductibles, copayments, and coinsurance.

The ACA offers plans in four "metal" categories based on how much cost-sharing you pay.

Bronze Plans: These plans have the lowest monthly premiums but the highest out-of-pocket costs when you need care. The insurance company pays roughly 60 percent of your average medical costs. You pay 40 percent. A Bronze plan might have a $7,000 individual deductible. This means you pay $7,000 out of pocket for covered healthcare before the insurance company starts paying most of your bills (except preventive care, which is always free). Bronze plans are best for people who are generally healthy and rarely need medical care (Centers for Medicare & Medicaid Services, 2025)[36].

Silver Plans: These plans have moderate monthly premiums and moderate out-of-pocket costs. The insurance company pays roughly 70 percent of your average medical costs. You pay 30 percent. A Silver plan might have a $4,000 individual deductible. Silver plans are the most popular on the ACA Marketplace. In 2025, 13.7 million people enrolled in Silver plans. This is important: Silver plans are the only metal tier that qualifies for cost-sharing reductions. If you have a low or moderate income and choose a Silver plan, the government reduces your deductible and out-of-pocket maximums (Centers for Medicare & Medicaid Services, 2025)[37].

Gold Plans: These plans have higher monthly premiums but lower out-of-pocket costs when you need care. The insurance company pays roughly 80 percent of your average medical costs. You pay 20 percent. A Gold plan might have a $2,000 individual deductible. Gold plans are best for people who expect to use healthcare frequently or who have chronic conditions requiring ongoing treatment (Centers for Medicare & Medicaid Services, 2025)[38].

Platinum Plans: These plans have the highest monthly premiums but the lowest out-of-pocket costs. The insurance company pays roughly 90 percent of your average medical costs. You pay 10 percent. A Platinum plan might have a $500 or lower deductible. However, very few people choose Platinum plans because the high monthly premiums make them unaffordable even with subsidies. In 2025, only 1 percent of Marketplace enrollees selected Platinum plans (Centers for Medicare & Medicaid Services, 2025)[39].

For all plans in 2025, the maximum out-of-pocket limit is $9,200 for an individual and $18,400 for a family. This means regardless of which metal tier you choose, you will never pay more than this amount for covered healthcare in a single year. This maximum protects people from financial catastrophe (Centers for Medicare & Medicaid Services, 2025)[40].

COST-SHARING REDUCTIONS: THE SECRET TO AFFORDABILITY FOR LOW-INCOME PEOPLE

There is something critical that most people do not understand about the ACA: if you have a low or moderate income and you choose a Silver plan, the government automatically reduces your deductible and out-of-pocket costs. This is called a "cost-sharing reduction."

These reductions are extraordinary.

For a person earning between 100 and 150 percent of the federal poverty level who chooses a Silver plan, the insurance company effectively pays 94 percent of their average medical costs. This is better than a Platinum plan. For a single person earning $23,475 in 2025, this means their deductible might drop from $4,000 to $0, and their maximum out-of-pocket might drop from $9,200 to $3,050 (Center on Budget and Policy Priorities, 2025)[41].

For a person earning between 150 and 200 percent of the federal poverty level, the insurance company pays roughly 87 percent of costs. The deductible and out-of-pocket maximums are also significantly reduced.

For a person earning between 200 and 250 percent of the federal poverty level, the insurance company pays roughly 73 percent of costs, which is still better than a standard Silver plan.

In 2025, 12.3 million people enrolled in Silver plans qualified for cost-sharing reductions. This is 89 percent of Silver plan enrollees. For all these people, the government is not just paying their premiums. The government is also reducing their deductibles and out-of-pocket costs.

This is why the ACA works. This is why millions of people who previously had no access to affordable insurance now have coverage.

PRE-ACA VS. POST-ACA: WHAT ACTUALLY CHANGED

Before the ACA, the healthcare situation for uninsured people was dire.

In 2010, 48 million Americans under age 65 were uninsured. This was 16 percent of the non-elderly population (Centers for Disease Control and Prevention, 2024)[21]. For these people, healthcare was either impossible to access or financially catastrophic.

Before the ACA, several things were true:

People with pre-existing conditions were denied coverage or charged premiums two to three times higher than healthy people. An asthmatic was charged double the premium of a non-asthmatic. A person with diabetes was denied coverage entirely. If you had any health condition, you were marked for financial punishment. An insurance company could simply refuse to insure you.

Young adults aged 19 to 26 had an uninsured rate of 32 percent. They aged out of their parents' insurance and could not afford individual plans. A healthy 25-year-old might pay $150-300 per month for coverage on the individual market.

Women were charged more than men for the same coverage. This was standard. Insurance companies charged women up to 50 percent more than men for identical plans.

Insurance companies could impose annual and lifetime limits on coverage. A person could receive a certain amount of care and then be cut off entirely. If you had a serious illness requiring $500,000 in treatment, your insurance company could deny coverage for the remaining costs.

Emergency room visits were the primary source of care for uninsured people. Without preventive care, conditions became worse and more expensive to treat. An uninsured person would wait until their condition was critical, then go to the emergency room. This cost the healthcare system far more than preventive care would have (Kaiser Family Foundation, 2024)[42].

After the ACA, all of this changed.

Pre-existing conditions can no longer be used to deny coverage or charge higher premiums. A person with diabetes pays the same premium as a healthy person their age. A person with cancer, heart disease, or any other condition cannot be denied coverage.

The ACA allowed young adults to stay on their parents' insurance until age 26. The uninsured rate for young adults fell from 32 percent in 2010 to 14 percent by 2017. Millions of young people gained coverage.

Women cannot be charged more than men for the same coverage. Insurance companies must charge the same premium to men and women of the same age.

Annual and lifetime limits on coverage are prohibited. Your insurance company cannot cut you off after paying a certain amount. Coverage continues for as long as you need it.

Preventive care is free. People can see doctors for checkups, screenings, and vaccinations without paying anything out of pocket. This prevents diseases from progressing to more serious stages.

The Marketplace provides an affordable way to purchase coverage. For the first time, people without employer-sponsored insurance could shop for plans and receive subsidies based on their income.

These changes directly improved people's health and financial security.

Research shows that gaining health insurance through the ACA leads to: Improved access to care. People with insurance visit doctors more frequently, have regular prescriptions filled, and receive timely treatment for chronic conditions. Better health outcomes. Studies document improved blood pressure control, better management of diabetes, and reduced rates of preventable hospitalization among newly insured people. Greater financial security. People with insurance are less likely to experience medical debt, bankruptcy, or delayed care due to cost. Increased preventive care. People with insurance receive cancer screenings, blood pressure checks, and other preventive services that identify problems early. Early detection saves lives and reduces the cost of treatment (Commonwealth Fund, 2024)[43].

THE LIMITATIONS OF THE ACA: AN HONEST ASSESSMENT

The ACA is not perfect. It has significant limitations that future reforms should address.

First, deductibles remain high even with subsidies. A person with a $4,000 deductible still must pay $4,000 out of pocket before their insurance covers most care. For people with low incomes, this is still a substantial barrier to getting care. Cost-sharing reductions lower these deductibles significantly, but they do not eliminate them. For people who do not qualify for cost-sharing reductions, deductibles are a real problem.

Second, insurance networks remain narrow. Many ACA plans do not include all hospitals and doctors in a region. This limits people's choices and sometimes forces them to travel long distances for care. A person might discover that their favorite doctor is not in their plan's network, or their local hospital is not covered.

Third, most ACA plans offer limited mental health and dental coverage. A person might have comprehensive health insurance but no dental insurance. This is a design flaw that creates a gap in care. Dental disease can cause serious health problems, yet dental care is not covered.

Fourth, the ACA relies on private insurance companies to deliver coverage. Insurance companies respond to profit incentives, which sometimes conflict with providing high-quality care. Studies show that ACA insurers reject about 1 in 5 claims, leaving people with unpaid medical bills. Insurance companies deny treatments, refuse referrals to specialists, and delay care to reduce their costs (MoneyGeek, 2025)[44].

Fifth, the ACA does nothing to control the underlying cost of healthcare. Premiums continue to rise faster than wages. Without subsidies, health insurance remains unaffordable for many Americans. The cost of healthcare itself is not addressed by the ACA. The law assumes that healthcare will be expensive and tries to subsidize people so they can afford it. But healthcare in America is deliberately expensive, and the ACA does not change that.

These limitations exist not because the ACA is poorly designed but because it was designed as a compromise. The ACA expanded coverage using the private insurance system rather than creating a public healthcare program. This was a political decision, not a health policy decision. When the ACA was being negotiated in 2009-2010, the insurance industry lobbied heavily to ensure that a government healthcare option would not be created. The result is that the ACA uses private insurance companies as the delivery mechanism. This saves the insurance industry billions of dollars in profits. But it means the ACA will never fully solve healthcare affordability.

THE BOTTOM LINE: WHAT THE ACA ACTUALLY DOES

The ACA serves one specific function: it provides affordable health insurance to people who do not have access to employer-sponsored coverage and do not qualify for Medicaid or Medicare.

It accomplishes this through three main mechanisms:

First, it establishes minimum standards for coverage. Insurers must cover essential health benefits. They cannot deny coverage based on pre-existing conditions. They cannot impose lifetime limits. Every plan must cover preventive care at no cost.

Second, it provides financial assistance through premium tax credits and cost-sharing reductions. These subsidies are the reason the ACA works. Without subsidies, millions of people still could not afford coverage. With subsidies, coverage is affordable. A person earning $30,000 per year can find a plan for under $100 per month. This is transformative.

Third, it creates a Marketplace where people can compare plans and enroll in coverage. The Marketplace is a tool. It allows people to see all available plans in their area, compare costs, and choose the plan that works best for them. Before the Marketplace, people in the individual market had no easy way to compare plans. They had to contact multiple insurance companies separately. Now they can see all options in one place.

Through these mechanisms, the ACA has reduced the uninsured rate by nearly 50 percent and provided coverage to over 45 million Americans.

The ACA is not perfect. But it works. And millions of Americans depend on it.

CHAPTER 3
ACA SHORTCOMINGS—HONEST ASSESSMENT

The Affordable Care Act is not perfect. It was never designed to be. It was designed to expand coverage to millions of uninsured Americans while preserving the existing private insurance market.

That choice, to work within the employer-based and private insurance system rather than replace it, created structural limitations that persist today.

These limitations are real. They affect millions of people. They deserve honest analysis. But they also deserve honest context: these same limitations exist throughout American private insurance, and Congress has done nothing to fix them in either the ACA marketplace or the employer-based system.

HIGH DEDUCTIBLES AND OUT-OF-POCKET COSTS

ACA marketplace plans vary significantly in their cost-sharing structures. Bronze plans, which cover 60 percent of expected healthcare costs, often carry individual deductibles of $7,000 and family deductibles exceeding $14,000 (Kaiser Family Foundation, 2024)[45].

Silver plans, which cover 70 percent of costs, typically have deductibles ranging from $3,000 to $5,000 for individuals and $6,000 to $10,000 for families, depending on the insurer and geographic region. Gold and Platinum plans offer lower deductibles but higher monthly premiums. For many low-income Americans, even Silver plans create a choice between insurance and actual healthcare access.

A 2024 Commonwealth Fund study found that 41 percent of American adults with health insurance reported difficulty affording care in the past year (Commonwealth Fund, 2024)[46]. Among those with ACA marketplace coverage, the figure was similar: 39 percent reported cost-related barriers to care. High deductibles mean that people who buy insurance still cannot afford to use it. They pay premiums and still delay or skip necessary medical care.

This is a legitimate criticism of the current ACA marketplace design.

But here is the critical fact: this problem is not unique to the ACA.

Among Americans with employer-based insurance, 45 percent reported difficulty affording care in 2024 (Commonwealth Fund, 2024)[46]. The average employer-sponsored family plan carries a deductible of $1,735 (Kaiser Family Foundation, 2024)[47]. Since 2010, average employer plan deductibles have increased by 123 percent, while wages have increased by only 27 percent. Workers covered by their employers face the same barrier: insurance they cannot afford to use.

High-deductible health plans are now the fastest-growing health plan category in America, covering more than 30 million people (America's Health Insurance Plans, 2024)[48]. These plans were sold as a way to increase consumer engagement and lower premiums. Instead, they have created a system where people avoid seeking care, even preventive care, because they cannot afford to pay until they meet their deductible. Research from Harvard Medical School shows that high deductibles reduce preventive care utilization by 15 to 20 percent and do not reduce overall healthcare spending; they simply shift costs to individuals (Wharam et al., 2023)[49].

The ACA did not create this problem. Congress did, by failing to regulate deductible levels or cost-sharing across the entire insurance system. If Congress were serious about solving this problem, it would set reasonable maximum deductible limits for all health insurance plans, employer-sponsored and marketplace alike. It has not done so.

Congress had the opportunity to address deductibles when it passed the ACA. Congress chose not to. Congress had the opportunity to address deductibles in every budget negotiation since 2010. Congress chose not to. Instead, Congress allowed deductibles to rise across all insurance types while attacking only the ACA for having high deductibles.

This is selective outrage. This is deliberate deception.

When a member of Congress stands on the House floor and attacks ACA deductibles, that member is silent about the 160 million Americans with employer-sponsored insurance who face the same problem. When a member attacks marketplace plans for being unaffordable, that member votes to preserve tax subsidies for employer plans that are equally unaffordable. The criticism is targeted. The silence is strategic.

The truth is simple: Congress does not care about high deductibles. Congress cares about attacking the ACA. If Congress cared about deductibles, it would regulate them everywhere. It does not.

NARROW NETWORKS AND LIMITED PROVIDER ACCESS

ACA marketplace plans often use narrow networks as a cost-containment strategy. A narrow network plan limits enrollees to a smaller set of hospitals, specialists, and providers than traditional insurance plans (Avalere Health, 2023)[50]. In many cases, these networks exclude major medical centers, reduce specialist access, or require long commutes for care.

A 2023 Kaiser Family Foundation analysis found that 30 percent of ACA marketplace plans in major metropolitan areas had networks that excluded at least one major hospital system (Kaiser Family Foundation, 2023)[51]. In some regions, preferred provider networks exclude two or three major hospitals, forcing patients to choose between traveling significant distances or paying higher out-of-network costs. Rural areas face particularly severe limitations: in 45 counties, marketplace plans offer access to fewer than five in-network specialists in essential categories like cardiology or oncology.

For patients with chronic conditions, narrow networks are devastating. A patient whose preferred cardiologist or oncologist is out of network faces a choice: change doctors or pay substantially higher out-of-pocket costs. Some patients with complex medical needs are effectively trapped in plans they cannot use.

This is a real problem. It causes real suffering.

But again: this is not unique to the ACA.

Narrow networks are standard practice throughout American private insurance. Employer-sponsored plans increasingly use narrow networks as well, and employers actively promote these plans because they reduce premiums (National Association of Insurance Commissioners, 2024)[52]. In 2024, 38 percent of employer-sponsored plans used narrow or ultra-narrow networks. Workers covered through their employers face the same barriers: restricted provider access, mandatory referrals, and the choice between staying in-network or paying substantially higher costs.

HMO and PPO plans offered through employers routinely exclude major medical centers and limit specialist access. The difference is that these plans are rarely discussed in political debate about healthcare. When Congress attacks the ACA, it does not attack employer-sponsored plans for using the same network restrictions. When Congress attacks narrow networks in the ACA, it is selective criticism that ignores 160 million Americans covered through employers.

The reason for this selective criticism is obvious: employer-sponsored insurance is subsidized through the tax code. The federal government spends $280 billion per year subsidizing employer health insurance through tax exclusions (Congressional Budget Office, 2024)[14]. That subsidy is eight times larger than the entire ACA subsidy budget. Congress does not attack employer insurance because employer insurance represents the largest healthcare subsidy in the federal budget, and that subsidy flows primarily to middle-class and upper-middle-class workers who vote.

The ACA serves people without employer coverage. These people are more likely to be low-income, more likely to be self-employed, more likely to work in retail or food service. They have less political power. Congress attacks their insurance. Congress protects the insurance of people with employer coverage.

This is not about policy. This is about power.

LIMITED INSURER CHOICE IN RURAL COUNTIES

Perhaps the most acute ACA marketplace problem is insurer availability in rural America. Rural counties have fewer insurers participating in the marketplace, which reduces consumer choice and competition.

In 2024, 23 percent of counties had only one insurer participating in the ACA marketplace (Kaiser Family Foundation, 2024)[53]. In nine states, Alaska, Mississippi, Oklahoma, South Carolina, Tennessee, Texas, Utah, Wyoming, and West Virginia, the percentage of counties with only one marketplace insurer exceeded 50 percent. Rural Americans living in these regions have no choice. They buy the single available plan or go uninsured.

This creates pricing power for the single insurer. With no competition, that insurer faces no market pressure to hold down premiums or expand coverage. A rural patient cannot threaten to buy from a competitor. The single insurer charges what it wants.

This is a structural failure of the marketplace model. Markets require choice. Without choice, markets fail.

This problem demands a solution. Congress should address it.

But Congress has not addressed it. And rural counties did not become underserved by insurers because of the ACA.

Before the ACA, rural America was underserved by insurers. Rural counties with only one or two insurers have been the norm in American insurance for decades (Robert Wood Johnson Foundation, 2022)[54]. The difference is that before the ACA, rural residents had no marketplace option at all. They either bought coverage through employers, paid full price on the individual market, which was unregulated and often predatory, or went uninsured.

The ACA did not create rural insurer scarcity. It inherited it. Rural

America has always been expensive and difficult for insurers to serve, which is why they have always avoided it. The solution is not to eliminate the marketplace. The solution is for Congress to make rural insurance viable by directly subsidizing rural insurers or by allowing public options to enter rural markets.

Today, Congress does neither. Instead, it uses rural insurer scarcity as evidence that the entire ACA should be eliminated, a position that would make rural healthcare access even worse, not better.

Congress knows this. Congress does not care.

Rural Americans are among the most vulnerable populations in the healthcare system. They have higher rates of chronic disease, lower incomes, less access to specialists, and longer travel distances to hospitals (Centers for Disease Control and Prevention, 2023)[55]. Rural hospitals are closing at record rates. Between 2010 and 2023, 136 rural hospitals closed, leaving entire counties without inpatient care (University of North Carolina, 2023)[56]. Rural Americans die at higher rates from preventable causes than urban Americans. They have shorter life expectancies. They face worse health outcomes across nearly every category.

The ACA marketplace is one of the few mechanisms that provides rural Americans with subsidized access to health insurance. Eliminating the ACA would not solve the rural insurer problem. It would eliminate the only insurance option many rural Americans have.

Congress knows this. Congress is doing it anyway.

CLAIM DENIALS AND ADMINISTRATIVE BARRIERS

One of the most frustrating aspects of ACA marketplace plans, and all private insurance, is the frequency of claim denials and administrative barriers that prevent people from accessing care.

Studies show that ACA insurers reject about 18 percent of claims (MoneyGeek, 2025)[44]. This means nearly one in five times a person submits a claim for care, the insurer denies it. The person must then appeal, submit additional documentation, or pay out of pocket. This process is time-consuming, confusing, and often deliberately designed to discourage people from pursuing care.

Insurance companies deny claims for a variety of reasons. Some denials are legitimate: the service was not covered under the plan, or the claim was submitted incorrectly. But many denials are not legitimate. Insurers deny claims that should be covered, forcing patients to appeal. The appeal process is complex and requires detailed knowledge of insurance terminology, medical coding, and plan documents. Most people do not have this knowledge. Most people give up.

Research shows that fewer than 1 percent of denied claims are appealed (Patient Advocate Foundation, 2023)[57]. Of the claims that are appealed, approximately 40 percent are overturned in the patient's favor. This means that insurers routinely deny claims they know should be covered, betting that most patients will not appeal.

This is not accidental. This is strategy. Insurers save money by denying claims. If most patients do not appeal, the insurer keeps the money. If a patient appeals and wins, the insurer pays the claim it should have paid in the first place. The insurer risks nothing. The patient risks everything.

This problem exists across all private insurance, not just ACA plans. Employer-sponsored insurance uses the same claim denial tactics. Medicare Advantage plans, which are private insurance plans subsidized by Medicare, have some of the highest claim denial rates in the industry (U.S. Department of Health and Human Services, 2023)[58]. In 2022, Medicare Advantage plans denied 18 percent of prior authorization requests and 3 percent of payment requests, and federal audits found that many of these denials were improper.

The ACA did not create this problem. Private insurance created this problem. Congress allows it to continue because Congress serves the insurance industry, not the people.

MENTAL HEALTH AND DENTAL COVERAGE GAPS

Most ACA marketplace plans provide limited mental health coverage and no dental coverage. This creates a gap in care that affects millions of Americans.

The ACA requires all marketplace plans to cover mental health services as an essential health benefit. But the law does not specify the extent or quality of that coverage. Many plans cover only a limited number of therapy sessions per year, exclude certain types of therapy, or require high copayments that make regular treatment unaffordable (Mental Health America, 2024)[59]. People with serious mental health conditions often exhaust their coverage limits and must pay out of pocket or go without care.

Dental coverage is even more limited. The ACA requires marketplace plans to offer pediatric dental coverage, but adult dental coverage is optional. Most marketplace plans do not include adult dental coverage, and standalone dental plans are expensive and offer limited benefits (National Association of Dental Plans, 2024)[60]. A person with comprehensive health insurance through the ACA marketplace often has no dental insurance at all.

This is a serious problem. Dental disease is linked to heart disease, diabetes, and other chronic conditions. Poor dental health increases healthcare costs and worsens overall health outcomes. Yet Congress has done nothing to require dental coverage in marketplace plans or employer plans.

Mental health coverage is similarly inadequate across all insurance types. People with employer-sponsored insurance face the same mental health coverage limits, the same narrow networks of mental health providers, and the same high out-of-pocket costs (American Psychological Association, 2024)[61]. The difference is that Congress does not attack employer insurance for failing to provide adequate mental health coverage. Congress only attacks the ACA.

THE PREMIUM AFFORDABILITY PROBLEM

Even with subsidies, premiums remain unaffordable for many Americans. A single person earning $50,000 per year, approximately 319 percent of the federal poverty level, pays roughly 6.5 percent of their income toward a benchmark Silver plan (Kaiser Family Foundation,

2025)[27]. That amounts to approximately $3,250 per year, or $271 per month.

For a person earning $50,000, paying $271 per month for health insurance is a significant burden. That person still faces a deductible, copayments, and out-of-pocket costs when they need care. The insurance is affordable in the sense that the person can technically pay for it. But it is not affordable in the sense that it leaves the person with enough income to meet their other needs.

This problem is worse for people earning above 400 percent of the poverty level who do not qualify for enhanced subsidies in states where subsidies have not been expanded. A 60-year-old earning $70,000 per year might face premiums of $15,000 per year or more, even with the 8.5 percent income cap under enhanced subsidies (Kaiser Family Foundation, 2024)[28]. That is more than 21 percent of their income. This is not affordable. This is crushing.

The reason premiums are high is simple: healthcare in America is expensive. Hospitals charge more. Doctors charge more. Drug companies charge more. Medical device manufacturers charge more. Administrative costs are higher. Profit margins are higher. Every part of the healthcare system extracts more money than comparable systems in other countries.

The ACA subsidizes premiums to make insurance affordable. But it does not address the underlying cost of care. Congress could address underlying costs by regulating hospital prices, negotiating drug prices, capping administrative costs, or creating a public insurance option that competes with private insurers. Congress has done none of these things.

Instead, Congress attacks the subsidies. Congress says the subsidies are too expensive. Congress says America cannot afford them. Congress is lying.

The subsidies cost $33.5 billion per year (Congressional Budget Office, 2024)[14]. The subsidies make insurance affordable for 24 million people. That is $1,396 per person per year. For $1,396 per person, Congress ensures that millions of Americans have access to healthcare. Congress says this is unaffordable.

The same Congress spends $280 billion per year subsidizing

employer-sponsored insurance through tax exclusions (Congressional Budget Office, 2024)[14]. That subsidy costs eight times as much as the ACA subsidies. Congress does not call that unaffordable. Congress does not threaten to eliminate it. Congress protects it.

This is not about affordability. This is about who gets subsidized. Employer-sponsored insurance subsidizes people with stable, middle-class jobs. ACA subsidies go to people without employer coverage, people who are self-employed, people who work in retail or food service. Congress protects the subsidies for the middle class. Congress attacks the subsidies for the working class.

THE CRITICAL ARGUMENT: THESE PROBLEMS EXIST ACROSS ALL PRIVATE INSURANCE

The most important observation about ACA shortcomings is this: they are not unique to the ACA. They are structural features of American private insurance itself.

High deductibles, narrow networks, limited provider choice, insufficient coverage in underserved regions, claim denials, mental health gaps, dental coverage gaps, and premium affordability problems are not ACA problems. They are American healthcare problems. They exist in employer-sponsored plans, individual market plans outside the ACA, Medicare Advantage plans, and marketplace plans. They exist wherever private insurance is the primary mechanism for healthcare access.

Congress created this system. Congress could fix it. Congress has chosen not to.

When Congress attacks the ACA specifically, it implicitly endorses these same problems in employer-based insurance. It says: "High deductibles are unacceptable in the marketplace but acceptable for workers with employer plans." It says: "Narrow networks are a failure in the ACA but acceptable in employer insurance." It says: "Rural insurer scarcity is a reason to eliminate the marketplace but not a reason to regulate employer insurance."

This is intellectually dishonest.

If Congress were genuinely concerned about deductibles, it would regulate all deductibles, marketplace and employer plans alike (Center on Budget and Policy Priorities, 2024)[62]. If Congress were concerned about network adequacy, it would require all plans to meet network standards. If Congress were concerned about rural access, it would create incentives for insurers to serve underserved regions across the entire system.

Congress has not done any of this. Instead, it has allowed high deductibles to proliferate across all insurance types, watched network narrowing accelerate in employer plans, and ignored rural healthcare collapse. And then it blames the ACA for having the same problems.

Eliminating ACA subsidies does not solve these problems. It makes them worse.

A person who loses marketplace coverage does not gain access to employer insurance. They become uninsured. An uninsured person does not benefit from narrower networks or higher deductibles. They do not benefit from having those problems eliminated. They suffer from having no insurance at all. An uninsured person cannot see a cardiologist in-network or out-of-network. They cannot afford to see one at all.

The people harmed by ACA cuts are not harmed because the ACA was inadequate. They are harmed because Congress is refusing to fix the problems that affect all of private insurance, and then it is eliminating the one program that made insurance affordable for millions of people who had no other option.

WHAT CONGRESS REFUSES TO DO

Congress has the authority to fix every problem described in this chapter. Congress chooses not to.

Congress could cap deductibles at $1,000 for individuals and $2,000 for families across all insurance plans. It does not.

Congress could require all insurance plans to maintain adequate provider networks that include at least two major hospital systems in every region. It does not.

Congress could subsidize rural insurers or create a public option that operates in underserved counties. It does not.

Congress could require all insurers to cover mental health and dental care as essential benefits. It does not.

Congress could negotiate drug prices, cap hospital prices, regulate administrative costs, and create cost controls that reduce premiums. It does not.

Congress could do all of this. Congress refuses.

Instead, Congress attacks the ACA. Congress says the ACA is inadequate. Congress uses the ACA's limitations, limitations that exist across all private insurance, as justification to eliminate the program entirely.

This is not criticism. This is sabotage.

The honest assessment of ACA shortcomings is this: they exist, they matter, and they should be fixed. But they should be fixed for all Americans, not eliminated for some Americans while left untouched for others. The ACA should be expanded, not attacked. The entire private insurance system should be reformed, not just the ACA narrowed.

Congress refuses to do this. Congress refuses even to acknowledge that these problems exist everywhere, not just in the ACA. This refusal reveals the truth: Congress is not attacking the ACA because it is inadequate. Congress is attacking the ACA because it works. It expanded coverage. It reduced the uninsured rate. It created a functioning insurance system that does not require employer sponsorship. And healthcare corporations would prefer that this system not exist.

CHAPTER 4

WHY EMPLOYER-BASED INSURANCE EXISTS (HISTORICAL ACCIDENT)

The American healthcare system is built on a historical accident. It was never planned. It was never debated. It was never chosen as the best way to organize healthcare. It happened because of a wartime wage freeze, and then Congress locked it into place through tax policy. Today, 160 million Americans depend on a system that exists for no reason other than inertia and political capture.

Understanding this history is essential. It explains why the United States is the only major developed nation that ties health insurance to employment. It explains why millions of Americans lose coverage when they lose jobs. It explains why entrepreneurs, freelancers, and gig workers have no reliable path to affordable insurance. It explains why Congress has spent seventy years unable to build a national healthcare system: because an accidental system became institutionalized, and powerful interests grew wealthy protecting it.

Most importantly, it reveals a fundamental truth about American governance: when Congress had the power to choose a healthcare system, it chose nothing. And that choice, to let an accident become policy, has cost millions of lives and trillions of dollars.

THE WAGE FREEZE OF 1942 AND THE BIRTH OF EMPLOYER INSURANCE

During World War II, the federal government imposed strict wage and price controls to prevent inflation and redirect resources to military production (National War Labor Board, 1942)[63]. The War Labor Board, established by executive order in 1942, froze nominal wages at their January 1942 levels. This was economically necessary. The government needed to control inflation while mobilizing 16 million men and women for military service. But it created an immediate problem for employers: they could not raise wages to compete for scarce workers.

So employers got creative. They began offering non-wage benefits to attract and retain employees. Health insurance was one of those benefits. Since the wage freeze did not explicitly prohibit benefits, and since insurance premiums were not classified as wages under War Labor Board rules, employers could offer health insurance without violating the wage freeze (Blumberg & Holahan, 2019)[64].

This was a brilliant workaround. Employers could offer something of real value, access to healthcare, without technically violating wage controls. Workers got access to medical care they otherwise could not afford. Employers got the workers they needed. The War Labor Board tolerated it because it solved a wartime problem without appearing to circumvent wage controls.

By 1945, when the wage freeze ended, employer-sponsored health insurance had become standard practice. Major employers like General Motors, Ford, and US Steel had established health plans. Union contracts began including health benefits as a negotiating point. What started as a temporary wartime workaround had become institutionalized (Thomasson, 2003)[65].

But employer-based insurance was not the only model available. Other nations faced the same wartime pressures. Britain, Canada, and most of Western Europe chose different paths. Britain established the National Health Service in 1948, creating a tax-funded, universal system. Canada created a provincial public insurance system. Germany had established Bismarck-model social insurance decades earlier. These nations recognized that healthcare was a public responsibility, not a private benefit tied to employment.

America chose differently. Not because Americans debated and decided employer insurance was superior. America chose differently by accident.

THE TAX EXEMPTION: CEMENTING THE ACCIDENT INTO LAW

In 1943, the federal government made a critical decision that would shape American healthcare for the next eighty years. The Internal Revenue Service ruled that employer contributions to health insurance premiums were not taxable income to employees (Internal Revenue Service, 1943)[66]. This meant that a worker who received $500 in health insurance from their employer did not have to count that $500 as income for tax purposes.

This was extraordinary. No other benefit received this treatment. A worker who received $500 in cash wages had to pay income tax on that money. A worker who received $500 in housing, food, or transportation had to count it as taxable income. But a worker who received $500 in health insurance premiums did not.

The IRS did not explain why. There was no congressional debate. There was no public discussion of whether this made sense as policy. It was simply an administrative decision, made during wartime, that treated employer health insurance differently from every other form of compensation.

The tax exemption created an enormous incentive. Employers could offer health insurance and deduct the cost as a business expense. Employees could receive that insurance without paying income tax on it. Both parties benefited. And workers with employer coverage got a substantial tax subsidy that workers without employer coverage did not get.

The tax exemption was not small. In 2024, the employer health insurance tax exemption cost the federal government approximately $310 billion in foregone tax revenue (Congressional Budget Office, 2024)[14]. This is the single largest tax expenditure in the U.S. tax code, larger than the child tax credit, larger than the earned income tax credit, larger than the standard deduction itself (Joint Committee on Taxation, 2024)[67]. For seventy years, the federal government has been subsidizing employer-based insurance through the tax code. Not through direct appropriation, but through foregone revenue that workers and non-workers never see.

This subsidy is invisible and regressive. It benefits workers with employer coverage and ignores everyone else. A person working for a Fortune 500 company with a generous health plan receives a massive tax subsidy. A self-employed person, a freelancer, a gig worker, or an unemployed person receives no subsidy at all. A retiree under 65 receives no subsidy. A person working for a small business that cannot afford to offer insurance receives no subsidy.

The tax code thus locks millions of Americans out of affordable insurance by design.

The subsidy structure is also deeply unfair. Workers in higher tax brackets receive larger subsidies because the value of the tax exclusion increases with income. A worker earning $200,000 per year who receives $20,000 in employer health benefits avoids paying federal income tax at the 32 percent marginal rate, saving $6,400 in taxes. A worker earning $50,000 per year who receives $10,000 in employer health benefits avoids paying tax at the 22 percent rate, saving $2,200. The wealthy worker receives a subsidy three times larger in absolute dollars, simply because they earn more (Tax Policy Center, 2023)[68].

Meanwhile, the self-employed person earning $50,000 receives no federal subsidy for health insurance unless they qualify for ACA marketplace subsidies. The gig worker earning $30,000 receives ACA subsidies but still pays more out of pocket than the Fortune 500 employee. The unemployed person receives nothing.

Congress created this system. Congress maintains this system. Congress refuses to fix this system.

CONGRESS LOCKS IT IN: 1974 AND BEYOND

By the 1970s, employer-based insurance dominated American health-care. But it was not yet locked into law. Congress could have changed course. It could have created a national healthcare system. It could have expanded public insurance. It could have regulated employer plans out of existence. It had the power.

Instead, Congress actively cemented employer insurance into place.

In 1974, Congress passed the Employee Retirement Income Security Act (ERISA), a comprehensive federal law governing employer-sponsored benefits, including health insurance (Employee Retirement Income Security Act, 1974)[69]. ERISA preempted state insurance regulation, meaning states could not impose requirements on employer health plans. ERISA exempted self-insured employers from state insurance mandates, allowing large employers to avoid minimum coverage standards. ERISA created a federal regulatory structure specifically designed to preserve employer-based insurance.

Why? Because large employers, the Fortune 500 companies that had established health plans in the 1940s and 1950s, wanted federal protection from state regulation. They wanted to minimize costs. They wanted flexibility. Congress gave them what they wanted.

The result: employer-based insurance became legally entrenched. States could not impose network standards, deductible limits, or coverage mandates on employer plans. The federal government created a two-tier system: one set of rules for employer plans (minimal regulation through ERISA), and another set of rules for individual market plans (state regulation, much more stringent) (Jacobson & Parmet, 2007)[70].

This legal structure persists today. Employer plans operate under federal ERISA rules that prioritize cost containment and employer flexibility. Individual market plans operate under state insurance laws that impose network standards, coverage mandates, and consumer protections. As a result, employer plans can be cheaper because they have fewer regulatory requirements, and individual market plans must meet higher standards because states regulate them.

The irony is profound: the "free market" solution (employer insurance) is the heavily subsidized, lightly regulated option. The "government-run" solution (individual market insurance) is the one with more regulations and fewer subsidies.

Congress did this intentionally. In 1974, Congress chose to embed employer insurance into federal law rather than create a national alternative. Every year since, Congress has renewed this choice by maintaining ERISA, maintaining the tax exemption, and refusing to create a universal system.

The consequences are clear. Employer insurance is subsidized at $310 billion per year through the tax code (Congressional Budget Office, 2024)[14]. ACA marketplace subsidies cost $33.5 billion per year. Congress protects the $310 billion subsidy. Congress attacks the $33.5 billion subsidy. The larger subsidy goes to people with stable jobs and middle-class incomes. The smaller subsidy goes to people without employer coverage, people who are self-employed, people working in retail or food service. Congress protects the subsidy for the privileged. Congress eliminates the subsidy for the vulnerable.

This is not accident. This is policy.

HOW EMPLOYER INSURANCE CROWDED OUT NATIONAL HEALTHCARE REFORM

For seventy years, the existence of employer-based insurance has prevented Congress from building a national healthcare system.

This is not coincidence. It is structural. As long as millions of Americans have employer coverage, Congress faces a political barrier to national reform: those covered by employers believe they have "good" insurance and resist changes that might affect it. Insurance companies, hospital systems, and pharmaceutical corporations benefit from the current system and lobby aggressively to preserve it. Together, these forces have made healthcare reform politically impossible.

In 1945, President Harry Truman proposed the first comprehensive national health insurance plan in American history (Truman, 1945)[71]. Congress rejected it. The American Medical Association, pharmaceutical companies, and insurers opposed it vigorously. Truman could not overcome the opposition.

Why did reform fail? Because by 1945, millions of Americans already had employer insurance. They were satisfied with their coverage, or believed they were. Extending the same coverage to the uninsured felt like a government takeover. The status quo, employer-based insurance for some, nothing for others, proved politically defensible.

The AMA launched one of the most aggressive lobbying campaigns in American history to defeat Truman's plan (Starr, 1982)[72]. The campaign cost $1.5 million, an enormous sum in 1945 dollars. The AMA hired public relations firms to spread fear about "socialized medicine." Doctors were instructed to tell patients that national health insurance would destroy the doctor-patient relationship. The campaign worked. Congress killed the bill.

The defeat of Truman's plan established a pattern that would repeat for the next seventy years: whenever reformers proposed universal healthcare, the medical-industrial complex would mobilize to stop it. And the existence of employer insurance gave them a powerful argument: millions of Americans already had coverage, so why change the system?

In the 1960s, Congress created Medicare and Medicaid, establishing public insurance for the elderly and the poor (Social Security Amendments, 1965)[73]. These programs were necessary because millions of Americans had no coverage. But rather than extend the logic of Medicare to all Americans, Congress created a patchwork: Medicare for the elderly, Medicaid for the poor, employer insurance for workers, and the individual market for everyone else.

Why did Congress not create a universal system? Because employer insurance had become normal. Millions of working-age Americans had coverage. Congress could claim the problem was solved for workers, and address only the "gaps" (the elderly, the poor). This approach was politically easier than replacing the entire system.

The creation of Medicare and Medicaid was itself a compromise born from the failure to create universal coverage. Reformers had pushed for Medicare for All in the 1960s. Congress rejected it. Instead, Congress created two programs that left the employer-based system intact. The patchwork solution became permanent policy (Marmor, 2000)[74].

In 1993, the Clinton administration proposed healthcare reform that would have created a universal system while preserving employer insurance (Health Security Act, 1993)[75]. Congress rejected it. The insurance industry, pharmaceutical companies, and conservative politicians opposed the plan. Millions of Americans who had employer coverage feared the change. The employer insurance system, by existing, created a constituency opposed to reform.

The defeat of the Clinton plan was brutal. The Health Insurance Association of America spent $20 million on the "Harry and Louise" television ads that portrayed the plan as government overreach (Johnson & Broder, 1996)[76]. Republicans attacked the plan as socialism. Democrats who supported the plan lost their seats in the 1994 midterm elections. The message was clear: propose universal healthcare, lose power.

The same pattern repeated in 2009, when Congress debated the Affordable Care Act. The goal was to expand coverage to the uninsured without disrupting employer insurance. Congress preserved employer plans, subsidized employer coverage through the tax code, and created a marketplace only for those without employer access (Patient Protection and Affordable Care Act, 2010)[77].

Every healthcare reform attempt in American history has been constrained by the existence of employer insurance. Because millions of Americans already had coverage, however inadequate, Congress could not create a universal system. Instead, it created patches: Medicare, Medicaid, the ACA marketplace. Each patch addressed a specific group while leaving the underlying system intact.

This is the political trap of employer-based insurance. Once it exists, it becomes the baseline. Reformers must work around it, not replace it. And because it exists, there is always a constituency, the insured, who fear change more than they desire improvement.

The trap is self-reinforcing. Employer insurance creates a class of people with coverage. Those people resist reform because they fear losing what they have. Their resistance prevents universal coverage. The lack of universal coverage leaves millions uninsured. The uninsured have less political power than the insured. Congress ignores them. The system persists.

WHY THE UNITED STATES STANDS ALONE

The United States is the only major developed nation that ties health insurance to employment. This is not because employer-based insurance is superior. It is because of historical accident followed by political lock-in.

Canada, which borders the United States and shares similar wages and working conditions, created a universal public insurance system in the 1960s (Canadian Medicare, 1966)[78]. All Canadians have coverage regardless of employment status. No Canadian loses insurance because they change jobs, start a business, or retire before age 65. Canada spends 10.7 percent of GDP on healthcare and covers everyone. The United States spends 17.3 percent of GDP on healthcare and leaves 25 million people uninsured (OECD, 2024)[79].

Britain created the National Health Service in 1948, establishing that healthcare is a public good funded through taxation (National Health Service Act, 1946)[80]. Healthcare in Britain is not tied to employment. It is a right of citizenship. British workers do not lose coverage when they change jobs. British retirees do not fear medical bankruptcy. Britain spends 11.3 percent of GDP on healthcare and covers everyone (OECD, 2024)[79].

Germany, France, Japan, South Korea, and Australia all created universal or near-universal systems decades ago (World Health Organization, 2023)[81]. None of them tie insurance to employment. None of them tie healthcare access to job status. All of them cover their entire populations. All of them spend less per capita than the United States while delivering better health outcomes.

The data is unambiguous. Countries with universal healthcare systems achieve better health outcomes at lower cost than the United States. Life expectancy is higher. Infant mortality is lower. Maternal mortality is lower. Preventable deaths are fewer. Medical bankruptcy does not exist. And yet these countries spend 30 to 50 percent less per capita on healthcare than the United States (Commonwealth Fund, 2023)[82].

The United States is an outlier not because American workers preferred employment-based insurance. It is an outlier because a wartime wage freeze created a workaround, a tax exemption institutionalized it, and Congress locked it into law through ERISA. By the time Americans could have chosen a different system, the existing system was too powerful to dislodge.

The international comparison reveals the full scale of American failure. Every other wealthy nation provides universal healthcare. Every other wealthy nation spends less per capita. Every other wealthy nation achieves better outcomes. The United States spends more, covers fewer people, and produces worse results. This is not because Americans are sicker or because American doctors are less skilled. This is because the American system is designed to extract profit, not deliver care.

THE ABDICATION OF GOVERNMENT RESPONSIBILITY

This history reveals something fundamental about American governance: when faced with a major policy choice, Congress chose not to choose.

Healthcare is not a trivial issue. It is a matter of life and death. It determines whether a person can afford to see a doctor, whether a family faces bankruptcy because of illness, whether a child gets vaccinated or goes without. Every other major developed nation recognized this and decided that healthcare was a public responsibility, that government had an obligation to ensure all citizens had access to care.

Congress did not make this choice. Congress allowed an accidental system to persist. And when that accidental system proved inadequate, when millions of Americans remained uninsured, Congress created temporary patches instead of solving the problem.

This pattern repeats throughout American policy. Congress built the most powerful military in human history, spending $886 billion annually to defend against foreign threats (U.S. Department of Defense, 2024)[16]. Congress spent trillions building highways, airports, and ports as national infrastructure. Congress subsidized agriculture, energy, manufacturing, and finance. Congress took responsibility for national defense, national infrastructure, and national economic development.

But on healthcare, Congress abdicated responsibility. It allowed employers to provide insurance as an accident of wartime policy. It subsidized that accident through the tax code. It locked it into law through ERISA. And then it stepped back and claimed the problem was solved because some Americans had employer coverage.

Seventy years later, 25 million Americans remain uninsured (Centers for Disease Control and Prevention, 2024)[21]. Millions more have inadequate coverage. Medical debt is the leading cause of bankruptcy. Americans die from treatable conditions because they cannot afford care. Meanwhile, healthcare corporations extract trillions in profit from a system Congress refused to govern.

This is not a failure of policy design. It is a failure of government responsibility.

Congress had the power to build a national healthcare system. Every other major nation did. Congress refused. Congress could still do it today. Congress still refuses. Not because such a system is impossible or unaffordable. Canada, Britain, Germany, Japan, and dozens of other nations prove it is neither. Congress refuses because healthcare corporations have captured Congress, and those corporations profit from the current chaos.

The employer-based system was born from accident. It was cemented into law through political choice. And it persists today because Congress has chosen to protect corporate profit over human health.

The historical record is damning. In 1942, employers offered health insurance as a wartime workaround. In 1943, the IRS made that workaround tax-free. In 1974, Congress made it permanent through ERISA. At every decision point, Congress chose to preserve the accidental system rather than create a deliberate one. At every decision point, Congress chose corporate interests over public health.

Seventy years of failure. Seventy years of patches and compromises. Seventy years of refusal to govern. And the result is 25 million uninsured Americans, medical bankruptcy, preventable deaths, and the highest healthcare costs in the world.

This is what happens when Congress abdicates responsibility. This is what happens when government serves corporations instead of people. This is what happens when an accident becomes policy, and policy becomes capture.

The American healthcare system is not broken. It is working exactly as Congress designed it: to extract maximum profit while providing minimum coverage, to subsidize the privileged while abandoning the vulnerable, to preserve corporate power while betraying the public trust.

Congress created this system. Congress maintains this system. Congress could end this system. Congress refuses.

CHAPTER 5
THE ECONOMICS OF ACA CUTS—MYTHS VS. REALITY

The political argument for cutting the Affordable Care Act rests on a single economic claim: the ACA is unsustainable and drains federal resources that could be used for other purposes. This claim is false. It is not supported by federal budget data, economic analysis, or honest accounting.

The real economic question is not whether America can afford the ACA. The real question is whether America can afford to eliminate it. The answer is that cutting the ACA will increase federal spending, not decrease it, and will shift healthcare costs from the federal government to individuals, hospitals, and the broader economy in ways that damage national economic growth.

Congress knows this. Congress does not care. The attack on the ACA is not about fiscal responsibility. It is about ideology and corporate profit.

ACA Costs as a Percentage of the Federal Budget

The Affordable Care Act costs the federal government approximately $125 to $130 billion annually in marketplace subsidies and expanded Medicaid coverage (Congressional Budget Office, 2024)[14]. This figure includes tax credits to help individuals purchase insurance, cost-sharing reductions for low-income enrollees, and federal funding for state Medicaid expansions.

The total federal budget for fiscal year 2024 was $6.75 trillion (Congressional Budget Office, 2024)[83]. The ACA marketplace and Medicaid expansion represents approximately 1.8 percent of total federal spending.

To put this in perspective: the United States spends $886 billion annually on defense (U.S. Department of Defense, 2024)[16]. It spends $1.4 trillion on Social Security (Social Security Administration, 2024)[84]. It spends $874 billion on Medicare for the elderly (Centers for Medicare & Medicaid Services, 2024)[85]. The ACA costs less than the defense budget, less than one-tenth of Social Security, and roughly one-seventh of Medicare.

The political claim that the ACA is bankrupting America is economically absurd. The ACA represents a smaller share of the federal budget than military spending. No credible economist argues that 1.8 percent of federal spending is unsustainable. No credible economist argues that reducing this spending would meaningfully improve federal fiscal health.

Yet Congress treats the ACA as a fiscal emergency while appropriating unlimited funds for military spending that exceeds inflation by 3 to 5 percent annually (Congressional Research Service, 2024)[86]. Congress treats the ACA as a priority for cuts while maintaining tax expenditures for employer-sponsored insurance that cost the federal government $310 billion annually (Congressional Budget Office, 2024)[14]. That subsidy is more than twice the size of the entire ACA budget.

This reveals the truth: the argument for cutting the ACA is not fiscal. It is political and ideological.

Congress protects the $310 billion subsidy for employer insurance because it benefits middle-class workers who vote. Congress attacks the $125 billion ACA subsidy because it benefits people without employer coverage, people who work in retail and food service, people who are self-employed. The difference is not economics. The difference is power.

REAL FISCAL SAVINGS FROM CUTS: NEGLIGIBLE

If the ACA were eliminated entirely, not reformed, not adjusted, but completely eliminated, the federal government would save approximately $125 to $130 billion annually (Congressional Budget Office, 2024)[14]. This would reduce the federal budget deficit by less than 2 percent (Committee for a Responsible Federal Budget, 2024)[87].

But this savings figure assumes that no other federal spending would replace it. This assumption is false.

When the ACA is cut, people do not simply accept being uninsured and stop using healthcare. They continue to require emergency care, hospital treatment, and medical attention. The cost does not disappear. It is simply paid differently.

A person who loses ACA marketplace coverage and becomes uninsured will still visit the emergency room when they have a heart attack, a serious infection, or a traumatic injury. The emergency room is required by federal law to treat them regardless of ability to pay (Emergency Medical Treatment and Labor Act, 1986)[88]. That treatment is still federally funded, but it is paid for through hospital uncompensated care programs, Medicaid emergency services, and federal emergency medical programs. The federal government still bears the cost. The individual bears it as well, through medical debt and bankruptcy.

Research from the Commonwealth Fund and the Urban Institute shows that uninsured people receive less preventive care, have worse health outcomes, and incur higher emergency and inpatient costs than insured people (Commonwealth Fund, 2024)[43]. When people lose insurance coverage, they delay care until conditions become acute. An uninsured diabetic who cannot afford insulin will eventually require hospitalization for diabetic ketoacidosis, a condition that costs $15,000 to $25,000 to treat in a hospital emergency department (American Diabetes Association, 2023)[89]. An insured person with the same diabetes who takes regular insulin might incur $3,000 to $5,000 in annual medication costs.

Eliminating the ACA does not eliminate healthcare costs. It shifts them. The federal government would save on marketplace subsidies while paying more for emergency Medicaid, uncompensated hospital care, and federal emergency medical programs. The individual would pay through medical debt and bankruptcy. The hospital would pay through uncompensated care write-offs.

Federal analysis suggests that the net federal savings from ACA elimination would be close to zero, perhaps $20 to $30 billion at most, after accounting for increased emergency care costs (Urban Institute, 2023)[90]. This is less than 0.5 percent of the federal budget. From a fiscal perspective, eliminating the ACA saves almost nothing.

From an economic perspective, eliminating the ACA costs America far more.

HOW CUTS INCREASE NATIONAL MEDICAL DEBT AND ECONOMIC DAMAGE

Medical debt is the leading cause of personal bankruptcy in the United States. Approximately 66 percent of all bankruptcies are tied to medical debt or medical events (American Journal of Public Health, 2019)[91]. Medical debt exceeds $195 billion in outstanding balances held by collection agencies (Consumer Financial Protection Bureau, 2022)[92].

When people lose health insurance, medical debt increases dramatically. Research from Harvard Law School and the American Journal of Public Health shows that uninsured adults accumulate medical debt at rates 3 to 4 times higher than insured adults (Himmelstein et al., 2019)[93]. When a person is uninsured and requires serious medical treatment, they typically cannot pay the full bill. They are sent to debt collection. Their credit score is damaged. Their ability to borrow money, buy a home, or finance education is compromised.

The ACA reduced medical bankruptcy by approximately 40 percent in states that expanded Medicaid (Health Affairs, 2020)[94]. Patients with insurance coverage could access preventive care, manage chronic conditions, and avoid the catastrophic medical bills that trigger bankruptcy. When people have insurance, they build wealth instead of accumulating debt.

Eliminating the ACA would reverse this trend. Millions of people who currently have insurance would become uninsured. They would incur catastrophic medical bills. They would accumulate medical debt. They would file for bankruptcy. The total medical debt outstanding in America would increase.

This is not abstract economic harm. Medical debt directly damages individual economic security and national economic growth.

When people are managing medical debt, they are not buying homes. When they are not buying homes, the housing market contracts. When the housing market contracts, construction employment falls, property tax revenue falls, and state and local governments lose funding. A 2022 study from the Federal Reserve found that medical debt reduces homeownership rates by 4 to 6 percentage points among affected households (Federal Reserve Board, 2022)[95].

When people are managing medical debt, they are not starting small businesses. When they are not starting businesses, entrepreneurship falls, job creation falls, and economic dynamism falls. Research from the Kauffman Foundation shows that medical debt is among the leading barriers to entrepreneurship in America (Kauffman Foundation, 2021)[96]. Entrepreneurs with medical debt are 35 percent less likely to secure startup financing than entrepreneurs without medical debt.

When people are managing medical debt, they are not investing in their children's education. When they are not investing in education, workforce skills decline, productivity declines, and long-term economic competitiveness declines (National Bureau of Economic Research, 2022)[97].

Medical debt is not just a personal problem. It is a macroeconomic problem. It suppresses consumer spending, business investment, and capital formation. Every dollar spent managing medical debt is a dollar not spent in the broader economy.

The ACA reduced medical debt. Eliminating it would increase medical debt, which would suppress economic growth, reduce business formation, lower home purchases, and damage long-term prosperity.

Congress knows this. Congress does not care. The people harmed by medical debt do not fund congressional campaigns. The insurance companies that profit from unaffordable healthcare do.

HEALTHCARE AS NATIONAL ECONOMIC INFRASTRUCTURE

The United States spends $4.5 trillion annually on healthcare, 17.3 percent of gross domestic product (Centers for Medicare & Medicaid Services, 2024)[98]. This is by far the highest healthcare spending per capita in the world (OECD, 2024)[79]. Healthcare spending exceeds spending on transportation, education, and defense combined.

This spending is not waste. Healthcare is infrastructure. It is as essential to economic function as roads, ports, electricity, and telecommunications. A nation without functioning healthcare cannot function economically.

Consider the basic economic logic: a workforce must be healthy to be productive. Workers with untreated illness are absent more frequently, work with reduced productivity, and suffer shorter working lives than healthy workers (Journal of Occupational and Environmental Medicine, 2023)[99]. Employers benefit from having a healthy workforce, which is why enlightened employers offer health insurance. The entire economy benefits from having a healthy workforce, which is why public healthcare investment is economically rational.

The ACA expanded healthcare access to 24 million people who had been uninsured (Centers for Medicare & Medicaid Services, 2025)[17]. These people are now healthier, more productive, and contribute more to the economy than they did when uninsured. A worker who has insurance and regular preventive care produces more output, earns more income, and pays more taxes than an uninsured worker. An economy with higher health insurance coverage is a more productive economy.

Eliminating the ACA would remove insurance coverage from millions of people. These people would become less healthy, less productive, and contribute less to the economy. The economy would shrink. Tax revenues would fall. Economic growth would decline.

A 2021 study from the RAND Corporation found that expanding health insurance coverage increases labor force participation by 2 to 3 percent among working-age adults (RAND Corporation, 2021)[100]. People with insurance are more willing to work, more able to work, and more productive when they work. They are not missing shifts because of untreated illness. They are not quitting jobs because they fear losing employer coverage. They have the security to change jobs, start businesses, and pursue economic opportunities.

Eliminating the ACA would reduce labor force participation, reduce productivity, and reduce economic output. The Congressional Budget Office estimates that eliminating the ACA would reduce GDP growth by 0.3 to 0.5 percent annually (Congressional Budget Office, 2024)[14]. Over ten years, that amounts to $1.5 to $2.5 trillion in lost economic output.

From the perspective of national economic infrastructure, the ACA is an investment in productivity and growth. The argument for cutting it is not that it is economically inefficient. The argument is ideological: some policymakers believe that healthcare should be purchased privately, not provided through government programs, even if private provision is less efficient.

This is a legitimate political argument. It is not an economic argument. It should not be dressed in fiscal language.

But Congress does dress it in fiscal language. Congress claims the ACA is unaffordable. Congress claims fiscal responsibility requires cuts. Congress is lying. The economic case for the ACA is overwhelming. The fiscal case for eliminating it is nonexistent.

THE FEDERAL BUDGET DEFICIT AND DISHONEST ACCOUNTING

Congress often argues that the ACA must be cut to reduce the federal deficit. This argument is misleading in two ways.

First, it assumes that eliminating government spending on healthcare reduces overall healthcare spending. It does not. It shifts who pays. When the federal government stops paying for ACA marketplace coverage, individuals, hospitals, and state governments pay instead. The total spending does not change. The distribution of burden changes.

If Congress truly wanted to reduce national healthcare spending, it would regulate healthcare prices, control pharmaceutical costs, and enforce antitrust law against healthcare monopolies. Instead, Congress attacks the ACA, the only significant federal healthcare program that actually works within the constraints of the private insurance market. Congress protects healthcare corporate profits while attacking the program that makes insurance affordable for millions of people.

Second, the deficit argument ignores the fact that cutting the ACA would increase other federal healthcare spending. When uninsured people require emergency care, the federal government pays through Medicaid emergency services, federal emergency medical programs, and hospital uncompensated care funding. When elderly people lose insurance and age into Medicare, they have worse health outcomes and cost Medicare more to treat. When working-age people lose insurance and later become disabled, they cost the federal government more through the Social Security Disability Insurance program (Social Security Administration, 2023)[101].

The net federal deficit reduction from cutting the ACA is negligible. The human cost is immense.

The deficit argument is particularly dishonest when one examines what Congress chooses to fund and what Congress chooses to cut. Congress had no problem passing the Tax Cuts and Jobs Act in 2017, which reduced federal revenue by $1.9 trillion over ten years (Committee for a Responsible Federal Budget, 2017)[15]. Congress did not demand offsets. Congress did not claim fiscal crisis. Congress simply gave corporations and wealthy individuals a massive tax cut.

The ACA costs $125 billion per year. The 2017 tax cuts cost $190 billion per year. Congress claims it cannot afford the ACA. Congress had no problem affording tax cuts that were 50 percent larger.

This is not fiscal responsibility. This is class warfare. Congress cuts programs that benefit working people while protecting tax cuts that benefit corporations and the wealthy.

WHY THE ACA IS THE MOST COST-EFFECTIVE HEALTHCARE POLICY CONGRESS HAS ENACTED

The ACA expanded coverage to 24 million people at a cost of $125 to $130 billion annually (Congressional Budget Office, 2024)[14]. This is approximately $5,200 to $5,400 per insured person per year.

For comparison, the cost of employer-sponsored insurance is approximately $23,968 per insured person per year (Kaiser Family Foundation, 2024)[47]. Medicare spends approximately $15,726 per beneficiary per year (Centers for Medicare & Medicaid Services, 2024)[85]. Even Medicaid, America's low-cost insurance program, spends approximately $8,439 per beneficiary per year (Kaiser Family Foundation, 2024)[102].

The ACA achieves coverage at a cost per person that is lower than every other major insurance program in America. This is because ACA marketplace plans have lower overhead costs than employer plans, because marketplace enrollees are younger on average than Medicare beneficiaries, and because competition among insurers in many marketplaces has held down costs (Health Affairs, 2023)[103].

The ACA is not a fiscal burden. It is a fiscal achievement. It expanded coverage more efficiently than any alternative policy Congress has considered.

Eliminating the ACA in the name of fiscal responsibility is economically illiterate. It would eliminate the most cost-effective healthcare program Congress has created and replace it with nothing, leaving 24 million people uninsured and the federal government paying higher costs for emergency care, disability benefits, and other safety-net programs.

The honest economic assessment is this: the federal government cannot afford to cut the ACA. It can only afford to maintain it and expand it further.

But honesty is not the standard Congress applies to healthcare policy. Congress applies one standard to programs that benefit working people and another standard to programs that benefit corporations and the wealthy. Programs for working people must justify every dollar. Programs for corporations are funded without question.

The ACA subsidizes health insurance for 24 million people at $125 billion per year. Congress calls this unaffordable. The tax code subsidizes employer insurance for 160 million people at $310 billion per year (Congressional Budget Office, 2024)[14]. Congress calls this essential.

The difference is not economics. The difference is who benefits. Employer insurance benefits people with stable jobs and middle-class incomes. ACA insurance benefits people without employer coverage, people who are self-employed, people who work in retail and food service. Congress protects the subsidy for the middle class. Congress attacks the subsidy for the working class.

This is not fiscal responsibility. This is betrayal.

THE REAL COST OF ELIMINATING THE ACA

Congress frames the debate as a question of affordability. Can America afford the ACA? The answer is yes. The real question is: can America afford to eliminate it?

The answer is no.

Eliminating the ACA would:

Increase medical debt by tens of billions of dollars annually (American Journal of Public Health, 2019)[91]. Medical debt would rise from $195 billion to well over $250 billion within five years. Bankruptcies would increase by 40 percent. Credit scores would fall. Homeownership would decline. Small business formation would drop.

Reduce labor force participation by 2 to 3 percent (RAND Corporation, 2021)[100]. Millions of workers would leave the workforce or reduce hours because they lack insurance. Productivity would fall. Economic output would decline. GDP growth would slow by 0.3 to 0.5 percent annually, costing the economy $1.5 to $2.5 trillion over ten years (Congressional Budget Office, 2024)[14].

Increase emergency room utilization and hospital uncompensated care (Urban Institute, 2023)[90]. Hospitals would absorb billions in unpaid bills. Rural hospitals, already on the brink of closure, would close at accelerated rates. Access to care would decline, particularly in underserved areas.

Shift healthcare costs from the federal government to individuals, hospitals, and state governments (Commonwealth Fund, 2024)[43]. The federal government would save $125 billion in marketplace subsidies. It would pay $100 billion more in emergency Medicaid, hospital subsidies, and disability programs. The net federal savings would be $20 to $30 billion. Individuals would pay $200 billion more in out-of-pocket costs and medical debt. This is not savings. This is cost-shifting.

Increase preventable deaths by thousands annually (Centers for Disease Control and Prevention, 2024)[21]. Uninsured people delay care. They skip preventive screenings. They ration medications. They die from treatable conditions. Studies estimate that lack of insurance causes 45,000 preventable deaths per year in the United States (American Journal of Public Health, 2009)[104]. Eliminating the ACA would push that number higher.

This is the real cost of eliminating the ACA. Not the fiscal savings Congress claims. The human cost. The economic cost. The cost measured in bankruptcies, business failures, preventable deaths, and economic decline.

Congress knows this. Congress does not care. The people who would die from lack of insurance do not fund congressional campaigns. The insurance companies that profit from unaffordable healthcare do.

The economics of ACA cuts are clear. Eliminating the ACA would damage the American economy, increase medical debt, reduce productivity, and kill thousands of people. The fiscal savings would be negligible. The human cost would be catastrophic.

Congress claims it cannot afford the ACA. The truth is that America cannot afford to eliminate it.

CHAPTER 6
WHEN CONGRESS PROTECTED PEOPLE, NOT MONOPOLIES—THE SHERMAN ACT BETRAYAL

There was a time when Congress acted for the people. There was a time when the federal government broke up monopolies instead of protecting them. There was a time when concentrated corporate power faced consequences instead of campaign contributions.

That time is over.

The Sherman Antitrust Act of 1890 stands as one of the foundational laws of American economic life (Sherman Antitrust Act, 1890)[105]. Congress passed it for one purpose: to stop powerful corporations from dominating entire sectors of the economy, eliminating competition, fixing prices, and strangling the free market. The law prohibits "every contract, combination, or conspiracy in restraint of trade" and addresses any attempt to "monopolize or attempt to monopolize" interstate commerce (U.S. Department of Justice, 2023)[106].

The intent was explicit and unambiguous. Congress understood that concentrated economic power threatened democratic self-governance. When a single corporation controls an entire market, that corporation wields power equal to or greater than state and local governments. The Sherman Act was written to prevent this concentration. It established a principle that remains central to American law: in a democracy, no private corporation should have the power to control a market more completely than the people's elected government (Kovacic & Shapiro, 2000)[107].

The Sherman Act was a promise to the American public that Congress would act as a shield against concentrated economic power. It was a vow that the federal government, not private monopolies, would protect the public interest and ensure that markets remained competitive, prices remained fair, and innovation remained possible.

Today, that promise is being broken.

Healthcare companies now control their markets to a degree that would have made the 1890 Congress recoil in horror. In numerous states, single companies control 75 to 90 percent of entire insurance markets (American Medical Association, 2024)[18]. Hospital systems have consolidated into regional monopolies that have eliminated competition and driven prices upward (Beaulieu et al., 2020)[19]. Three pharmacy benefit managers control 80 percent of all prescription drug negotiations for the entire nation (American Medical Association, 2024)[18]. These are not competitive markets. These are monopolistic markets by any historical or legal standard.

And yet, Congress does nothing.

This is not a failure of law. American antitrust law remains powerful and, when enforced, effective. This is a failure of leadership. Congress has chosen not to enforce the Sherman Act in healthcare while aggressively enforcing it in every other sector of the economy. That choice reveals the fundamental truth: Congress is no longer acting as trustee of the people. Congress is acting as agent of industry.

WHEN GOVERNMENT PROTECTED PEOPLE: THE GREAT ANTITRUST CASES

To understand how far Congress has fallen from its constitutional responsibilities, we must revisit the great antitrust cases of American history. These were moments when the federal government acted with clarity, conviction, and moral courage to dismantle concentrated economic power and restore competition.

Standard Oil (1911): When Congress Had Courage

John D. Rockefeller's Standard Oil Company controlled roughly 90 percent of America's oil refining capacity by 1900 (Yergin, 1991)[108]. It was the most powerful private corporation in American history to that point. Standard Oil did not achieve this dominance through superior efficiency or innovation. It achieved it through ruthless monopolistic practices.

Standard Oil dictated prices to every oil retailer in America. It crushed competitors by undercutting their prices below cost in markets where they competed, while raising prices above cost in markets where they had no competition, a practice called predatory pricing (McGee, 1958)[109]. It manipulated railroad transportation rates, making deals with rail companies to charge competitors higher rates than Standard Oil paid. It acquired refineries not to operate them, but to shut them down and eliminate competition. It abused its dominant position to control one of the most essential industries in the nation.

President Theodore Roosevelt's administration, working with state attorneys general, brought suit against Standard Oil under the Sherman Act. The case reached the Supreme Court in 1911. The Court found that Standard Oil had engaged in a conspiracy in restraint of trade and had illegally monopolized the oil refining market (Standard Oil Co. v. United States, 1911)[110]. The Supreme Court ordered Standard Oil to be broken into 34 independent companies.

The result was dramatic and economically significant.

Prices fell sharply. Competition soared among the newly independent companies. New technologies and innovations emerged. The industry diversified. Consumer welfare improved. The American oil industry became competitive again (Granitz & Klein, 1996)[111].

That is what happens when monopolies are confronted, not coddled. That is what federal enforcement of antitrust law achieves.

Compare this to today. Three pharmacy benefit managers control 80 percent of prescription drug pricing (American Medical Association, 2024)[18]. They dictate which medications Americans can access. They extract profit at every step. They operate with complete impunity. Congress does nothing. The Department of Justice does nothing. The

Federal Trade Commission challenges hospital mergers but leaves PBMs untouched.

In 1911, Congress broke up Standard Oil for controlling 90 percent of one market. In 2025, Congress protects three companies that control 80 percent of prescription drug access for the entire nation.

The law has not changed. Congress has changed.

AT&T (1982): When Government Chose Innovation Over Corporate Power

For most of the twentieth century, AT&T controlled nearly every telephone line in America through its subsidiary, the Bell System (Temin, 1987)[112]. It was the most powerful private communications monopoly in world history. At its peak, AT&T controlled approximately 80 percent of all telephone lines in the United States (Noll & Owen, 1989)[113].

AT&T's monopoly over telecommunications infrastructure gave it power over fundamental communication. It could dictate the terms on which people and businesses communicated. It could set prices without competitive pressure. It could control what technologies were developed and deployed. Consumers had no choice: they could accept AT&T's terms or have no telephone service.

The Department of Justice brought an antitrust suit against AT&T in 1974, alleging that the company had illegally monopolized telecommunications (United States v. AT&T, 1982)[114]. The case took eight years to litigate. In 1982, AT&T agreed to a settlement requiring the breakup of the Bell System into seven independent regional phone companies.

When the federal government forced AT&T's breakup, the results were transformative.

Telecommunication prices plummeted. Long-distance service became affordable. Innovation exploded in telecommunications technology. Mobile technologies were born. Satellite communications developed. Cable companies entered the telecommunications market. Competition drove prices down and innovation up (Crandall & Waverman, 2000)[115].

The modern digital age, the internet, mobile phones, wireless networks, exists because the federal government had the courage and commitment to enforce antitrust law against one of the most powerful corporations in America. Within two decades of AT&T's breakup, technologies that would have been impossible under AT&T's monopoly became standard features of American life.

Compare this to today. Five health insurance companies control coverage for more than 150 million Americans (American Medical Association, 2024)[18]. In 14 states, a single insurer controls more than 75 percent of the entire market. These insurers dictate which doctors Americans can see, which hospitals they can use, which treatments they can receive. They set prices without competitive pressure. They deny claims at rates approaching 20 percent (MoneyGeek, 2025)[44].

In 1982, Congress forced AT&T to break up because it controlled 80 percent of telephone lines. In 2025, Congress protects health insurers that control 75 to 90 percent of entire state markets.

The law has not changed. Congress has changed.

Microsoft (2001): When Government Defended the Digital Future

Microsoft, founded in 1975, became one of the most successful corporations in American history. By the 1990s, it dominated personal computer software and operating systems. Windows was the dominant operating system; Microsoft Office was the dominant productivity suite (Evans et al., 2000)[116].

But Microsoft leveraged this dominance to extend its monopoly into web browsers. The company developed Internet Explorer and then engaged in what the Department of Justice would later describe as anticompetitive practices. Microsoft bundled Internet Explorer with Windows in a way that choked off competition from Netscape Navigator, the leading independent browser at the time (United States v. Microsoft Corp., 2001)[117]. Companies could not easily remove Internet Explorer from Windows. Manufacturers of personal computers faced pressure to distribute Internet Explorer exclusively. Microsoft used its operating system monopoly to create a browser monopoly, and threatened to use both to exclude competitors from emerging web-based technologies.

The Department of Justice, under the Clinton administration, and the Federal Trade Commission brought antitrust suits against Microsoft in 1998. The trial revealed extensive evidence of anticompetitive conduct. The government argued that Microsoft was attempting to monopolize not just operating systems, but the entire software market, including browsers, web services, and media players (Gilbert & Katz, 2001)[118].

While the case settled rather than reaching a final judgment, Microsoft was forced to change its practices. The company was required to make Internet Explorer removable from Windows. It was required to provide access to application programming interfaces that would allow competitors to compete. It was prohibited from using predatory bundling practices.

The outcome was innovation.

Competitive browsers emerged, Firefox, Chrome, Safari, and others, each competing on features and performance rather than leveraging control of the operating system. Web-based technologies flourished. Companies could develop web applications without worrying that Microsoft would leverage its monopoly to exclude them. The tech ecosystem diversified. New technologies, cloud computing, mobile applications, software-as-a-service, emerged from a competitive marketplace rather than being controlled by a single monopolist (Bresnahan & Greenstein, 2014)[119].

Once again, the government acted. Once again, innovation won. Once again, consumers benefited.

Compare this to today. UnitedHealth Group, through its subsidiary Optum, now directly controls more than 90,000 physicians nationwide through owned medical practices (Mathews, 2024)[120]. This represents unprecedented vertical integration in healthcare, a single company controlling both insurance (through UnitedHealth) and the delivery of care (through Optum and its physician practices). UnitedHealth uses this integration to exclude competitors, control referrals, and dictate treatment decisions. The Department of Justice is reviewing the acquisitions but has taken no enforcement action.

In 2001, the federal government sued Microsoft for bundling Internet Explorer with Windows. In 2025, the federal government allows UnitedHealth to bundle insurance with physician practices, hospitals, and pharmacy benefit management, creating a vertically integrated monopoly that controls every aspect of healthcare for millions of Americans.

The law has not changed. Congress has changed.

The Pattern Is Clear and Inescapable

When monopolies threatened innovation, consumer welfare, or national economic health, the government acted, and acted decisively. When corporations acquired too much market power, the federal government used antitrust law to restore competition (Baker, 2019)[121]. The results were consistent: prices fell, innovation accelerated, consumer welfare improved, and new technologies emerged.

Which raises one unavoidable question:

If Congress and the courts would break up oil, telecom, and technology monopolies, why do they allow healthcare monopolies to grow unchecked?

If the Sherman Act applies to Standard Oil, AT&T, and Microsoft, why does it not apply to UnitedHealth, CVS Aetna, and Optum?

If federal antitrust enforcement is legitimate in energy, telecommunications, and software, why is it illegitimate in healthcare, the sector where Americans spend more money than anywhere else on earth?

The only honest answer is that Congress has stopped enforcing antitrust law in healthcare because healthcare corporations have captured Congress through lobbying, campaign contributions, and the promise of post-congressional employment.

CONGRESS STILL ENFORCES ANTITRUST LAW —JUST NOT IN HEALTHCARE

Even today, in 2024 and 2025, the Department of Justice and the Federal Trade Commission are actively litigating major antitrust cases against some of the largest corporations in America. The laws remain strong. The enforcement machinery remains in place. The courts remain willing to act.

United States v. Google (2023–Present)

The federal government successfully proved in federal court that Google illegally maintained a monopoly in online search through exclusionary contracts and market manipulation (United States v. Google LLC, 2023)[122]. Google controls more than 90 percent of the search market. The DOJ alleged that Google paid billions of dollars to device manufacturers and browsers to make Google the default search engine, thereby excluding competitors and maintaining its monopoly (U.S. Department of Justice, 2023)[123].

The case has significant implications for competition and innovation in the digital economy. The government is seeking structural remedies, potentially including the breakup of Google, to restore competition in search and digital advertising.

United States v. Apple (2024–Present)

The Department of Justice alleges that Apple maintains an illegal monopoly in smartphones and app distribution through restrictive App Store rules, anticompetitive fees, and ecosystem lock-in (U.S. Department of Justice, 2024)[124]. Apple's App Store takes a 30 percent commission on purchases made through the store, which the DOJ argues is possible only because Apple has monopoly power that prevents consumers from easily switching to alternative platforms. The case alleges that Apple uses its control of the App Store to exclude competitors and maintain its dominant market position.

FTC v. Amazon (2023–Present)

The Federal Trade Commission accuses Amazon of predatory pricing, using marketplace data to unfairly compete against third-party sellers, and structuring its marketplace to trap both buyers and sellers in anti-competitive arrangements (Federal Trade Commission, 2023)[125].

Amazon's marketplace dominance in e-commerce gives it power to exclude competitors and control prices.

Meta (Facebook) Enforcement Actions

Ongoing regulatory challenges and proposed actions focus on Meta acquiring emerging competitors, particularly Instagram and WhatsApp, to eliminate future threats to its dominance in social media (Federal Trade Commission, 2020)[126]. Regulators argue that Meta is attempting to monopolize social media by acquiring potential competitors rather than competing on features and performance.

So the government still acts. The courts still care about competition. The laws still work in sector after sector of the American economy.

But not in healthcare insurance.

Healthcare insurers have consolidated their markets so aggressively that in nearly every state, only one or two carriers control the majority of the market. In several states, one insurer controls more than 75 percent of the entire market (American Medical Association, 2024)[18]. This level of concentration would trigger federal action in any other sector. This level of concentration would spark investigations, legal challenges, and potential enforcement actions in energy, technology, telecommunications, and transportation.

In healthcare?

Nothing happens. Congress remains silent. The FTC and DOJ remain inactive in the insurance market itself, though they challenge hospital mergers. Healthcare corporations continue consolidating, raising prices, and reducing consumer choice with complete impunity.

HEALTHCARE MONOPOLIES: THE MOST DANGEROUS AND MOST IGNORED

Here is the reality Congress does not want to confront, does not discuss publicly, and does not act upon.

Insurer Market Concentration: Monopoly Power by State

In 47 states, the top two health insurers control more than 50 percent of the market. In 14 states, a single insurer controls more than 75 percent of the entire market (American Medical Association, 2024)[18]. In some states, the concentration is even more extreme: in Wisconsin, UnitedHealth controls approximately 40 percent of the market and Anthem controls approximately 30 percent, meaning two companies control 70 percent of health insurance for the entire state's population.

The national landscape is dominated by five companies: UnitedHealth Group, Anthem, Aetna (now CVS Aetna), Cigna, and Humana. Together, these five companies insure more than 150 million Americans, more than half the population. This level of concentration would trigger federal action in any other sector.

In healthcare?

Nothing happens.

A person living in a state with 75 percent insurer concentration has essentially no choice. They can accept the dominant insurer's terms or go uninsured. There is no meaningful market. There is no competition. There is no choice. The insurer can set prices without competitive pressure because consumers have nowhere else to go.

This is textbook monopoly. This is exactly what the Sherman Act was written to prevent. And Congress does nothing.

Hospital Consolidation: Prices Rise, Quality Stagnates, Workers Suffer

Between 2010 and 2024, nearly 1,600 hospitals merged into larger systems or were acquired by existing hospital chains (American Hospital Association, 2024)[127]. This represents an unprecedented consolidation of the nation's hospital infrastructure. Hospitals that had been independent are now part of massive regional or national hospital systems.

Post-merger studies consistently show the same pattern.

Prices rise by 20 to 50 percent after hospital mergers (Cooper et al.,

2019)[128]. Patients in consolidated hospital markets pay significantly more for the same procedures than patients in competitive markets. A study published in the American Economic Review found that hospital consolidation in a single market resulted in price increases of 5 to 30 percent for the same procedures, without any corresponding improvement in patient outcomes. Another study found that mergers between large hospital systems resulted in price increases averaging 30 percent within five years.

Patient outcomes do not improve after hospital consolidation (Beaulieu et al., 2020)[19]. In fact, some studies show that consolidation may reduce quality. When hospitals merge, they often eliminate redundancies, including cutting back on specialists, consolidating services, and closing facilities in less profitable areas. This harms patients by reducing access and reducing the breadth of services available.

Wages for nurses and hospital staff stagnate or decline after consolidation (Prager & Schmitt, 2021)[129]. When hospitals consolidate, they often use their enhanced market power to suppress wages. Consolidated hospital systems are in a stronger negotiating position with respect to labor, and they often use this position to hold down wages. Meanwhile, administrators and executives at consolidated hospital systems see their compensation increase substantially.

Congress has watched this consolidation accelerate for over a decade and taken no action to stop it. The Federal Trade Commission has challenged some hospital mergers, but many have been allowed to proceed. The pattern is clear: hospital consolidation raises prices, reduces quality, suppresses wages, and enriches executives. It is textbook monopolistic behavior.

And Congress does nothing.

Pharmacy Benefit Managers: Life-and-Death Decisions Made by Unaccountable Monopolies

Three pharmacy benefit managers, CVS Caremark, Express Scripts (owned by Cigna), and Optum Rx (owned by UnitedHealth), control more than 80 percent of all prescription drug negotiations in America (American Medical Association, 2024)[18]. PBMs are middlemen between insurance companies, pharmaceutical manufacturers, hospitals, and pharmacies. They decide which drugs are covered, which drugs are excluded, and how much patients pay at the pharmacy.

This is monopoly power with life-and-death consequences.

A patient whose medication is not on a PBM's formulary (the list of covered drugs) cannot afford to buy it. They must either accept a different medication that the PBM has approved or pay thousands of dollars out of pocket. The PBM's decision about which drugs to cover directly affects which drugs patients take and, therefore, affects patient health outcomes.

PBMs also negotiate rebates from pharmaceutical manufacturers. These rebates are supposed to lower drug costs for patients. Instead, PBMs often keep the rebates for themselves and raise patient copayments and coinsurance (Fein, 2023)[130]. The result is that manufacturers offer large rebates to PBMs, PBMs keep the money, and patients pay high prices at the pharmacy.

The consolidation of PBMs into three companies with combined market share of more than 80 percent has created a system where three corporations make healthcare decisions for hundreds of millions of Americans. These decisions are made without transparency, without accountability, and without recourse for patients who disagree.

This is monopoly power. This meets every legal definition of monopoly under the Sherman Act. And Congress does nothing.

WHY IS HEALTHCARE EXEMPT FROM ANTITRUST ACCOUNTABILITY?

There is one honest answer to why healthcare monopolies are tolerated while technology, energy, and telecommunications monopolies are prosecuted.

Healthcare corporations have the largest lobbying presence in Washington of any industry sector.

The health sector, including insurance companies, pharmaceutical manufacturers, hospital systems, and PBMs, spent $743.9 million on federal lobbying in 2024 (OpenSecrets, 2025)[1]. This outspends defense contractors, technology companies, energy companies, Wall Street, agriculture, transportation, and telecommunications.

Healthcare is the most powerful corporate lobby in America. The American Hospital Association, America's Health Insurance Plans (AHIP), the Pharmaceutical Research and Manufacturers of America (PhRMA), the American Medical Association, and various PBM lobbying groups collectively represent hundreds of thousands of healthcare industry employees and interests.

Pharmaceutical manufacturers alone have spent over $6.1 billion on federal lobbying since 1999 (OpenSecrets, 2025)[2]. The pharmaceutical lobby has been among the most successful in congressional history, winning nearly every legislative battle it has fought.

And Congress is captured by it.

Not captured in a philosophical sense or a rhetorical sense. Captured in a literal, financial, measurable sense.

Campaign Donations: Healthcare industry employees, executives, and PACs donate hundreds of millions of dollars to political campaigns every election cycle. Members of Congress who vote against healthcare industry interests face well-funded primary opponents. Members of Congress who vote for healthcare industry interests receive substantial campaign support.

Super PAC Contributions: Healthcare corporations fund Super PACs that support or oppose specific candidates based on their voting record on healthcare issues. A member of Congress who votes to regulate healthcare corporations faces well-funded Super PAC opposition in their next election.

Post-Congressional Employment: Hundreds of former members of Congress work as lobbyists, consultants, and executives for healthcare corporations after leaving office (Public Citizen, 2019)[9]. A member of Congress who votes against healthcare industry interests reduces their post-congressional earning potential. This creates a direct financial incentive to vote for healthcare industry interests while in office.

Sponsored Research: Healthcare corporations fund research at universities, think tanks, and policy organizations that produce conclusions favorable to the healthcare industry. Research funded by the pharmaceutical industry consistently finds that drug prices are justified. Research funded by insurance companies consistently finds that consolidation is beneficial. This creates intellectual infrastructure supporting industry positions.

Industry-Written Legislation: Healthcare industry lobbyists draft legislation that Congress then passes into law with minimal modification. Some provisions of the Affordable Care Act, for example, were drafted by insurance industry lobbyists. The result is legislation that appears to regulate the industry but actually benefits the industry.

Lobbyist-Crafted Talking Points: Members of Congress use talking points prepared by healthcare industry lobbyists when defending healthcare industry positions on the floor of Congress or in public statements. These talking points are not the member's own analysis. They are industry talking points designed to defend industry profits.

This is why healthcare monopolies are tolerated. This is why ACA subsidies are attacked while insurer profits soar. This is why Americans pay more for healthcare than any nation on earth, despite having no better health outcomes than other developed nations.

Healthcare monopolies exist today for the same reason Standard Oil existed in 1900: Congress stopped protecting the people and started protecting the monopolies.

The Sherman Act has not weakened. The laws are still on the books. The courts are still willing to enforce them. The Department of Justice and Federal Trade Commission still have the power to bring cases.

What has changed is Congress. Congress has chosen not to enforce antitrust law in healthcare. Congress has chosen to tolerate monopolies in healthcare that it would never tolerate in any other sector. Congress has chosen to prioritize healthcare industry profits over consumer welfare, affordability, and choice.

THE REFRAIN THAT MUST BE REPEATED: CONGRESS IS THE CRISIS

In each chapter of this book, one conclusion repeats with painful consistency.

Congress is no longer acting as steward, trustee, or guardian of the American people. Instead, Congress is acting as agent of industry.

Congress legislates for donors, not voters. Congress preserves monopolies that raise prices instead of breaking them up. Congress sabotages programs that help the public and defends programs that enrich the wealthy. Congress dismantles policies that protect families and preserves the power of corporations over the health of the nation.

This is not a failure of the ACA. The ACA works. It expanded coverage. It reduced the uninsured rate. It created a functioning marketplace for health insurance.

This is not a failure of the American people. Americans want affordable healthcare. Americans want competition. Americans want choice. Americans want Congress to enforce the law.

This is not a failure of policy. American antitrust law is among the most powerful and effective antitrust laws in the world. When Congress enforces it, it works.

This is a failure of representation. Congress is not representing the people. Congress is representing the corporations.

Democracy is not at risk because of bad presidents or bad policies. Democracy is at risk because the people we elect no longer represent us. Democracy is at risk because Congress has been captured by corporate interests. Democracy is at risk because the representatives of the people have become agents of industry.

If Congress enforced the Sherman Act in healthcare the way it enforces it in technology, energy, and communications, the American healthcare crisis would be over. Healthcare prices would fall. Healthcare quality would improve. Healthcare innovation would accelerate. Patients would have choice and competition would protect consumer interests.

If Congress acted as trustees of the people's money, healthcare would be affordable. Federal spending on healthcare would decrease because unnecessary administrative overhead, excessive executive compensation, and monopolistic pricing would disappear. Healthcare corporations would compete on efficiency and quality instead of competing on how to manipulate the system to maximize profits.

If Congress acted with the courage of 1911 (Standard Oil), 1982 (AT&T), or 2001 (Microsoft), healthcare monopolies would fall. These are precedents from American history, not distant fantasies. Congress has broken up monopolies before. Congress knows how to do this. Congress simply chooses not to.

If Congress acted at all on healthcare monopolies, millions of Americans would not be one illness away from bankruptcy. They would have a choice. They would have affordable care. They would have the security that comes with knowing that competition is protecting their interests and that their government is protecting their welfare.

Congress is the crisis. Congress is the reason healthcare is broken. Congress is the barrier to reform. And until Congress changes, until members of Congress start representing voters instead of donors, until Congress stops being captured by industry, until Congress starts enforcing laws instead of protecting monopolies, nothing else will change.

The law is ready. The courts are ready. The precedent is clear. What is missing is the political will of Congress to act.

That political will will not emerge until the American people demand it. Until the people who are being harmed by healthcare monopolies make it clear to Congress that they will not tolerate a government that protects monopolies. Until the people vote out members of Congress who vote to protect healthcare industry profits. Until the people reclaim their democracy from the corporations that have captured it.

CHAPTER 7

INSURER, HOSPITAL, AND PBM CONSOLIDATION —MARKET POWER BY THE NUMBERS

The debate over healthcare reform circles back to the same tired refrain: "Let the private market fix it." That argument assumes a market that functions like a market. What exists is not a competitive ecosystem. It is a consolidated structure of insurers, hospital systems, and pharmacy benefit managers operating with systemic market power that no employer, small business, or individual patient can counter.

Competition requires meaningful choice. Healthcare has been systematically stripped of it. In region after region, one or two insurers dominate enrollment, one or two hospital systems dominate care delivery, and three PBMs control the prescription drug pipeline. These entities do not compete on price. They set the price environment itself. Consumers do not negotiate. Employers absorb the increases. Workers lose wages. Patients absorb the shock.

If prior chapters exposed the ideological contradictions and policy failures that produced this landscape, this chapter exposes the machine underneath. Who controls the levers. How concentrated that control has become. Why this structure makes authentic market regulation mathematically impossible. What appears to be a fragmented system of thousands of hospitals and plans is a small cluster of corporate networks coordinating pricing, access, and reimbursement behind closed doors.

Private healthcare is not failing because government intruded into a functional market. Private healthcare is failing because government abandoned its duty to preserve competition and allowed consolidation to metastasize into dominance.

This was not an accident. It was a policy choice.

MARKET CONCENTRATION TABLES: WHO CONTROLS THE INSURANCE MARKET

Employer-based health insurance did not arise from consumer preference, market innovation, or democratic choice. It was a policy accident of World War II. Federal wage controls prevented employers from raising salaries to compete for scarce labor, so businesses began offering health benefits instead. The Internal Revenue Service later ruled those benefits tax-exempt, locking the system into place (Internal Revenue Service, 1943)[64]. What began as a temporary wartime workaround hardened into a permanent financing structure that the private insurance industry would eventually dominate, consolidate, and weaponize for profit.

This matters because it dismantles the central myth of American healthcare: that today's private insurance system evolved through rational market choice. It did not. It evolved through regulatory silence and political neglect. From that moment forward, insurers gained a structurally protected role between the public and medical care, one no other developed nation ever intentionally created at national scale.

Over the next eighty years, insurers followed a predictable corporate playbook: acquire regional competitors, eliminate local plans, lock in employer groups, vertically integrate into pharmacy, data, and provider ownership. The end result is not a market. It is an oligopoly with monopoly behavior at the state level, the same pattern that defined the railroad, oil, and steel trusts of the early 1900s.

The American Medical Association's 2023 "Competition in Health Insurance" report provides one of the clearest empirical pictures of this concentration. In 383 of 384 U.S. metropolitan statistical areas, at least one insurer controls 30 percent or more of the market (American Medical Association, 2024)[18]. In nearly half of all metro areas, a single insurer controls over 50 percent. In Alabama, Blue Cross Blue Shield controls 86 percent of the entire commercial insurance market. In Michigan, a single carrier commands nearly 70 percent. In North Dakota, concentration exceeds 80 percent.

Under the Department of Justice and Federal Trade Commission's Horizontal Merger Guidelines, any market with a Herfindahl-Hirschman Index above 2,500 is considered highly concentrated (U.S. Department of Justice, 2010)[131]. Markets above 4,000 are considered functionally monopolistic. Most state insurance markets now exceed 5,000.

No sector meeting these thresholds would escape antitrust scrutiny unless it is healthcare.

No neutral economist would describe this environment as competitive. It is dominance, sustained by regulatory omission and political protection.

The same policymakers who attack the ACA for "limiting choice" remain silent as private insurers eliminate that choice in nearly every U.S. state. The contradiction is not academic. It is operational. The government is condemned for expanding access, while private dominance goes unchallenged for eliminating alternatives.

Market share alone no longer captures the real structure of control. The modern insurer is no longer just an insurer. It is a data broker, care provider, PBM, pharmacy chain, and risk manager rolled into one corporate entity.

The five dominant firms—UnitedHealth Group, Elevance Health (Anthem), CVS Health/Aetna, Cigna, and Humana—now control most of the commercial insurance market and most of the drug pricing infrastructure and an expanding share of physician practices and outpatient facilities.

UnitedHealth Group alone controls 152 million patient records through Optum's data platforms, more than 70,000 physicians through Optum Health, and the nation's largest PBM, OptumRx, which manages prescriptions for roughly one-third of all Americans (Mathews, 2024)[120].

This structure allows one corporation to design the insurance product, set the provider network, control the pharmacy benefit, manage the physician group, process the claims, and own the data generated at every step.

That is not insurance. That is vertical market capture across the full healthcare supply chain.

When one firm can both deny your claim and employ your doctor, the consumer has no leverage. When that same firm also controls the pharmacy benefit and drug access, it extracts revenue at every transaction point with no competitive pressure to reduce cost or improve quality.

This is the opposite of a free market. It is a closed economic loop.

Even where two or three insurers technically operate, consumers do not exercise real choice. Most Americans receive insurance only through their employer. Employers choose plans based on premium cost, not network breadth or clinical quality. Employees inherit whatever network, deductible structure, and formulary the employer selected.

A so-called "choice" among three insurers becomes meaningless when all three share the same hospital systems, all three use the same dominant PBMs, and all three restrict networks to the same consolidated provider groups.

This is why premiums rise even when multiple insurers are present. They are not independent competitors. They are participants in the same consolidated ecosystem.

When lawmakers claim that government involvement "threatens choice," they are addressing a hypothetical future while ignoring a documented present. The monopolies already exist. The data is not speculative. The concentration is not marginal. It is overwhelming.

The United States does not suffer from too much government control of healthcare. It suffers from too little market discipline imposed on private healthcare power.

Congress did not merely allow this to happen. Congress structured the legal and regulatory environment that made it inevitable and then looked away as the market collapsed into permanent dominance.

HOSPITAL MERGER MAPS: A DECADE OF CONSOLIDATION

Hospitals have followed the same path as insurers, PBMs, and pharmaceutical distributors. Scale first. Market power second. Price control last. Since 2010, the United States has lived through one of the most aggressive waves of hospital consolidation in modern history. What once looked like a mixed ecology of nonprofit community hospitals, faith-based providers, and regional medical centers has hardened into a landscape dominated by a small number of multi-state corporate systems.

More than 1,600 hospital mergers occurred between 2010 and 2022 (Gaynor, Mostashari & Ginsburg, 2017)[132]. Nearly two-thirds of all U.S. hospitals are now owned by a system rather than operating independently (American Hospital Association, 2024)[127]. Most telling of all, 90 percent of metropolitan hospital markets are now classified as "highly concentrated" under DOJ and FTC antitrust guidelines (Fulton, 2017)[133].

Under federal standards, a highly concentrated market is not merely competitive with a few large players. It is a market in which competition no longer disciplines price or behavior. A small number of firms dictate contract terms, shape reimbursement rates, block new entrants, and control referral patterns across entire regions.

When hospital ownership is mapped geographically, consolidation is not abstract; it is spatial and structural. Entire regions are now controlled by two or three systems that operate hospitals, outpatient clinics, ambulatory surgery centers, imaging facilities, physician groups, and urgent-care networks under a single corporate umbrella.

In the Southeast, a handful of systems dominate multi-state territories. In the Midwest, once-independent rural hospitals are now controlled by distant urban conglomerates. In states such as California, Texas, Florida, and New York, mega-systems own dense webs of facilities that stretch across dozens of counties. In many metropolitan areas, the top two systems now control more than 70 to 80 percent of all inpatient capacity (Berenson, Ginsburg & Christianson, 2012)[134].

This level of concentration transforms how healthcare markets function. Employers lose leverage in negotiations. Insurers lose credible threats of network exclusion. Physicians become economically dependent on a single dominant employer. Patients retain the illusion of choice, but the underlying ownership is the same. Prices cease to be disciplined by competition and instead become administratively set by market power.

Hospitals no longer operate as community institutions embedded in local accountability. They operate as financial networks optimized for revenue extraction across geography.

Hospital systems defend consolidation with three recurring claims: survival, efficiency, and quality. Mergers, they argue, allow struggling hospitals to stay open, reduce duplicated services, and improve care through shared infrastructure and expertise. These claims dominate regulatory filings and media statements. They do not survive contact with the data.

Independent research tells a far less generous story. After hospital mergers, inpatient prices rise between 6 and 18 percent on average (Cooper et al., 2019)[128]. Outpatient prices increase even more sharply, between 9 and 45 percent depending on market structure and physician acquisition patterns. Yet across these same post-merger periods, core quality metrics—mortality rates, readmissions, and hospital-acquired infection rates—remain flat or deteriorate (Beaulieu et al., 2020)[19].

The pattern is consistent and durable across states, payer mixes, and ownership models. Prices rise. Quality does not improve in proportion. Sometimes it worsens.

What follows logically is unavoidable: the primary effect of consolidation is not clinical improvement. It is greater pricing leverage over payers. The economic value of the merger is not generated by better medicine. It is generated by enhanced bargaining power.

Hospital mergers do not primarily optimize care delivery. They optimize negotiating position. Once systems reach regional dominance, they gain the power to impose take-it-or-leave-it contracts on insurers and employers. Networks become non-excludable. Payers must accept higher rates because there is no viable alternative hospital system with sufficient geographic coverage.

Facility fees proliferate. Site-of-service billing strategies shift ordinary outpatient care into higher-paid hospital settings. Physician practices, once independent, become vertically integrated extensions of hospital billing structures. The same office visit that once generated a modest professional fee now produces a combined physician charge plus a hospital facility charge without any change in the care delivered.

Revenue growth after consolidation does not come from operational breakthroughs. It comes from reclassification, contract leverage, and billing intensity. The hospital becomes not only a site of care, but a toll gate within a controlled network.

Consolidation also reshapes which services survive within a community. After acquisitions, systems routinely conduct profitability audits of service lines. Units that fail to meet margin thresholds are closed or consolidated elsewhere. This logic applies even when the service is medically essential to the surrounding population.

Labor and delivery units disappear in rural counties. Behavioral health wards close in poor urban regions. Emergency departments shrink or vanish in areas where reimbursement is weak and payer mix is unfavorable. Trauma services migrate toward wealthier catchment areas with better commercial insurance penetration.

Once a hospital becomes a node in a distant corporate network, community health needs lose priority to system-wide return on investment. Access follows capital. Care deserts form not because medicine is impossible, but because it is insufficiently profitable.

This is how the United States, the highest-spending healthcare system in the world, simultaneously produces world-class tertiary care and widespread primary-care scarcity.

Hospital consolidation also reshapes labor markets in ways that rarely enter public discussion. When one or two systems dominate an entire region, the hospital labor market becomes functionally monopsonistic. Nurses, technicians, therapists, and even physicians face a single dominant buyer of labor.

In such markets, wages stagnate despite rising hospital revenues (Prager & Schmitt, 2021)[129]. Worker mobility collapses because switching employers no longer changes the employer in any meaningful sense. Contract terms become standardized downward. Staffing ratios tighten. Burnout accelerates. Meanwhile, corporate overhead and executive compensation expand in parallel with system size and revenue.

The paradox is striking. Healthcare employment grows. Healthcare revenue grows faster. Yet the frontline workforce loses bargaining power as consolidation deepens. The financial surplus generated by market dominance does not flow toward patient care or clinical labor. It flows upward into administrative layers and capital expansion.

The DOJ and FTC possess full legal authority to block anticompetitive hospital mergers. Yet for decades, enforcement remained weak, fragmented, and largely reactive. From 2000 through 2020, only a small fraction of hospital mergers faced serious federal challenge (Dafny, 2014)[135]. Most were approved with minimal conditions. Many proceeded without any formal opposition at all.

Even when agencies intervened, challenges often occurred after consolidation effects had already materialized. Courts frequently accepted hospital claims of financial distress, rural necessity, or speculative efficiency gains. Behavioral remedies, when imposed, proved difficult to monitor and easy to evade.

Meanwhile, hospital systems invested heavily in lobbying, state-level certificate-of-need protections, and public narratives of fragility. Regulators moved slowly. Capital moved quickly. By the time antitrust scrutiny intensified in the late 2010s, the damage was no longer episodic. It was structural.

The political contradiction is now impossible to ignore. The same voices that insist government regulation destroys innovation have spent decades observing a largely unregulated wave of private hospital consolidation. During that same period, private systems acquired competitors, centralized billing power, closed unprofitable services, expanded market dominance, and raised prices at a pace far exceeding inflation.

If consolidation worked as advertised, insurance premiums would have stabilized or fallen. Instead, premiums doubled. Employer-sponsored coverage absorbed the shock through higher deductibles and cost shifting. Households paid the rest through stagnant wages and rising out-of-pocket exposure.

Premium inflation tracks hospital price growth far more closely than it tracks medical innovation, workforce expansion, or demographic change. This is not a technology-driven cost curve. It is a market-power-driven cost curve.

Hospital consolidation did not emerge by accident. It emerged because antitrust enforcement was weakened, corporate healthcare was ideologically protected, community hospitals were financially starved, and private equity capital was given unrestricted entry into essential infrastructure. Policy did not merely fail to stop consolidation. It actively enabled it through neglect and permissiveness.

The United States now operates inside a hospital marketplace where dominant systems dictate prices, suppress labor competition, restrict access, and re-engineer care delivery around revenue optimization rather than public health.

This is not a failure of "too much government." It is the long-term outcome of government choosing not to govern market power.

PBM DOMINANCE CHARTS: THE HIDDEN GIANTS BEHIND DRUG PRICES

If insurers control the front end of healthcare, pharmacy benefit managers control the back end, the drug pipeline that determines which medications Americans can access, how much they pay at the counter, and which manufacturers survive in the marketplace. Most patients have never heard of PBMs. Most policymakers barely understand how they function. Yet these entities now sit at the financial choke point of the entire pharmaceutical system.

Today, three PBMs control nearly 80 percent of all prescriptions in the United States: CVS Caremark, Express Scripts, and OptumRx (Fein, 2023)[130]. Each is owned by or formally integrated into a major health insurance conglomerate. Each operates at a scale that would trigger antitrust alarms in nearly any other sector of the economy. Each touches the majority of Americans every time they fill a prescription, often without their knowledge.

This level of concentration is not incidental. It is structural. It is the result of two decades of vertical integration, regulatory blind spots, and financial engineering that transformed PBMs from administrative processors into central price-setting institutions.

PBMs were originally created to perform modest administrative functions: processing claims, managing pharmacy networks, and negotiating limited discounts on behalf of insurers. They were not designed to control formularies, shape market competition, or extract multi-billion-dollar revenue streams from opaque financial spreads. Yet that is precisely what they now do.

They are no longer middlemen. They are market governors.

Because three firms manage almost four out of every five prescriptions, drug manufacturers no longer negotiate with a competitive field of buyers. They negotiate with a triopoly. Access to patients flows through a narrow set of corporate gates. A manufacturer can develop a clinically superior drug, receive FDA approval, and still be effectively locked out of the U.S. market if it fails to satisfy the pricing demands of a dominant PBM.

Formularies—the lists of drugs that insurance plans will cover—are designed and controlled by PBMs. Placement on a preferred tier means commercial survival. Exclusion means rapid market death. The decision is not governed purely by therapeutic value. It is governed by rebate maximization.

Rebates are the quiet engine of PBM power. Manufacturers pay PBMs large after-the-fact payments in exchange for favorable formulary placement. These payments do not reduce the price at the pharmacy counter. They flow backward through the PBM to insurers and corporate parents, often never reaching patients at all. The higher the list price, the larger the rebate base. The incentive structure rewards inflation, not restraint.

This is the central paradox of the modern drug market: PBMs profit when drug prices rise, not when they fall.

Patients experience only the surface outcome—higher list prices and rising out-of-pocket costs. Employers experience rising drug spend. Governments experience expanding Medicaid and Medicare Part D obligations. The financial internals remain sealed behind contractual confidentiality and non-disclosure agreements that block public auditing.

The negotiating leverage of dominant PBMs is often described as "market bargaining." That description is too gentle. What exists in practice is closer to coercive purchasing power enabled by consolidated market access.

A manufacturer that refuses to provide the requested rebate risks exclusion from major formularies that control enormous pools of covered lives. In practical terms, that exclusion means the loss of tens of millions of patients overnight. For specialty drugs, the consequences are even more severe. PBMs increasingly control the specialty pharmacy channel as well, allowing them to steer high-cost therapies through their own captive distribution systems.

This is not a neutral market interaction between buyer and seller. It is the exercise of gatekeeping authority over population-level access to medicine. It transforms PBMs from negotiators into private regulatory entities with the power to shape which therapies reach the public and under what financial terms.

The manufacturer that pays more wins access. The manufacturer that pays less loses visibility. The patient pays the difference.

The PBM market would already be dangerously concentrated even if these firms were independent. They are not. Each dominant PBM is embedded within a vertically integrated health conglomerate that controls multiple layers of the healthcare delivery and financing stack.

CVS Caremark sits inside CVS Health, which owns a national retail pharmacy chain, an insurance company (Aetna), specialty pharmacies, data analytics platforms, and clinical service networks. Express Scripts is owned by Cigna. OptumRx is part of UnitedHealth Group, the largest health insurer in the country and the parent of Optum's vast physician, data, and care-delivery subsidiaries.

This integration collapses traditional market boundaries. The same corporate entity now designs insurance benefits, decides which drugs are covered, dispenses those drugs through captive pharmacies, analyzes patient data, and negotiates manufacturer pricing. Each layer reinforces the others. Each narrows external competition.

What once were separate negotiating interests—insurer versus PBM, PBM versus pharmacy, pharmacy versus manufacturer—now operate under the same corporate roof. Internal transfer pricing replaces arm's-length market discipline. Market checks dissolve into internal accounting.

The result is not efficiency in the public-interest sense. It is corporate self-dealing at scale.

Independent pharmacies stand on the frontline of this power shift. As PBMs consolidated, reimbursement rates to community pharmacies declined. Spread pricing—where PBMs bill insurers one amount while reimbursing pharmacies a lower amount and capture the difference—became a primary profit center (Sood et al., 2017)[136]. Thousands of independent pharmacies closed as margins collapsed under opaque and non-negotiable contracts.

Manufacturers are squeezed from the opposite side. They face a narrow buyer field that demands ever-larger rebates to access the same patient populations. Development costs rise. Prices are inflated to fund rebates. The patient, employer, and taxpayer absorb the consequences.

The system becomes a circular extraction loop. Higher list prices fund higher rebates. Higher rebates reinforce PBM dominance. Dominance ensures that prices never fall.

In a functioning competitive market, multiple buyers discipline seller pricing. In the PBM market, three dominant buyers distort pricing upward because their profit is linked to price differentials rather than net cost containment.

Even when multiple therapeutic alternatives exist, PBMs do not select the lowest-cost option for patients. They select the option that offers the most lucrative rebate stream. Over time, this behavior warps manufacturer pricing strategies. Drug companies do not compete primarily on net price. They compete on rebate generosity coupled with inflated list pricing.

This inversion would be illegal in most regulated procurement markets. It persists here because PBMs operate in a regulatory gray zone, classified neither as insurers nor as manufacturers nor as fiduciaries with transparent duties to patients.

They operate as private financial arbitrage engines inside a public health system.

Beyond pricing, PBMs now control unmatched volumes of patient data. Through integrated insurance and pharmacy platforms, they track prescribing behavior, medication adherence, treatment switching, and long-term utilization patterns across millions of lives. This data informs more aggressive formulary engineering, prior authorization algorithms, and step-therapy requirements that shape clinical behavior.

Physicians experience this as "utilization management." Patients experience it as delayed access, forced drug switching, and administrative exhaustion. Underneath both experiences sits a data-driven financial optimization model directed not by clinical boards but by corporate revenue strategies.

Medicine becomes actuarialized. Not optimized for outcome. Optimized for margin.

Despite this scale of consolidation and control, PBMs operate with surprisingly limited direct regulatory oversight. Congressional hearings occur episodically. Industry executives testify, promise transparency, then retreat behind proprietary confidentiality. State-level reforms chip at narrow practices such as spread pricing in Medicaid networks, but fail to confront national dominance.

Meanwhile, the same political voices that describe government healthcare as inherently inefficient accept without objection the existence of private administrative monopolies that actively engineer drug prices upward. This contradiction is rarely confronted directly.

When government sets prices, it is called "interference." When three private corporations set prices behind closed doors, it is called "the market."

The distinction is rhetorical, not economic.

THE IMPACT ON PREMIUMS AND OUTCOMES

Once healthcare market power concentrates to this degree, the results are no longer speculative. They are mechanical. Prices rise because they can. Access narrows because it must. Risk shifts downward because the dominant players are structurally insulated from it. What remains is a system that privatizes profit while socializing instability across households, employers, and state budgets.

Healthcare did not become expensive because Americans

suddenly became sicker. It became expensive because the entities that control pricing no longer face functional competition. What we are observing is not the failure of markets in theory. It is the predictable behavior of markets once they are no longer competitive in fact.

The modern American premium is no longer a fringe expense. It is now one of the largest fixed costs in the household and business balance sheet. According to the 2024 Kaiser Family Foundation Employer Health Benefits Survey, the average annual premium for employer-sponsored family coverage now exceeds $24,000 per year (Kaiser Family Foundation, 2024)[137].

That number alone should end any serious debate about affordability.

Premium growth has persistently outpaced both inflation and wage growth for more than two decades. This divergence did not coincide with dramatic improvements in population health. It coincided with the consolidation of hospitals, insurers, and PBMs into pricing oligopolies. The premium is not the price of care. It is the price of market power.

Employers absorb this first. Workers absorb what remains. The household never sees the full cost because the premium is fragmented between paycheck deductions, employer contributions, and foregone wage increases. Economically, it is the same burden. A $24,000 premium is still a $24,000 premium, regardless of how it is disguised on a pay stub.

What consolidation produced was not lower operating costs passed on to consumers, but higher negotiating leverage passed on as higher premiums.

As premiums rose beyond political tolerance, insurers did not reduce their margins. They shifted risk downward. The modern insurance product is no longer designed primarily to protect against routine medical cost. It is designed to protect the insurer from paying.

Since 2006, the average deductible for covered workers has increased nearly fourfold (Kaiser Family Foundation, 2024)[47]. The typical family now carries multiple thousands of dollars in out-of-pocket exposure before insurance meaningfully activates. In practical terms, millions of insured Americans are functionally self-insured for most routine and even moderately serious care.

This is not cost sharing in the classical insurance sense. It is risk offloading. The rising deductible converts insurance from a financial shield into a conditional reimbursement mechanism. The household fronts the cost. The insurer reimburses selectively, later, and often partially.

Deductibles did not rise because medical care suddenly became four times more unpredictable. They rose because insurers, facing concentrated hospital pricing power, protected their margins by transferring instability to consumers.

Narrow networks did not emerge from clinical research or patient-centered design. They emerged from pricing warfare between consolidated insurers and consolidated hospital systems. When hospitals refuse to lower rates, insurers respond by excluding them. When dominant hospital systems are non-excludable, insurers compress networks further around secondary providers.

The stated purpose is cost control. The operational result is access restriction.

Patients now routinely discover that the nearest hospital, the best cancer center, or the only trauma facility in their region is out-of-network. Care decisions become financial triage exercises. Patients delay treatment. They shop for physicians under emergency conditions. They accept inferior options to avoid catastrophic billing exposure.

Narrow networks are not evidence of efficient markets. They are evidence of market failure managed through consumer rationing. Access is no longer a function of medical need alone. It is a derivative of network design optimized for profit containment.

Health insurance did not simply become more expensive. It absorbed the wage growth of the American middle class.

For twenty years, productivity increased. Corporate profits expanded. Executive compensation soared. Yet median real wages stagnated. The missing income did not vanish. It was quietly reallocated into healthcare premiums paid on behalf of workers.

Every dollar an employer spends on health insurance is a dollar not available for wages, retirement contributions, training, or workforce expansion. Economically, the worker still pays. The payment is simply routed through a benefits ledger rather than a paycheck.

This is why Americans feel poorer even when "total compensation" statistics appear stable. Their labor is purchased, but an increasing share of its value is captured by healthcare intermediaries before it ever reaches the household.

Healthcare did not merely grow as a sector of the economy. It crowded out wage growth as a competing claim on national income.

The final consequence is the collapse of financial protection itself. More than 100 million Americans now carry medical debt (Consumer Financial Protection Bureau, 2022)[90]. This includes households across income levels, employment categories, and insurance status. Crucially, the majority of medical debtors were insured at the time their debt was incurred.

This fact alone dismantles the core promise of private insurance. Medical bankruptcy is no longer associated primarily with the uninsured poor. It is a routine risk for the insured middle class. Insurance now frequently fails at its most basic function: preventing financial devastation after illness.

Medical debt damages credit scores, blocks mortgage access, delays education, and destabilizes retirement. It follows families for decades. It affects labor mobility by trapping workers in jobs purely for coverage continuity. It weakens consumer demand across the economy. What was once a health crisis becomes a macroeconomic drag.

Medical debt is no longer an anomaly. It is a system output.

Private markets promised efficiency. They promised innovation. They promised consumer choice. They promised that competition would discipline prices and reward value. Instead, consolidation absorbed competition, innovation aligned to billing optimization, and consumers lost both price transparency and bargaining power.

The last twenty years settled the question empirically. The private healthcare market in its current form does not self-correct toward affordability. It consolidates toward dominance. It shifts risk downward. It monetizes essential care. It protects capital first and patients last.

We did not arrive at this outcome because the market was allowed to function freely. We arrived here because the market was allowed to abandon competition while retaining profit protection.

Higher premiums. Higher deductibles. Narrower access. Stagnant wages. Exploding medical debt.

WHY HEALTHCARE QUALIFIES AS A MONOPOLY UNDER EXISTING LAW

American antitrust law does not require absolute control to establish monopoly power. Under the Sherman Act and the Clayton Act, monopoly is defined by three functional conditions: dominant market share, significant barriers to entry, and the power to raise prices without losing customers (Sherman Antitrust Act, 1890)[105]. Total ownership is not required. Market command is.

By these legal standards, modern U.S. healthcare does not merely flirt with monopoly conditions. It squarely satisfies them.

What complicates public understanding is not the law. It is the structure. Monopolies in healthcare do not appear as single firms controlling 100 percent of a market. They appear as interlocking regional monopolies, systems so concentrated within defined geographies that effective competition disappears even while multiple brand names remain in view.

The law was designed to address exactly this condition. The political system has simply failed to apply it.

Healthcare markets are not national in function. They are regional. Patients do not shop across state lines for routine care. Employers must source networks where their workers live. Emergency services are local by definition. Because geography bounds the market, dominance inside a metropolitan area or state carries the same legal weight as national ownership.

Within these bounded markets, insurer groups, hospital systems, and PBMs routinely control between 50 and 80 percent of total activity. In many metropolitan regions, two hospital systems account for nearly all inpatient capacity. In several states, one insurer dominates the employer market while a second controls Medicaid managed care.

PBMs, operating nationally, concentrate even more aggressively, with three firms controlling the overwhelming majority of prescription drug processing.

This is not textbook competition. It is effective market command.

When one or two hospital systems determine where most doctors work, which services exist, and which facilities insurers must include, all downstream pricing becomes captive. When one insurer controls the majority of covered lives in a region, providers negotiate under coercion. When one PBM controls the majority of pharmacy transactions, drug access becomes contingent on compliance with opaque rebate structures.

Market share at this scale rewrites the rules. At this scale, firms no longer respond to competition. They discipline it.

In ordinary industries, new competitors emerge when prices rise high enough to attract alternative supply. In healthcare, that self-correcting mechanism is largely blocked by structural barriers so severe that entry becomes functionally impossible for all but the largest corporations on earth.

A new insurer cannot simply appear and begin offering coverage. It requires enormous initial capitalization to satisfy state solvency requirements. It must negotiate contracts with hospitals that are already locked into exclusive or dominant system agreements. It must secure pharmacy access through PBMs that are owned by its largest competitors. It must build claims infrastructure, compliance systems, actuarial capacity, risk pools, and regulatory reporting frameworks before it can issue a single policy.

A new hospital cannot enter a market without navigating certificate-of-need restrictions in many states, acquiring land, building capital-intensive facilities, and then persuading insurers already tied to dominant systems to include it in their networks. Even if it succeeds clinically, it must survive long enough under unfavorable reimbursement to achieve scale, something most cannot do independently.

A new PBM cannot survive without access to existing pharmacy networks, which are already contractually bound to dominant incumbents. Nor can it compete on price when the incumbents control formulary placement, rebate access, and vertically integrated insurers.

This is not a free market with high difficulty. It is a gated market designed for incumbents.

In antitrust terms, these are classic structural barriers to entry. They prevent price discipline. They prevent innovation at scale. They prevent meaningful competition from arising even when demand is immense and prices are historically high.

The final and decisive test of monopoly is not market share alone. It is whether a firm can raise prices without losing customers. In healthcare, this condition is met with brutal consistency.

Insurance premiums rise every year regardless of public satisfaction. Deductibles climb even when wage growth stalls. Out-of-pocket exposure expands even as coverage shrinks. Consumers do not leave in response. They cannot. Employment-based coverage locks workers into the network chosen by their employer. Medicare and Medicaid beneficiaries are bound by geography and program rules. Individual market consumers face the same dominant carriers across every exchange tier.

Hospitals raise prices through mechanisms almost invisible to patients. Facility fees appear on routine outpatient visits even when no hospital infrastructure is used. System ownership quietly converts once-independent physician offices into hospital billing sites, triggering higher reimbursement without changing care delivery. Patients protest only after the bill arrives, long after exit has become impossible.

PBMs escalate list prices indirectly by forcing manufacturers into rebate structures that reward higher sticker prices in exchange for formulary access. The consumer experiences only the result: higher copays, higher coinsurance, and rising premiums. Switching PBMs is impossible for the individual. Even employers lack leverage once PBM consolidation reaches national scale.

This is the functional definition of monopoly behavior. Prices rise. Customers stay. There is nowhere else to go.

Healthcare preserves the outward appearance of competition. Multiple logos line hospital campuses. Several insurers advertise during football games. Dozens of drug brands crowd pharmacy shelves. But this is brand diversity without ownership diversity.

Behind the curtain, the ownership networks converge. The same hospital systems operate under different facility names. The same insurers own the same PBMs. The same PBMs control the same formularies across competing health plans. The consumer perceives choice. The market experiences concentration.

Antitrust law recognizes this condition as oligopolistic monopoly, a market in which coordination and dominance replace rivalry, even without explicit collusion (Baker, 2019)[121]. Pricing power becomes stabilized. Innovation decouples from consumer benefit. Access bends toward profitability rather than public need.

Healthcare now operates inside that structure nationwide.

The legal framework exists. The economic thresholds have been crossed. The empirical indicators are public. What has failed is not doctrine. It is political will.

For decades, policymakers accepted a narrative that healthcare was too complex, too fragile, or too socially important to subject to ordinary antitrust discipline. That exemption, informal but real, became a shield for consolidation. Regulators deferred. Courts hesitated. Legislatures remained silent. Lobbyists filled the vacuum.

Market ideology replaced market supervision. Law was treated as optional restraint rather than mandatory boundary. The result is the contradiction now embedded in American health policy: a publicly financed healthcare system operating through privately concentrated monopolies.

In ordinary monopolies, price regulation or public ownership often follows once market failure becomes undeniable. In healthcare, neither has occurred at sufficient scale. Instead, public money floods private monopolies without public control. Medicare, Medicaid, employer tax exclusions, and federal subsidies finance the system while leaving pricing authority in private hands.

Under existing antitrust law, the healthcare industry satisfies every operational condition of monopoly. Regional dominance replaces national ownership but achieves the same effect. Barriers to entry prevent corrective competition from forming. Price-setting power persists without consumer exit.

What remains missing is not legal standing. It is political enforcement.

Healthcare is not monopolistic because the law is unclear. It is monopolistic because the law has not been applied to those powerful enough to evade it.

And the price of that failure is paid not in abstract economic terms but in premiums, medical debt, delayed care, closed hospitals, abandoned rural communities, and households one diagnosis away from financial collapse.

CHAPTER 8
THE VA HEALTHCARE SYSTEM —PROOF GOVERNMENT CAN DELIVER, PROOF CONGRESS WON'T DEFEND IT

The United States operates the largest integrated healthcare delivery system in the world. It is not run by private insurers. It is not operated by hospital corporations. It is run by the federal government. It serves 9 million veterans across 1,293 medical facilities. It employs 450,000 people. It has an annual budget of approximately $301 billion when accounting for all veteran benefits, though direct medical care spending is approximately $87 billion annually (U.S. Department of Veterans Affairs, 2024)[138].

The Veterans Health Administration is living proof that the government can run healthcare effectively. It proves that integrated public healthcare works. It proves that when the government acts without the constraint of profit extraction, healthcare becomes better, more efficient, and more innovative.

Yet the VHA has been under relentless attack by private healthcare industries. Insurance companies, pharmaceutical manufacturers, hospital corporations, and private equity firms have spent decades funding negative media coverage, commissioning studies designed to undermine confidence in VA care, and promoting a narrative that government healthcare is inherently inferior.

This is not analysis. This is propaganda. And it is designed to protect one thing: private sector profits.

This chapter establishes one foundational truth: the VA is not broken. The VA is a threat to the private healthcare industry. Which is precisely why the private healthcare industry has waged a decades-long campaign to discredit it. And Congress, captured by that same industry, has allowed the assault to continue unchallenged.

THE VA'S REPUTATION CRISIS: MANUFACTURED, NOT EARNED

The Veterans Health Administration has a reputation crisis. The public believes the VA provides inferior care. The public believes the VA is inefficient. The public believes the VA is mismanaged. The public believes long wait times are routine. The public believes veterans are neglected.

Most of this is false.

The reputation problem is not a reflection of actual VA performance. The reputation problem is a reflection of decades of coordinated messaging designed to undermine public confidence in government healthcare. The reputation problem exists because private healthcare corporations have invested heavily in creating it.

In 2009, the VA faced genuine capacity constraints. Aging facilities, staffing shortages, and rising demand created real wait times for some appointments in some regions. This was a legitimate problem requiring real solutions.

The challenge intensified rapidly: average processing times for disability claims surged from 161 days in fiscal 2009 to 260 days by fiscal 2012, while the backlog of claims awaiting decisions for over 125 days more than tripled (Government Accountability Office, 2015)[139]. The Government Accountability Office and VA Office of Inspector General had been issuing reports since 2005 documenting unreliable wait time data and calling for improved scheduling practices (U.S. Department of Veterans Affairs Office of Inspector General, 2014)[140].

The private healthcare industry seized this moment. Media outlets ran countless stories about VA wait times. Congressional hearings were held. Investigations were launched. The narrative became: government healthcare is broken; only private markets can deliver care.

The crisis reached its peak in 2014 when investigations revealed that staff at approximately 40 locations had falsified appointment records to appear to meet the 14-day target, with the Phoenix facility accounting for one-fifth of the overall cases (U.S. Department of Veterans Affairs Office of Inspector General, 2014)[141]. An Inspector General report later clarified that while scheduling manipulation occurred, only six veterans had died experiencing clinically significant delays while on waiting lists, and in these cases the absence of timely care could not be conclusively linked to their deaths (U.S. Department of Veterans Affairs Office of Inspector General, 2015)[142].

What went unmentioned: during the same 2009-2015 period, private insurance companies systematically denied coverage for necessary treatments to millions of people. Pre-authorization delays in private insurance routinely reached weeks or months. Patients in private networks were denied access to specialists they needed. Emergency departments turned away uninsured patients.

Research from 2009 found that prior authorization requests consumed roughly 20 hours per week for each medical practice, with practices spending an average of $68,274 per physician annually on interactions with health plans (Casalino et al., 2009)[143]. Between 2009 and 2019, the use of prior authorization requirements in Medicare Advantage plans increased dramatically, with approximately 75 percent of enrollees eventually placed in plans mandating prior approval for certain services (Kaiser Family Foundation, 2019)[144].

The private sector faced the same or worse access problems as the VA. But these problems received a fraction of the media attention.

After 2015, the VA implemented systemic improvements. Wait times declined significantly in most regions. Quality metrics improved. Patient satisfaction increased. Yet the narrative persisted: the VA is dysfunctional.

This is the hallmark of successful propaganda. The facts change but the message does not. The narrative becomes detached from reality and sustains itself through repetition.

By April 2024, the VA achieved an 11 percent reduction in average wait times for new primary care patients and a 7 percent reduction for mental health appointments compared to the previous year (U.S. Department of Veterans Affairs, 2024)[138]. Between October 2023 and February 2024, the VA completed approximately 25,000 more new patient appointments than the same period the previous year, representing an 11 percent increase (U.S. Department of Veterans Affairs, 2024)[138]. The average wait time from request to mental health appointment fell to just 17.4 days (U.S. Department of Veterans Affairs, 2024)[138].

By 2023-2024, VA wait times in most markets were comparable to or better than private insurance access times. But the public still believed the VA had a wait time problem. The reputation problem outlasted the actual problem.

When private healthcare fails, the failures are treated as isolated incidents. When the VA faces challenges, the challenges are treated as systemic dysfunction.

A single hospital denies care to an uninsured patient. This is reported as a story about that hospital. Multiply this across thousands of private hospitals and millions of uninsured patients. Aggregate it nationally. This is not treated as a crisis. This is treated as how markets work.

But when the VA faces delayed appointments in multiple regions, this is treated as proof that government cannot manage healthcare.

A 2024 survey found that 16 percent of all insured adults experienced prior authorization problems in the past year, with those enrolled in Medicaid facing even higher rates at 22 percent (Commonwealth Fund, 2024)[145]. One-quarter of adults whose insurance problems included prior authorization issues reported that their health status declined as a direct result, while one-third experienced delayed or denied access to needed care (Commonwealth Fund, 2024)[145].

These systematic failures in private insurance received minimal investigative attention compared to the intense scrutiny directed at the VA. No congressional hearing examined private insurance access failures with comparable thoroughness. No major news organization launched multi-part investigative series on insurance company denials equivalent to their coverage of VA wait times.

Today, the VA's actual performance exceeds the public's perception of it. This gap exists because reputation lags reality. But it also exists because the forces that created the initial negative reputation have ongoing incentive to maintain it.

In 2024, the VA outperformed non-VA hospitals in major nationwide reviews: 79 percent of VA facilities received 4- or 5-star ratings in the Centers for Medicare & Medicaid Services Hospital Consumer Assessment survey, compared to only 40 percent of non-VA hospitals (U.S. Department of Veterans Affairs, 2024)[138]. This represented the ninth consecutive quarter in which VA facilities outperformed non-VA counterparts (U.S. Department of Veterans Affairs, 2024)[138].

Patient trust in VA outpatient healthcare reached an all-time high of 91.8 percent in 2024, up from 85.6 percent in 2018 (U.S. Department of Veterans Affairs, 2024)[138]. Nearly 92 percent of veterans reported trusting the outpatient healthcare they receive from the VA (U.S. Department of Veterans Affairs, 2024)[138]. These metrics demonstrate care quality and patient satisfaction that match or exceed private sector benchmarks.

Yet public perception remains anchored to narratives established during the 2014 crisis. The disconnect between measurable performance and public understanding represents one of the most successful propaganda campaigns in recent American healthcare policy, one that continues to shape debates about the future of veteran care and government-provided healthcare more broadly.

HOW PRIVATE INDUSTRIES FUND THE ATTACK: A COORDINATED, DOCUMENTED CAMPAIGN

The attack on the VA is not random. It is not organic. It is funded, coordinated, and deliberate. Private healthcare corporations have direct financial interest in undermining public confidence in government healthcare. They have invested substantially in making this happen.

The health sector spent $752.9 million on federal lobbying in 2024 (OpenSecrets, 2025)[1]. This is the single largest lobbying presence in Washington by sector. This spending funds not just direct legislative advocacy but also messaging, media relations, think tank research, and public relations campaigns designed to shape opinion.

The pharmaceutical and health products industry alone accounted for $294 million of this total in 2024 (OpenSecrets, 2025)[2]. America's Health Insurance Plans, the insurance industry's primary trade association, spent millions more on lobbying activities specifically related to healthcare policy. The American Hospital Association dedicated $24 million to lobbying in 2024. These figures represent only what is disclosed under federal law. The actual influence spending through indirect channels is substantially higher.

Lobbying spending surged at critical policy moments. PhRMA increased spending from $27 million in 2023 to $31 million in 2024, with $7.6 million spent in the fourth quarter alone as Congress negotiated year-end healthcare provisions. The Pharmaceutical Care Management Association nearly doubled its lobbying expenditure from $9 million in 2022 to $18 million in 2024 as lawmakers considered PBM reform legislation.

A portion of this spending goes directly to discrediting government healthcare. Insurance companies fund messaging campaigns about VA failures. Pharmaceutical manufacturers fund research questioning government drug price negotiation. Hospital corporations fund think tank papers arguing that public healthcare is inefficient.

This spending is tracked. It is documented. It can be itemized.

Healthcare corporations fund think tanks. These think tanks produce research critical of government healthcare. This research is cited by media outlets as objective analysis. It is presented to policymakers as independent expertise. But it is funded by the industries being discussed.

The mechanism is straightforward: pharmaceutical companies, insurance corporations, and hospital systems provide grants and donations to policy research organizations. These organizations then produce studies, white papers, and policy briefs that align with industry interests. The funding relationship is often disclosed in fine print or annual reports, but rarely emphasized when the research is cited publicly.

Specific example: A think tank funded primarily by pharmaceutical and insurance industry grants produces a study concluding that VA drug prices are unsustainable. The study is published. Media outlets report on it. Congress cites it. The study is presented as objective analysis. What is not reported is the funding source.

This is standard practice. It is legal. But it is propaganda.

The research output from industry-funded think tanks systematically emphasizes the failures of government healthcare while minimizing or ignoring comparable failures in private systems. Studies document VA wait times in granular detail while treating private insurance pre-authorization delays as inevitable market features. Research quantifies VA operational costs while treating private sector administrative overhead as necessary business expense.

Major media corporations have healthcare industry connections. News outlets are owned by conglomerates that own other businesses. Some of these conglomerates have financial interest in healthcare industry performance.

Additionally, media outlets depend on pharmaceutical and healthcare industry advertising revenue. Healthcare and pharmaceutical companies spent over $30 billion on advertising in 2024, representing one of the largest advertising categories in the United States. The pharmaceutical industry alone spent approximately $13.8 billion on advertising and promotion in 2023 (Schwartz & Woloshin, 2019)[146]. During the first quarter of 2025, drugmakers spent $729.4 million on commercials for just the top 10 drug brands. Twenty-five percent of evening news advertising minutes in early 2025 came from pharmaceutical companies.

A news organization that consistently criticizes the healthcare industry risks losing significant advertising revenue. This creates structural incentive toward favorable coverage of private healthcare.

This is not conspiracy. This is economics. Media outlets respond to incentives like any other business.

The result is systematic coverage imbalance. Private healthcare failures are reported as isolated incidents. Government healthcare failures are reported as systemic dysfunction. When a private hospital denies coverage, it's a story about one hospital. When the VA faces appointment delays, it's evidence that government cannot manage healthcare.

Members of Congress who vote against healthcare industry interests can expect primary opposition funded by healthcare industry Super PACs. Members of Congress who vote for healthcare industry interests can expect lucrative post-congressional employment.

This is the revolving door. It operates systematically in healthcare policy. Former members of Congress and their staffers become healthcare industry lobbyists, consultants, and executives. They earn substantially more after leaving office than they earned in Congress.

Research on Department of Health and Human Services appointees between 2004 and 2020 reveals the scope of this phenomenon: 32 percent of HHS appointees exited to private industry positions after their government service, compared to only 15 percent who came from industry before their appointments, a net increase of 17 percentage points (Jain et al., 2022)[147]. At the Centers for Disease Control and Prevention, 54 percent of appointees departed for industry jobs (Jain et al., 2022)[147]. More than half of appointees at the Centers for Medicare and Medicaid Services also left for private sector employment (Jain et al., 2022)[147].

Former FDA Commissioner Scott Gottlieb joined Pfizer's Board of Directors within four months of resigning as FDA commissioner in 2019. During his tenure, Gottlieb promoted biosimilar policies that directly affected Pfizer's business interests. A 2007 study of FDA medical examiners found that 11 of 16 took jobs with companies they had previously regulated (Lurie et al., 2006)[148].

This creates incentive for members of Congress to support healthcare industry interests while in office. The reward is waiting on the other side of the revolving door.

Healthcare industry employees, executives, and political action committees donate hundreds of millions of dollars to political campaigns. Members of Congress who vote against healthcare industry interests face well-funded primary opposition. Members of Congress who vote for healthcare industry interests receive campaign support.

During the 2023-2024 election cycle, the health sector gave substantial contributions to federal candidates. The pharmaceutical and health products industry specifically contributed tens of millions to candidates, with contributions increasing dramatically during presidential election cycles. Between 2012 and 2020, pharmaceutical industry contributions to federal candidates jumped 170 percent, reaching $89 million in the 2020 cycle (Wouters et al., 2020)[3].

These contributions correlate with legislative outcomes. Members who vote for industry-favorable positions receive continued support. Members who vote against industry interests face coordinated opposition. Primary challengers receive funding from industry-aligned Super PACs. The mechanism is measurable and documented.

This is measurable. This is documented. This is the mechanism through which political capture occurs.

VA SUCCESS METRICS: THE DATA CONGRESS IGNORES

The Veterans Health Administration achieves outcomes that exceed private sector averages across multiple clinical categories. This is not anecdotal. This is documented in peer-reviewed literature, government audits, and longitudinal comparative studies. The narrative that the VA provides inferior care is empirically false.

VA patients with diabetes achieve better glycemic control than comparable patients in private insurance networks. Hemoglobin A1C levels are lower in VA patients than in Medicare beneficiaries or commercially insured patients with diabetes. Better glucose control means fewer emergency hospitalizations, fewer amputations, fewer kidney failures, and longer life expectancy.

Research demonstrates that VA patients were significantly more likely to receive diabetes education classes and HbA1c testing than those covered by private insurance (Kerr et al., 2004)[149]. The VA's Advanced Comprehensive Diabetes Care program shows remarkable results: veterans achieve an average HbA1c reduction of 1.65 percent, and they maintain this improvement for as long as four years after completing the program (Crowley et al., 2013)[150].

A comparative study of medicine residents practicing in both VA and academic health systems found that VA patients were substantially more likely to receive comprehensive diabetes care: 94 percent received annual eye exam referrals compared to 78 percent in academic settings, 88 percent received lipid screening versus 74 percent, 63 percent received proteinuria screening versus 34 percent, and 85 percent received complete foot exams versus only 32 percent in non-VA settings (Stevens et al., 2004)[151].

VA patients with high blood pressure achieve superior blood pressure control compared to patients in private insurance networks. This translates to fewer strokes, fewer heart attacks, and fewer end-organ complications.

The VA's blood pressure control rate of 76.3 percent based on the treatment goal of less than 140/90 mm Hg exceeded that reported in the general population (Hyre et al., 2007)[152]. Among veterans with hypertension and high cardiovascular disease risk, approximately 46.7 percent of those with the most complex conditions achieved blood pressure control below 130/80 mmHg, despite having the highest disease burden (Carey et al., 2018)[153].

VA patients receive preventive services at higher rates than privately insured Americans. Colonoscopy screening rates, mammography rates, immunization rates, and other preventive services are more accessible in the VA system. Early detection prevents disease progression and reduces emergency care costs.

The VA explicitly exceeds the private sector in mammography screening rates (Weiner et al., 2012)[154]. VA facilities have breast cancer screening coordinators who proactively contact women due for mammograms, follow up on abnormal results, and help patients navigate the screening process, a level of coordinated care uncommon in private practice settings (Haggstrom & Schapira, 2006)[155].

For colonoscopy screening, a study at White River Junction VA Medical Center found that the detection rate for potentially precancerous polyps, a key quality measure, was substantially higher among patients whose procedures were performed within the VA compared to similar VA patients referred out to private facilities (Lieberman et al., 2012)[210]. This quality differential occurred despite both groups being VA patients with comparable risk profiles, suggesting superior technical quality in VA-performed procedures.

The VA pioneered evidence-based mental health treatment for

trauma. Veterans have access to cognitive processing therapy, prolonged exposure therapy, and integrated dual-diagnosis treatment for PTSD and substance abuse. The VA achieved suicide prevention improvements that exceed private sector outcomes for comparable populations.

A landmark VA study comparing the two leading trauma-focused psychotherapies found that both cognitive processing therapy and prolonged exposure therapy produce meaningful improvements for veterans with PTSD (Resick et al., 2015)[156]. In the study of 916 veterans across 17 VA medical centers, PTSD severity improved substantially in both prolonged exposure and cognitive processing therapy groups. More than 70 percent of participants reported combat exposure, over one-third reported military sexual trauma, and more than 90 percent had experienced a psychiatric disorder other than PTSD, demonstrating effectiveness in complex, real-world cases (Resick et al., 2015)[156].

Evidence-based treatments for PTSD often produce significant symptom reduction within eight sessions (Steenkamp et al., 2015)[157]. Among all VA patients with PTSD who received at least eight sessions of documented evidence-based treatment, 14 percent achieved meaningful change within the first eight sessions, and 10 percent subsequently (Steenkamp et al., 2015)[157].

The VA's mental health infrastructure is unmatched in American healthcare. Integrated care means a veteran with PTSD and substance abuse disorder receives coordinated treatment rather than being bounced between separate providers.

Despite the media narrative of VA dysfunction, veteran satisfaction with VA care is comparable to or exceeds patient satisfaction in private healthcare. Multiple surveys document this. Veterans who use VA services report satisfaction levels on par with or better than commercially insured Americans.

This contradicts the public perception. The gap between perception and reality is evidence of propaganda success.

The VA spends approximately $9,600 per veteran per year for comprehensive healthcare (Congressional Budget Office, 2024)[14]. This includes primary care, specialty care, mental health services, prescriptions, rehabilitation, and long-term care. Universal coverage. No medical bankruptcy. No rationing of care based on ability to pay.

For comparison, Medicare spends approximately $15,000 per beneficiary annually (Centers for Medicare & Medicaid Services, 2024)[85]. Employer-sponsored insurance costs approximately $22,500 per beneficiary annually (Kaiser Family Foundation, 2024)[137]. Medicaid spends approximately $8,000 per beneficiary annually (Kaiser Family Foundation, 2024)[103].

The VA achieves lower cost per person than Medicare while delivering superior clinical outcomes. This is not coincidental. It results from integrated care delivery, direct pharmaceutical negotiation, minimal administrative overhead, and elimination of billing complexity.

The VA negotiates drug prices directly with pharmaceutical manufacturers. Because the VA purchases on behalf of millions of veterans and has authority to exclude drugs from formulary if pricing is unreasonable, manufacturers negotiate seriously. VA prices are substantially lower than private sector prices for identical medications.

Example: A medication costing $300 per month in private insurance might cost $60 per month in the VA system. This is not regulatory imposition. This is market discipline. Large purchaser leverage equals lower prices.

Simultaneously, the VA funds pharmaceutical research. VA researchers develop drugs. VA hospitals participate in clinical trials. The VA contributes to pharmaceutical innovation while constraining prices. This disproves the claim that innovation requires high prices.

The VA employs 450,000 people. These are stable, well-compensated positions with benefits, retirement security, and job stability. The VA retains clinical staff at higher rates than many private healthcare employers. Physician burnout and turnover are lower in the VA than in comparable private healthcare settings.

This matters because workforce stability improves care quality. Continuity of provider relationships improves outcomes. Staff retention reduces training costs and improves institutional knowledge.

VA patients with diabetes have similar health outcomes regardless of whether their primary provider is a physician, nurse practitioner, or physician assistant, with no clinically important differences in intermediate diabetes outcomes (Pogach et al., 2010)[158]. This finding demonstrates the effectiveness of VA's team-based care model and its ability to maximize the capabilities of its diverse clinical workforce.

INNOVATIONS PIONEERED AT VA HOSPITALS: GOVERNMENT DRIVES MEDICAL PROGRESS

The claim that government healthcare stifles innovation is directly contradicted by VA history. The VA has pioneered medical innovations now standard throughout American healthcare. Private providers later adopted these innovations. This proves that innovation emerges from public sector research and that profit is not necessary for advancement.

VA researchers pioneered cognitive processing therapy for PTSD. This evidence-based approach is now the gold standard trauma treatment taught in graduate programs nationwide. Private hospitals employ therapists trained in CPT. This innovation originated at the VA.

Patricia Resick developed Cognitive Processing Therapy in 1988 while on the faculty at the University of Missouri-St. Louis (Resick & Schnicke, 1992)[159]. CPT was originally developed as a treatment for female survivors of sexual trauma (Resick & Schnicke, 1993)[160] and later adapted to address the experiences of military personnel and veterans (Monson et al., 2006)[161].

The therapy's foundational randomized controlled trial demonstrated its effectiveness in treating PTSD among female rape victims by comparing CPT to supportive counseling and other interventions, showing superior symptom reduction in the CPT group (Resick & Schnicke, 1992)[159]. By 2024, CPT had been translated into multiple languages including Spanish, Arabic, Chinese, Norwegian, Russian, and Italian. The 2023 VA/DoD Clinical Practice Guideline for the Management of Posttraumatic Stress Disorder and Acute Stress Disorder gave CPT a "Strong For" recommendation as a treatment for PTSD (U.S. Department of Veterans Affairs & U.S. Department of Defense, 2023)[162].

VA researchers developed prolonged exposure therapy, another evidence-based trauma treatment now standard nationwide. Again, a VA innovation later adopted by private providers.

Prolonged Exposure therapy was developed by Edna Foa and colleagues in the 1980s, shortly after PTSD was first introduced to the DSM-III (Foa et al., 1991)[163]. The first randomized controlled trials of PE were led by Foa and conducted with civilian women, demonstrating significant symptom reductions compared to supportive counseling and stress inoculation training (Foa et al., 2005)[164].

Following validation in civilian populations, the 2004 VA/DoD Clinical Practice Guideline for the Management of Post-Traumatic Stress strongly recommended PE as a first-line treatment for PTSD among military personnel and veterans (U.S. Department of Veterans Affairs & U.S. Department of Defense, 2004)[165]. PE produces clinically significant improvement in about 80 percent of patients with chronic PTSD (Powers et al., 2010)[166]. More than 40 randomized clinical trials of PE with adults have been conducted, establishing it as one of the most well-supported treatments for PTSD (Cusack et al., 2016)[167].

The VA developed integrated dual-diagnosis treatment for veterans with PTSD and substance abuse disorders. This coordinated approach reduced suicide rates and improved functional outcomes. Private healthcare systems are attempting to replicate this model but lack the integration infrastructure the VA provides.

VA hospitals serve patients with service-related amputations. This complex patient population drove innovation in prosthetic technology. VA researchers and engineers developed advanced prosthetics that improved mobility and function. Some innovations were licensed to private manufacturers.

The VA began the first human study in the United States to investigate osseointegrated prosthetics, a system that allows a prosthetic leg to be attached directly to the remaining bone of an amputated lower limb (Hagberg et al., 2014)[168]. In 2013, VA researchers published a study of amputees' and clinicians' feedback using the DEKA arm, the first prosthetic arm capable of performing multiple simultaneous powered movements (Resnik et al., 2014)[169].

DARPA invested over $100 million in the Revolutionizing Prosthetics program between 2005 and 2018 (Defense Advanced Research Projects Agency, 2018)[170]. The LUKE/DEKA prosthetic limb improved on existing prostheses by including a simpler and more flexible control system and a range of pre-programmed grips of varying strength (Perry et al., 2018)[171]. After eight years of research and development, the FDA approved the DEKA arm in May 2014 (U.S. Food and Drug Administration, 2014)[172].

The VA developed VistA, one of the most advanced integrated electronic health record systems in American healthcare. VistA was developed internally at VA hospitals, predating most private healthcare EHR systems and remaining more functionally integrated than many private systems.

Early in the 1970s, the National Center for Health Services Research and Development began planning for development of what would become Electronic Health Records (Brown et al., 2003)[173]. The VA Massachusetts General Hospital Utility Multi-Programming System, a precursor to VistA, was developed by the Computer Assisted System Staff Team (Brown et al., 2003)[173].

In the early 1980s, VA made its software available without restriction in the public domain to other government and private sector organizations, in compliance with the Freedom of Information Act (Brown et al., 2003)[173]. VA's Under Secretary for Health, Kenneth Kizer, renamed DHCP as VistA, the Veterans Health Information Systems and Technology Architecture, in the 1990s (Kizer, 1999)[174].

The adoption of VistA allowed the VA to achieve a pharmacy prescription accuracy rate of 99.997 percent, and the VA outperformed most public sector hospitals on many other quality metrics, all attributable to VistA (Evans et al., 1998)[175]. For development of VistA, the United States Department of Veterans Affairs was named the recipient of the Innovations in American Government Award presented by the Ash Institute of the John F. Kennedy School of Government at Harvard University in July 2006 (Ash Center for Democratic Governance and Innovation, 2006)[176].

Because all VA facilities use the same EHR, patient information is instantly available at any VA location. A veteran can receive care in New York with complete medical history instantly accessible. Private healthcare networks cannot achieve this integration because they operate independently.

VistA has been deployed internationally, running the healthcare information system of entire national healthcare systems, such as the Kingdom of Jordan (Kolodner et al., 2008)[177]. Some United States universities, such as UC Davis and Texas Tech, have implemented VistA (Kolodner et al., 2008)[177].

The VA launched the Whole Health initiative, integrating traditional medicine, mental health services, physical rehabilitation, and patient engagement into coordinated care plans. This treats the person, not just the disease. It incorporates evidence-based complementary approaches alongside conventional medicine.

VA's Office of Patient Centered Care and Cultural Transformation began the development of VA's Whole Health model in 2011 (U.S. Department of Veterans Affairs, 2016)[178]. VHA established the Integrative Health Coordinating Center within the Office of Patient Centered Care and Cultural Transformation in 2014 (U.S. Department of Veterans Affairs, 2017)[179].

In 2018, VHA initiated a demonstration program in 18 VA Medical Centers to implement its Whole Health System (Kligler et al., 2022)[180]. Research partners from Health Systems Research & Development and Quality Enhancement Research Initiative examine patient-reported health outcomes, clinical outcomes, cost impact, and Veteran satisfaction measures (Kligler et al., 2022)[180].

Among veterans with chronic musculoskeletal pain receiving health care at Flagship sites, 9.7 percent used a complementary and integrative health therapy before the Flagship program initiation, whereas 14.2 percent used a therapy in the second year of the program, a 46.0 percent increase (Taylor et al., 2021)[181]. In comparison, CIH therapy use among Veterans at non-Flagship sites increased from 10.3 to 12.0 percent over the same period, only a 16.5 percent increase (Taylor et al., 2021)[181].

This model is now being adopted by private health systems. Mayo Clinic, Cleveland Clinic, and other leading private providers are implementing integrative care models based on the VA's Whole Health framework. The innovation originated in the public sector. Private providers followed.

The VA serves rural veterans across geographically dispersed areas. This drove innovation in telemedicine and remote care delivery. VA clinicians developed approaches to deliver specialty care to rural patients through video consultation and remote monitoring.

The Veterans Health Administration has been an early adopter of telehealth, starting in 2003 when it pioneered the testing and implementation of telehealth on a national scale (Darkins et al., 2008)[182]. The VHA's early adoption was driven by its commitment to providing veterans access to specialized medical and mental health care, particularly for those in rural areas (Darkins et al., 2008)[182].

Before the COVID-19 pandemic, 34 percent of rural VA healthcare systems used telemedicine for primary care services compared to 30 percent use in urban areas, demonstrating VA's prioritization of rural access (Heyworth et al., 2020)[183].

During COVID-19, the VA's existing telemedicine infrastructure allowed rapid expansion of remote care. Veterans continued receiving treatment. Private healthcare systems scrambled to implement telemedicine. The VA already had it.

At the onset of COVID-19, the likelihood of telemedicine use was approximately 12 times higher than it was pre-COVID-19 (Ferguson et al., 2021)[184]. As the United States scrambled to deliver health care during the COVID-19 pandemic, current projections estimated there could be 1 billion telehealth appointments conducted in 2020, compared to the original pre-COVID projection of 36 million virtual visits for 2020 (Bestsennyy et al., 2020)[185].

WHY THE VA IS A PROVEN MODEL: SCALE, SCOPE, AND OPERATIONAL SUCCESS

The VA is not a theoretical pilot program or proof-of-concept. The VA is the largest integrated healthcare delivery system on earth, operating at massive scale, serving millions of people daily, achieving documented superior clinical and financial outcomes.

If the federal government cannot manage the VA, the entire premise of federal government management is false. But the government does manage the VA. Successfully. At scale. This is the most damning evidence against the claim that government cannot run healthcare.

The VA operates 1,380 healthcare facilities, including 170 medical centers and 1,193 outpatient sites of care (U.S. Department of Veterans Affairs, 2024)[138]. It serves 9.1 million enrolled veterans (U.S. Department of Veterans Affairs, 2024)[138]. As of September 2024, the Department of Veterans Affairs employed 482,831 people, making it the second-largest federal employer and accounting for 20.9 percent of the overall federal civilian workforce (U.S. Office of Personnel Management, 2024)[186].

The VA is larger than any private hospital system in America. It is larger than the combined healthcare operations of UnitedHealth Group, Anthem, and CVS Aetna. It is larger than Kaiser Permanente. UnitedHealth Group provides health insurance services to roughly 85 million individuals but does not operate a comparable integrated delivery system. Kaiser Permanente, often considered the gold standard for integrated care, operates in only eight states plus Washington D.C., while the VA operates in every state and territory.

The VA serves more than 9 million veterans annually through more than 16.2 million patient interactions (U.S. Department of Veterans Affairs, 2024)[138]. The VA was on pace to provide more than 127 million appointments in fiscal 2024, exceeding the previous year's record of 120 million appointments (U.S. Department of Veterans Affairs, 2024)[138].

If government can operate this scale, the argument that government is too incompetent to manage a public healthcare system becomes indefensible. The government already manages it. This proves government can do it.

The VA demonstrates government capability to hire and retain clinical staff at unprecedented scales, manage complex medical facilities across all 50 states, coordinate care across multiple locations with integrated information systems, negotiate with pharmaceutical suppliers to achieve substantial cost savings, maintain quality standards that exceed private sector benchmarks, innovate in medical practice, serve vulnerable populations with complex, high-acuity medical needs, operate at massive scale with 1,380 facilities serving 9.1 million people, and control costs while maintaining quality spending less per beneficiary than Medicare.

The VA employs 482,831 people as of September 2024 (U.S. Office of Personnel Management, 2024)[186]. This represents a 56.4 percent increase from 2010, when the VA employed 308,814 workers. These are good jobs with competitive salaries, benefits, retirement packages, and job security. The VA is one of the largest employers in the United States.

If the VA healthcare system were expanded to serve the entire population, employment would expand accordingly. Millions of additional jobs would be created. These would be jobs in healthcare delivery, not insurance administration. These would be productive jobs that contribute to public health, not rent-seeking positions that extract value from patients.

The job creation potential of expanded public healthcare is enormous and largely unrecognized in policy debates.

VA patients are among the most complex patient populations in American healthcare. They include aging veterans with multiple chronic conditions, young veterans with service-related disabilities, veterans with mental health challenges including PTSD, veterans with substance abuse disorders, and veterans with polytrauma requiring multidisciplinary care.

This is not a young, healthy population. This is not a population with simple healthcare needs. This is a population that requires complex, coordinated, comprehensive care. The VA serves this population successfully.

The VA has demonstrated its capacity to expand services rapidly in response to legislative mandates. Following passage of the PACT Act in 2022, which expanded VA healthcare and benefits eligibility for veterans exposed to toxic substances during military service, more than 400,000 veterans enrolled in VA care, a 30 percent increase over the previous year (U.S. Department of Veterans Affairs, 2024)[138]. The department successfully scaled operations to accommodate this surge while maintaining quality metrics and reducing wait times.

If government can manage healthcare for this complex population, the argument that government cannot manage healthcare for the general population becomes absurd. The VA population is harder to serve than the general population. Yet the VA serves them well.

The VA operates at lower cost per beneficiary than any comparable healthcare system while achieving superior outcomes. This is sustainable. The VA has operated sustainably for decades. The VA continues to expand capacity while controlling costs.

The Department of Veterans Affairs spent $324.9 billion in fiscal year 2024, representing 4.8 percent of the $6.78 trillion in overall federal spending (Congressional Budget Office, 2024)[14]. Adjusting for inflation, VA federal spending has increased from $82.3 billion in 1980 to $324.9 billion in 2024, reflecting both the expansion of services and the growth of the veteran population (Congressional Budget Office, 2024)[14].

Despite this substantial budget, the VA achieves remarkable cost efficiency. The per-veteran annual spending of approximately $9,600 for comprehensive healthcare, including primary care, specialty care, mental health services, prescriptions, rehabilitation, and long-term care, compares favorably to Medicare and far exceeds the cost-efficiency of employer-sponsored insurance.

If the VA cannot achieve financial sustainability, no public healthcare system can. But the VA is financially sustainable. This proves public healthcare systems can be fiscally sound.

The VA operates medical facilities in every state. Rural veterans have access to VA care. The VA has solved the rural access problem that private healthcare continues to struggle with.

As the largest telehealth provider in the United States, the VA conducted over one million telehealth visits in 2018, with more than half of these visits serving veterans in rural areas (Darkins et al., 2019)[187]. In fiscal year 2023, approximately 40 percent of veterans who used VA healthcare received some of their care through telehealth. More than 770,000 veterans living in rural communities participated in over 2.9 million telehealth episodes of care.

Private healthcare abandons rural areas because rural populations are not profitable enough. The VA serves rural areas because the mission is healthcare access, not profit maximization. This is proof that public systems can achieve access in areas private markets fail.

The VA operates as a unified system. Veterans receive care across multiple VA facilities with complete information sharing. Accountability is clear. Management is accountable to Congress and the American people. Performance is measured and reported.

The VA's integrated electronic health record system, VistA, enables instant access to complete medical histories at any VA location nationwide. A veteran can receive care in New York with their complete medical history instantly accessible. This level of integration is unmatched in American healthcare and impossible to achieve in fragmented private markets where different insurers, hospitals, and providers operate independently.

Private healthcare is fragmented. Different insurers, different hospitals, different providers. Accountability is diffused. Performance measurement is inconsistent. Coordination is difficult. When a patient transitions between providers or insurers, information is lost, care is duplicated, and quality suffers.

The VA proves that integrated public systems provide better continuity than fragmented private markets.

CONGRESS IS THE BARRIER, NOT THE SOLUTION

The VA works. The data proves it. The outcomes prove it. The scale proves it. The innovation proves it. The cost efficiency proves it.

Congress knows this. Congress has access to every report, every study, every metric documented in this chapter. Congress receives testimony from VA leadership. Congress conducts oversight hearings. Congress reviews budget requests.

Congress knows the VA outperforms private healthcare on clinical outcomes, patient satisfaction, cost per beneficiary, preventive care utilization, mental health treatment, pharmaceutical pricing, workforce retention, innovation, rural access, and system integration.

And yet Congress continues to underfund the VA. Congress continues to allow private healthcare corporations to attack the VA through propaganda campaigns. Congress continues to propose privatization schemes that would dismantle the VA and hand veterans over to the same private insurers and hospital systems that have failed the rest of America.

Why?

Because Congress is captured by the healthcare industry. Because members of Congress receive campaign contributions from insurance companies, pharmaceutical manufacturers, and hospital corporations. Because members of Congress leave office to become healthcare industry lobbyists. Because the revolving door between Congress and healthcare industry ensures that industry interests are protected while public interests are sacrificed.

The VA is not broken. Congress is broken. The VA does not need to be privatized. Congress needs to be held accountable. The VA does not threaten American healthcare. Congress's capture by industry threatens American healthcare.

Every argument against government healthcare collapses when confronted with VA performance data. Every claim that private markets deliver better care is refuted by VA clinical outcomes. Every assertion that government cannot manage large systems is disproven by VA's scale and scope. Every prediction that public healthcare stifles innovation is contradicted by VA's track record of medical breakthroughs.

The VA is the proof that government healthcare works. Congress is the proof that political capture prevents it from being expanded. The crisis is not healthcare delivery. The crisis is representation. The crisis is Congress.

CHAPTER 9
THE AMERICAN HOSPITAL PROPOSAL

THE INFRASTRUCTURE CONGRESS REFUSES TO SEE

Congress loves declaring war. Iraq. Afghanistan. The War on Terror. The War on Drugs. But when veterans come home needing care, Congress suddenly discovers fiscal restraint. Meanwhile, 735 VA buildings sit underutilized and 400 more sit completely vacant.(188)

These aren't crumbling shacks. Some date back to the Revolutionary and Civil Wars. They represent billions in taxpayer investment gathering dust while Congress debates whether Americans "deserve" healthcare. The answer sits empty across all 50 states.

The VA owns 449 buildings from the Revolutionary and Civil War eras. Ninety-six stand vacant. Only half of all VA facilities were built since 1920. The average VA building is 60 years old. This isn't a resource problem. It's a political choice problem.

When Congress Tried to Close VA Facilities

In 2018, Congress created the Asset and Infrastructure Review Commission. The mission: modernize VA infrastructure. The reality: gut rural healthcare access while claiming fiscal responsibility.

VA developed 1,400 recommendations for infrastructure changes. Of these, 540 targeted facility closures, replacements, or updates. The pattern was predictable. VA recommended closing rural facilities 60% of the time compared to 35% for urban facilities. Replace urban facilities 38% of the time versus 31% for rural. Update urban facilities 27% versus 9% for rural.

Translation: abandon rural America while polishing urban showpieces.

Veterans, VA employees, and lawmakers across party lines revolted. Congress defunded the Commission in 2022. For once, public outcry stopped a terrible idea. VA leadership got the message. Undersecretary for Health Shereef Elnahal committed to "focus much more diligently and upfront on the build agenda" rather than closures.

The lesson: Americans will fight to keep healthcare infrastructure. They just need someone willing to expand it rather than destroy it.

The PACT Act Proved Capacity Exists

The PACT Act of 2022 opened VA healthcare to millions of veterans exposed to toxic burn pits. Lobbyists and fiscal hawks predicted disaster. The VA would collapse under the weight. Wait times would explode. Quality would crater.

None of it happened.

Between October 2023 and February 2024, VA completed 25,000 more new patient appointments than the same period the previous year. An 11% increase. Wait times didn't explode. They dropped. Average wait times for new primary care patients fell 11%. Mental health appointments fell 7%.

More than 400,000 veterans enrolled in VA care following the PACT Act—a 30% enrollment increase (Centers for Medicare & Medicaid Services, 2025)[17]. The VA absorbed this surge while improving access and maintaining quality metrics. This proves institutional capacity for rapid expansion exists.

The VA workforce grew 56.4% between 2010 and 2024, from 308,814 employees to 482,831.(189) When Congress actually funds healthcare instead of tax cuts for pharmaceutical executives, the system scales.

The Cost of Inaction

VA estimates addressing infrastructure needs would cost $76 billion as of fiscal year 2021.(190) Congress calls this unaffordable. The same Congress that approved $1.5 trillion in tax cuts in 2017 (Committee for a Responsible Federal Budget, 2017)[15] and $858 billion for defense in 2024 (U.S. Department of Defense, 2024)[16].

Let's be clear about priorities. Congress finds money when defense contractors need it. Congress finds money when pharmaceutical companies want patent extensions. Congress finds money when hospital chains want merger approvals. But modernizing healthcare infrastructure for veterans and civilians? Suddenly we're broke.

The PACT Act provided $5.5 billion for 31 new facilities across 19 states. That's $177 million per facility. Building from scratch. Now consider repurposing the 735 underutilized buildings and 400 vacant buildings already owned by taxpayers. The cost advantage is obvious. The political will is absent.

B. REBRAND AS AN AMERICAN HOSPITAL SYSTEM

Core concept: Remove veteran-only restriction, rebrand as universal public healthcare option

What Americans Actually Want

Sixty-eight percent of voters support a public health insurance option. (191) This includes 80% of Democrats and 56% of Republicans. These numbers rose during COVID-19 as Americans watched their employer-sponsored insurance evaporate with their jobs.

Compare this to Medicare for All: 55% support, with 79% of Democrats but only 28% of Republicans. The difference matters. Americans want choice. They want the option to choose public coverage without forcing everyone into it. This isn't complicated.

Congress ignores this consensus. Both parties. Democrats talk about public options during campaigns, then abandon them during negotiations. Republicans scream about socialism while their constituents beg for affordable healthcare. The insurance industry wins either way.

The Framing That Terrifies Insurance Companies

Healthcare industry lobbyists spend millions testing messages. They know what works. Call it "government-controlled healthcare" and support drops. Frame it as "losing your current coverage" and people panic.

But describe it as expanding proven programs? Support surges. When proposals are framed as expansions of existing systems rather than new bureaucracies, Americans support them overwhelmingly.[(192)]

The VA has existed for 80 years. It delivers better diabetes care than private insurance (Kerr et al., 2004)[169]. Better hypertension management (Hyre et al., 2007)[173]. Higher patient satisfaction. Lower wait times than private insurance after reform.

This isn't theoretical. The VA already works. It just serves only 9 million people instead of 330 million.

Why Congress Won't Expand the VA

Follow the money. OpenSecrets tracks it religiously. In 2024, the health sector spent over $739 million lobbying Congress (OpenSecrets, 2025)[1]. Pharmaceutical and health product companies contributed $89 million to political campaigns (OpenSecrets, 2025)[2].

These companies don't donate out of civic duty. They buy access. They buy votes. They buy silence on proposals like VA expansion that would demolish their profit margins.

Kaiser Family Foundation research shows most Americans falsely believe they could keep their insurance under single-payer plans. Sixty-seven percent of Medicare for All supporters think they'd retain current coverage. This confusion benefits insurance companies. It creates fear of change even when change means better coverage at lower cost.

An American Hospital System public option would offer genuine choice. Keep your private insurance if you prefer. Or choose public coverage. Nobody loses access. Nobody gets forced into anything. The only losers are insurance executives whose business model depends on captive customers.

The Legal Changes Required

Opening VA facilities to non-veterans requires amending 38 U.S.C. Chapter 17, which establishes eligibility criteria limiting services to veterans and dependents.

The primary changes:

First, amend 38 U.S.C. § 1710 to add eligibility categories for U.S. citizens and residents regardless of veteran status. Veterans retain priority access during transition periods.

Second, modify 38 U.S.C. § 1722A to authorize non-veteran care without requiring specific medical conditions or emergencies.

Third, establish new funding mechanisms separate from veterans' appropriations. Veteran care funding cannot be diluted by expanded mission.

Fourth, amend 38 U.S.C. § 1701 definitions to include non-veteran populations while maintaining specific provisions for service-connected conditions.

Fifth, update facility use authorizations under 38 U.S.C. § 8110 to permit construction and alterations for civilian population services.

None of this is constitutionally complex. Congress has plenary authority to establish healthcare delivery systems. Medicare, Medicaid, Indian Health Service, and military health systems prove it. The question is purely statutory. The barrier is purely political.

The British Precedent Congress Pretends Doesn't Exist

The British National Health Service launched July 5, 1948 (National Health Service Act, 1946)[18]. It emerged directly from the Emergency Medical Service established in 1939 to handle military and civilian war casualties.

When Britain declared war on Germany in September 1939, the Emergency Medical Service activated immediately. This wasn't improvised. Pre-war planning began in 1926 when casualty analysis revealed Britain lacked ambulances and hospital capacity for anticipated air raids. By 1939, plans called for 300,000 beds to handle 25,000 casualties per day for the first ten days of war.

The Emergency Medical Service created a state-directed, centrally planned hospital system. It integrated previously independent voluntary hospitals and municipal hospitals under unified command. It standardized equipment and procedures. It trained thousands of auxiliary nurses. It coordinated evacuation and treatment at unprecedented scale.

By war's end, the system was "generally considered a success." It proved government could effectively manage large-scale healthcare delivery. This wartime experience directly informed postwar planning.

Labour's 1945 landslide victory was driven by returning soldiers' expectations that their wartime sacrifice would be rewarded with transformed social provision. The British class divide narrowed. Millions of battle-weary soldiers returned to civilian life. The "blitz mentality" created corporate altruism and sense that "we were all neighbours."

Aneurin Bevan, Minister of Health and son of a Welsh miner, led NHS creation. He extended to the entire British population the benefits his mining town enjoyed through its community-run medical scheme. "All I am doing is extending to the entire population of Britain the benefits we had in Tredegar for a generation or more. We are going to Tredegarise you."

The NHS launched by nationalizing 2,688 hospitals overnight—

1,143 voluntary hospitals with 90,000 beds and 1,545 municipal hospitals with 390,000 beds in England and Wales.

The British Medical Association initially threatened to boycott. One doctor called Bevan "a complete and uncontrolled dictator" and cooperative physicians "quislings." Bevan prevailed by allowing general practitioners to remain independent contractors rather than salaried employees.

The American context parallels Britain's 1945-1948 situation: proven government healthcare capability through VA, growing recognition of healthcare system failures, existing infrastructure and workforce, and a population demanding healthcare security.

Congress knows this history. They ignore it because insurance industry donations depend on them ignoring it.

Every Congressional District Benefits

Every U.S. state has VA facilities. Three hundred seventy-seven of 435 congressional districts contain at least one VA medical facility or outpatient clinic. This creates natural political constituencies for VA expansion in nearly every district.

Members of Congress representing districts with VA facilities would benefit from expanded patient volume through increased local employment, enhanced economic activity, improved constituent access to care, and reduced emergency department burden on local hospitals.

The VA employs 482,831 people across all 50 states. These employees and their families vote. Expanding VA facilities to serve broader populations creates substantial new employment opportunities. Direct economic benefits that members of Congress could deliver to constituents.

VA expansion doesn't require closing facilities or reducing services. This contrasts with the failed Asset and Infrastructure Review Commission, which generated fierce opposition because it proposed closures and consolidations.

The politics are straightforward. Offer members of Congress a way to deliver jobs and healthcare access to constituents. Or watch them continue taking insurance industry money while their districts' hospitals close and residents go bankrupt from medical debt.

C. HIRE CLINICIANS DIRECTLY

Core concept: Eliminate insurer/hospital middlemen, employ doctors/nurses as federal employees

What Doctors Actually Earn at VA

VA physicians earn competitive salaries under Title 38 authority, which provides flexibility beyond standard federal pay scales. Primary care physicians in high-cost areas earn $200,000-$280,000 annually. Specialists earn $250,000-$400,000+ depending on specialty and experience.

Direct salary comparison understates VA's total compensation value. Federal Employees Retirement System provides defined-benefit pension calculated as 1% of highest three-year average salary multiplied by years of service, guaranteed for life. A physician retiring after 30 years with $250,000 average salary receives $75,000 annually in pension income plus Social Security.

Thrift Savings Plan matching contributions up to 5% of salary provide additional retirement security. Federal Employees Health Benefits offers comprehensive insurance with government paying 72-75% of premiums.

Education Debt Reduction Program provides up to $200,000 in student loan repayment over five years for physicians committing to VA employment. Public Service Loan Forgiveness eligibility allows remaining federal student loan balances forgiven after 10 years of qualifying payments.

Paid leave includes 26 days annual leave plus 13 days sick leave and 11 federal holidays. Malpractice coverage provided by federal government through Federal Tort Claims Act eliminates malpractice insurance premiums of $20,000-$200,000+ annually and personal liability exposure.

Private practice physicians pay their own malpractice insurance, their own health insurance, and face income fluctuations with patient volume. They get no pension. They get no loan forgiveness. They spend 49.4% of their time on administrative tasks rather than patient care.[(193)]

The Burnout Crisis Congress Ignores

Sixty-three percent of U.S. physicians reported at least one symptom of burnout in 2021, up from 45.5% in 2011.[(194)] Emergency medicine physicians hit 65% burnout rates. Internal medicine 60%. Family medicine 58%. OB/GYN 58%.

The primary driver isn't patient care. It's administrative burden. Private practice physicians spend 14.6 hours weekly on prior authorization tasks (Commonwealth Fund, 2024)[24]. Insurance companies demand pre-approval for routine care. Doctors fill out forms justifying medications they prescribed. Insurers deny claims, forcing appeals. The cycle never ends.

VA physicians experience significantly reduced administrative burden. No insurance pre-authorization. VA physicians order necessary tests, prescribe medications, and refer to specialists without seeking insurance company approval. Simplified billing through single-payer infrastructure eliminates complexity of billing multiple insurers with different requirements, codes, and payment rates.

VistA's unified electronic health record eliminates information fragmentation (Brown et al., 2003)[183]. Private practice physicians work across multiple EHR systems that don't communicate, requiring duplicate data entry and manual records transfer.

Salary-based compensation eliminates pressure to maximize patient volume. Fee-for-service payment forces physicians to see more patients in less time to maintain income. VA physicians spend adequate time per encounter without financial penalty.

A 2022 study found physicians in integrated delivery systems like VA reported higher job satisfaction and lower burnout than fee-for-service private practice physicians, with administrative simplification identified as the primary driver.[(195)]

Congress watches physician burnout accelerate. They do nothing.

Insurance companies and hospital chains profit from the current system. Changing it would require courage Congress doesn't have.

Medical School Debt Makes Federal Employment Attractive

Median medical school debt for 2024 graduates was $250,000. Many graduates carry $300,000-$400,000 when undergraduate debt is included.[196] Seventy-three percent of 2023 graduates left school with education debt, median $200,000 for public institutions and $215,000 for private institutions.

This debt burden profoundly influences career decisions. Physicians carrying substantial debt often choose higher-paying specialties over primary care. Ninety percent of medical students report medical school debt as "a significant concern."

The calculation for debt-burdened physicians becomes straightforward:

Private practice: Higher gross salary of $280,000 for primary care. Medical school debt of $250,000 at 6.5% interest requires $2,839 monthly payments, $34,068 annually. Malpractice insurance costs $15,000-$30,000 annually. Health insurance costs $12,000-$20,000 annually. No pension. After debt service, insurance costs, and taxes: significantly reduced take-home income.

VA employment: Salary of $240,000 for primary care. EDRP provides $200,000 loan repayment over 5 years, $40,000 yearly tax-free. PSLF eligibility means remaining $50,000 forgiven after 10 years. Malpractice coverage: $0. Health insurance: 72-75% subsidized. Pension: guaranteed lifetime income. Federal job security. After benefits: comparable or superior financial position.

For early-career physicians with substantial debt, VA employment provides better long-term financial outcomes than private practice. Congress could expand this model. They won't because it would reduce physician dependence on high-paying specialties that serve wealthy patients rather than primary care that serves everyone.

D. PURCHASE UNDERUTILIZED HOSPITALS

Core concept: Buy struggling rural/urban hospitals, convert to public system

The Rural Hospital Slaughter

One hundred sixty-six rural hospitals closed between January 2010 and October 2024 (University of North Carolina, 2023)[40]. Nineteen closed in 2020. Sixteen in 2021. Seven in 2022. Five in 2023. Five more by October 2024.

Texas leads with 29 closures. Tennessee follows with 15. Oklahoma 11. Kansas 10. Notice the pattern. These states refused to expand Medicaid under the Affordable Care Act (Kaiser Family Foundation, 2024)[8]. Their hospitals serve low-income populations who can't pay. Federal Medicaid expansion would have covered those patients. Republican governors and legislatures rejected the money out of spite. Their rural hospitals died as intended.

The correlation is statistically significant. Rural hospitals in non-expansion states were 62% more likely to close than those in expansion states (Robert Wood Johnson Foundation, 2022)[39]. This wasn't market forces. This was political murder.

When rural hospitals close, entire communities lose essential services. Emergency departments shut down. Patients drive 30-60+ miles for emergency care. Labor and delivery units close. Pregnant women deliver babies 50-100 miles from home or give birth in cars.

Rural hospitals are often their communities' largest employers. A typical Critical Access Hospital employs 50-150 people with above-average wages. Closure triggers cascading economic damage: direct job losses, reduced commercial activity, declining tax revenue, and population decline as families relocate.

Congress watches this happen. They shrug. Rural voters keep electing representatives who let their hospitals die, then blame Democrats for government overreach.

Hospitals Selling for Pennies

Financially distressed hospitals sell at substantial discounts to replacement value. Hospitals in bankruptcy or facing imminent closure sell for $10-50 million—tiny fractions of their physical plant replacement cost.

Hahnemann University Hospital in Philadelphia, a 496-bed academic medical center, sold for $50 million in 2018.(197) The buyer, Joel Freedman, subsequently closed the hospital and attempted to profit from real estate. A major urban facility serving low-income populations, acquired for less than most suburban McMansion neighborhoods.

Rural Critical Access Hospitals typically sell for $5-25 million depending on facility condition and equipment. These prices reflect low revenue generation but include all physical infrastructure, medical equipment, and substantial land parcels.

For comparison, new hospital construction costs $250-500 million for a 100-bed facility.(198) A 300-bed urban hospital costs $750 million to $1.5 billion to build from scratch. Acquisition of existing facilities, even requiring substantial renovation, typically costs 20-40% of equivalent new construction.

The opportunity is obvious. The federal government could acquire struggling hospitals at distressed prices, convert them to public operation, and maintain essential community services. Congress won't do it because it would demonstrate that government healthcare works.

Private Equity Vultures

Private equity firms have aggressively acquired hospitals over the past decade, paying premium prices based on projected profit extraction rather than community healthcare value.

Steward Health Care, backed by private equity firm Cerberus Capital Management, acquired Caritas Christi Health Care's six Massachusetts hospitals for $895 million in 2010. Steward subsequently extracted value through sale-leaseback arrangements and operational changes that degraded care quality. Patients suffered. Communities suffered. Investors profited.

This is what Congress permits. Private equity can buy hospitals to strip assets. But the federal government acquiring hospitals to provide care? That's socialism. That's government overreach. That's unacceptable.

The hypocrisy would be laughable if people weren't dying from it.

Federal Authority Already Exists

Multiple legal frameworks provide federal authority to acquire healthcare facilities. 38 U.S.C. § 8110 grants VA authority to purchase, lease, or construct healthcare facilities. Legislative amendment could explicitly authorize acquisition of non-VA hospitals for conversion to federal operation.

The Public Health Service Act, 42 U.S.C. § 300, provides broad HHS authority for healthcare infrastructure development. This authority has funded Community Health Centers but could extend to hospital acquisition with Congressional authorization.

Congress could enact specific legislation authorizing a Federal Hospital Acquisition Program. The Resolution Trust Corporation, created to manage failed savings and loans in the 1980s-1990s, provides precedent for large-scale federal acquisition of distressed private sector assets.[(199)]

The legal authority exists. The financial opportunity exists. The public health need exists. Congressional will doesn't exist because insurance companies and hospital chains don't want competition from a public system that would expose their price gouging.

E. NEGOTIATE DRUG PRICES DIRECTLY

Core concept: Extend VA drug pricing power to entire public system

The 54% Discount Congress Won't Give You

The Department of Veterans Affairs pays 54% less per unit for prescription drugs than Medicare Part D.[200] Not 5%. Not 15%. Fifty-four percent less. For the same medications. Made by the same companies. Delivered to the same pharmacies.

Of 399 drugs analyzed by GAO, 233 were at least 50% cheaper in VA than Medicare. One hundred six were at least 75% cheaper. Only 43 drugs were cheaper in Medicare than VA.

Why does VA pay less? Because VA negotiates as a single entity representing 9 million people. Medicare Part D splits beneficiaries among numerous prescription drug plans that each negotiate separately. The largest Part D plan had approximately 5.6 million enrollees in 2017. Most were much smaller. VA's single unified plan represented 9 million.

Pharmaceutical companies face a choice with VA: accept our price or we exclude your drug from the formulary. That's called negotiation. Medicare Part D lacked this authority until the Inflation Reduction Act partially restored it for a tiny number of drugs.

Congress prohibited Medicare from negotiating drug prices for 15 years through the Medicare Part D "non-interference" clause. This wasn't an accident. This wasn't an oversight. Pharmaceutical companies paid for that prohibition. Congress delivered.

Pharmaceutical Profit Margins Expose the Lie

Pharmaceutical companies claim they need high U.S. prices to fund research and development. Their profit margins expose this as fiction.

A 2020 JAMA study analyzed 35 large pharmaceutical companies from 2000 to 2018 (Wouters et al., 2020)[3]. Median annual gross profit margin: 76.5% compared to 37.4% for S&P 500 companies. EBITDA margin: 29.4% versus 19%. Net income margin: 13.8% versus 7.7%.

Even after controlling for company size, year, and R&D expenses, pharmaceutical companies maintained significantly higher margins: gross profit margin difference of 30.5%, EBITDA margin difference of 9.2%, net income margin difference of 3.6%.

Recent analysis found pharmaceutical manufacturers' average annual net income margin was nearly 23%. Other sectors of the prescription drug supply chain—distributors, retail pharmacies, PBMs, health insurers—averaged only 2.3%. A tenfold differential.

Individual companies show even higher margins. Novo Nordisk's gross margin in 2022: nearly 83%. Gilead's and Eli Lilly's gross margins: approximately 77-79%.

These profit margins demonstrate substantial room for price reduction. Even if pharmaceutical companies' net income margins fell to the S&P 500 average of 7.7%, they would remain profitable while enabling dramatic consumer price reductions.

Congress knows these numbers. They don't care. Pharmaceutical companies contributed $89 million to political campaigns in 2024 (OpenSecrets, 2025)[2]. Those donations buy silence on price negotiation proposals.

What Americans Pay Versus What Other Countries Pay

A 2024 analysis of Medicare's first ten negotiated drug prices under the Inflation Reduction Act found that even after negotiation, Medicare's new prices average 2.8 times the average price in 11 comparable OECD countries.[(201)]

Americans pay more for identical drugs made by identical companies than every other developed nation. Not because our drugs are better. Not because our pharmacies provide superior service. Because Congress allows pharmaceutical companies to extract maximum profit from captive customers.

The Peterson-KFF Health System Tracker compared prices for identical drugs across countries. For Eliquis, used for blood clot prevention, the U.S. list price for a 30-day supply exceeded prices in Canada, Germany, United Kingdom, and other developed nations by orders of magnitude.

What explains international price differentials? Virtually all developed countries empower their national healthcare systems to negotiate drug prices on behalf of entire populations (OECD, 2024)[17]. The United

States historically prohibited such negotiation through the Medicare Part D "non-interference" clause.

The Inflation Reduction Act partially reversed this for a limited number of drugs. Medicare negotiated prices for ten drugs, effective January 2026. If these negotiated prices had been available in 2023, they would have generated $6 billion in savings.

Six billion sounds impressive until you remember Medicare Part D spent $93.9 billion in 2017 (CBO, 2019)[10]. Negotiating ten drugs out of thousands is theatre. It's designed to look like action while preserving pharmaceutical profit margins.

The Inflation Reduction Act's Pathetic Limitations

The Inflation Reduction Act allows Medicare to negotiate prices for ten drugs initially, expanding gradually to 20 drugs by 2029. Given that Medicare Part D covers thousands of drugs, this represents a fraction of total spending.

Small-molecule drugs aren't eligible for negotiation until 9 years after FDA approval. Biologics not until 13 years after approval. This protects manufacturers' pricing power during peak revenue years. Exactly as pharmaceutical lobbyists demanded.

The law establishes maximum fair price ceilings based on complex formulas rather than enabling true head-to-head negotiation comparable to VA's approach.

Congress could extend VA pricing to all government healthcare programs tomorrow. They won't because pharmaceutical companies own them. Democrats and Republicans both. The pharmaceutical industry doesn't discriminate in their donations. Neither party discriminates in accepting them.

What Full VA Pricing Would Save

If VA's 54% lower prices were applied to Medicare Part D's $93.9 billion in 2017 spending, this would generate approximately $50.7 billion in annual savings (CBO, 2019)[10]. Extending similar savings to

Medicaid and other federal programs would produce total savings exceeding $60-70 billion annually.

Medicare spending on retail prescription drugs was $121 billion in 2021, accounting for 32% of total U.S. retail prescription drug costs (CMS, 2024)[73]. Applying VA pricing to 2021 Medicare spending would generate approximately $65 billion in annual savings.

These savings would compound over time as pharmaceutical spending grows. They would also increase appropriate medication adherence, improving health outcomes and reducing downstream costs from undertreated conditions. High out-of-pocket costs cause patients to skip doses or abandon prescriptions, resulting in preventable hospitalizations and emergency department visits.

The money exists to provide every American with affordable medications. Congress chooses pharmaceutical profits over public health. Every single day.

F. COMPETE WITH PRIVATE INSURANCE

Core concept: Public option available alongside private plans, not mandatory replacement

Americans Want Choice, Not Mandates

Sixty-eight percent of voters support a public health insurance option. Eighty percent of Democrats. Fifty-six percent of Republicans. These numbers rose during COVID-19 as Americans watched employer-sponsored insurance evaporate with their jobs.

Compare to Medicare for All: 55% support, with 79% of Democrats but only 28% of Republicans. The ten-percentage-point difference matters. Americans want options. They don't want forced enrollment in government programs. They don't trust government enough for that. Fair enough given Congress's track record.

But offer Americans a choice between overpriced private insurance and affordable public coverage? They'll choose based on value. Insurance companies know this. That's why they spend millions fighting public option proposals.

The "Crowding Out" Myth

Healthcare industry lobbyists warn that public options would "crowd out" private insurance through adverse selection and unfair competition. This is projection. Private insurers "crowd out" sick patients every single day through network restrictions, prior authorization denials, and claim rejections.

Critics argue public options paying Medicare rates gain unfair cost advantages that private plans cannot match while paying higher provider rates. Yes. That's called efficiency. That's called eliminating profit extraction. That's called serving patients instead of shareholders.

If private insurance can't compete with public options on price and quality, that reveals private insurance's failure, not public options' unfairness. Markets work when consumers have genuine choices. Insurance companies want captive customers, not market competition.

Germany Proves Public-Private Competition Works

Germany has maintained mixed public-private competition for over a century.(202) Approximately 86-88% of Germans enroll in statutory health insurance provided by approximately 95-105 nonprofit sickness funds. About 11% have private health insurance. The remaining 1-2% are covered by government schemes for military, police, and refugees.

Germans earning below €73,800 annually must enroll in statutory insurance. Those earning above this threshold may opt into private insurance. Freelancers and self-employed may join either system regardless of income.

Statutory insurance is financed through income-based contributions—14.6% of wages plus supplementary contributions averaging 1%, split between employers and workers. Private insurance charges risk-based premiums unrelated to income, based on age and health status at enrollment.

Since the 1990s, Germany introduced competitive elements into its public system. Germans choose among statutory sickness funds, which compete on supplementary contribution rates, customer service, and additional benefits. Morbidity-based risk adjustment prevents funds from avoiding sick enrollees.

Despite predictions that private insurance would hollow out the statutory system, approximately 88% of Germans remain in public coverage. Robust public options maintain dominant market position while allowing private competition for high-income segments.

Both public and private sectors pay providers, though private insurers typically pay higher rates. This creates provider incentives to see private patients, but regulatory frameworks prevent complete abandonment of public patients.

Congress could adapt Germany's model. They won't because American insurance companies demand monopoly protection, not market competition. And Congress delivers what their donors demand.

The Votes Are There If Congress Had Courage

Three hundred seventy-seven of 435 congressional districts contain at least one VA medical facility or outpatient clinic. Expanding those facilities to serve all constituents creates jobs, economic activity, and healthcare access in nearly every district.

The politics are straightforward. Members could deliver tangible benefits to constituents: employment, healthcare access, economic development. Or they could continue taking insurance industry money while their constituents go bankrupt from medical debt and their rural hospitals close.

Most choose the money. That's the betrayal. That's the indictment. Congress knows what works. They know what Americans want. They know what other countries achieve. They choose corporate profits over public health because that's what their donors pay them to choose.

The ACA was supposed to be the compromise. Market-based reforms. Private insurance exchanges. Subsidies to make private coverage affordable. And what did Americans get? Bronze plans with $6,000 deductibles (Kaiser Family Foundation, 2024)[31]. Narrow networks that exclude necessary providers (Kaiser Family Foundation, 2023)[35]. Claim denial rates pushing 20% for some insurers (Money-

Geek, 2025)[25]. Medical bankruptcy continuing despite "universal coverage" (Himmelstein et al., 2019)[64].

The ACA failed because it preserved the system that caused the crisis. It regulated around the edges while leaving insurance companies and hospital chains in charge. Any solution that maintains private insurance dominance will fail the same way.

An American Hospital System offers a different path. Not mandatory enrollment. Not government control. Just a real alternative to private insurance's extraction and denial. Let Americans choose. Watch what happens when they actually have a choice that serves their interests instead of corporate profits.

Congress won't do it unless forced. They'll need to be forced.

CHAPTER 10
NATIONAL SECURITY, PATRIOTISM, AND PUBLIC HEALTH

A nation at war mobilizes everything. Factories retool for weapons production. Young people enlist. Resources concentrate on military objectives. No expense is spared. No sacrifice is considered too great.

Yet the United States treats peacetime differently. We refuse to mobilize for health the way we mobilize for war. We spend trillions on military infrastructure while allowing civilian healthcare to collapse. We train soldiers to be healthy and disciplined, then discharge them into a population too sick to sustain them. We build the strongest military on earth, then surround it with a civilian population drowning in preventable disease.

This is not policy. This is abdication.

National security begins with national health. A sick population cannot defend itself. Chronic disease erodes the economic capacity to fund defense. Untreated mental illness destabilizes communities. Substance abuse destroys families. Preventable illness creates dependency. A nation that cannot care for its own people cannot project power beyond its borders. A nation that cannot ensure basic health cannot survive long-term competition with healthier rivals.

Yet this fundamental truth remains absent from national security debates. Congress discusses defense spending in isolation from health outcomes. Military planners focus on weapons systems without acknowledging that the people operating them grow progressively less capable as disease advances. Strategic thinkers debate geopolitical competition while ignoring that healthier populations outcompete unhealthy ones across every meaningful dimension.

The Veterans Health Administration exists because we recognized a basic truth: the nation owes health security to those who sacrificed for national security. The VA receives billions annually to deliver comprehensive care to veterans because Congress understands that wounded soldiers deserve medical attention. This principle is sound. The application is truncated.

If healthcare is a debt owed to soldiers, why is it not an investment in civilians? Soldiers exist to protect the population. What is the purpose of protecting a population that cannot work, reproduce, or think clearly because of untreated disease? What is the strategic value of military superiority if the civilian base supporting that military is collapsing from preventable illness?

The answer is there is no strategic value. A military is only as strong as the population it defends and the economy that sustains it. Both are deteriorating.

AMERICAN MILITARY READINESS AND POPULATION HEALTH: THE CONNECTION CONGRESS IGNORES

The Department of Defense confronts a growing recruitment crisis driven by preventable health conditions in the civilian population. Among Americans aged 17-24, approximately 77 percent do not meet military entrance standards without requiring a waiver.[203] The leading causes of disqualification are obesity, mental health conditions, and substance abuse—all preventable through adequate healthcare access.

Obesity alone disqualifies approximately 9 percent of military-age Americans.[204] Type 2 diabetes, now epidemic among young people, creates additional disqualifications. Untreated depression and anxiety account for thousands of disqualifications annually. Prior drug use or ongoing substance abuse dependencies eliminate candidates. These are not rare conditions affecting marginal populations. They are widespread across the demographic that should form the foundation of military recruitment.

The Department of Defense has responded by lowering standards. The military has granted increasing numbers of waivers for recruits who do not meet historical fitness and health standards. Some of these waivers prove manageable. Others create soldiers who cannot meet deployment demands. Soldiers who are obese face higher injury rates. Soldiers with untreated mental health conditions have higher suicide rates. Soldiers with substance abuse histories have higher attrition rates.

This is not new. After the September 11, 2001 terrorist attacks, the military was forced to recruit and deploy soldiers with significant health limitations because the population of fully healthy candidates was insufficient. The wars in Iraq and Afghanistan depleted recruiting pools. The military adapted by accepting candidates it would have rejected during the Cold War.

The crisis persists today. As chronic disease continues advancing through the civilian population, recruitment will become more difficult. The pool of fully healthy recruits will shrink further. The military will either lower standards further or face recruitment shortfalls.

This is a national security problem. It is also a healthcare problem. These are the same problem.

A population with universal access to primary care, mental health services, and substance abuse treatment would produce more recruits who meet military standards. A population with systematic diabetes screening and early intervention would disqualify fewer young people. A population with access to mental health treatment would reduce depression and anxiety disqualifications. A population without epidemic obesity would have recruits with the physical capacity to meet military demands.

The calculation is straightforward: invest in civilian health now, or accept degraded military readiness later. Yet Congress treats these as separate domains. Healthcare policy is left to committees focused on insurance and cost. Military policy is left to committees focused on weapons systems and force structure. No committee is tasked with connecting them.

This is deliberate ignorance. Congress knows that healthcare affects military readiness. They choose not to connect them because connecting them would require spending money on civilians instead of defense contractors. Insurance companies and pharmaceutical firms donate to the same members who sit on Armed Services Committees. Those donations buy silence on the healthcare-military readiness connection.

The result: Congress appropriates $858 billion for defense in 2024 (U.S. Department of Defense, 2024)[16] while allowing the recruiting pool to deteriorate from preventable disease. They fund weapons systems while ignoring that fewer Americans are healthy enough to operate them. They authorize force expansion while the population capable of filling that force shrinks.

This is strategic malpractice. Enemy nations don't need to defeat American military technology. They just need to wait for the American population to become too sick to field a military.

THE ECONOMIC FOUNDATION OF MILITARY POWER

Military power rests on economic capacity. The United States spends $858 billion annually on defense because the underlying economy generates sufficient wealth to support that spending. If the economy deteriorates, defense spending capacity deteriorates with it.

Healthcare costs erode economic capacity. In 2024, the United States spent $4.8 trillion on healthcare—17.3 percent of gross domestic product (CMS, 2024)[73]. This represents the highest percentage of any developed nation. Germany spends 12.5 percent of GDP on healthcare and covers everyone (OECD, 2024)[17]. Japan spends 10.8 percent and covers everyone. Canada spends 10.7 percent and covers everyone. The United States spends substantially more while leaving millions uninsured and underinsured.

This excess spending does not produce superior outcomes. American life expectancy lags behind comparable nations.[(205)] American infant mortality exceeds comparable nations.[(206)] American rates of preventable disease exceed comparable nations. The additional spending produces bureaucratic overhead, insurance company profits, and healthcare executive compensation rather than superior health outcomes.

This inefficiency directly undermines military capacity. Every dollar spent on healthcare bureaucracy is a dollar not available for defense investment, infrastructure development, or economic growth. Every dollar extracted from the economy through healthcare cost inflation is a dollar not available for productive investment.

Consider the math: if the United States spent the same percentage of GDP on healthcare as Germany—12.5 percent instead of 17.3 percent—while covering the entire population with superior outcomes, the United States would save approximately $1.3 trillion annually.[(207)] That savings equals one and a half years of defense spending. That savings could modernize every weapon system, rebuild infrastructure, eliminate student debt, or reduce the deficit.

This is not theoretical calculation. It is budgetary reality. The healthcare system's inefficiency taxes the economy and therefore taxes military capacity.

Congress knows this. The Congressional Budget Office produces reports on healthcare spending's impact on federal budgets and economic growth (CBO, 2024)[61]. These reports demonstrate clearly that healthcare cost growth undermines fiscal capacity for all other spending including defense. Members of Congress receive these reports. They ignore them because acting on them would require confronting insurance companies and pharmaceutical firms that fund their campaigns.

Truman recognized this principle. His 1945 proposal for national health insurance was explicitly framed as a matter of national strength (Truman, 1945)[57]. Truman believed a healthy population was an economically productive population, and economically productive populations could support strong militaries. Universal healthcare was not a gift to the poor. It was an investment in national power.

Congress abandoned this principle. Healthcare is treated as a consumption item rather than a strategic investment. Healthcare costs are treated as fiscal problems rather than strategic weaknesses. This abandonment serves corporate interests at the expense of national interests.

A strategic reframing is necessary. Healthcare investment should be evaluated primarily on national security and economic productivity grounds, not on healthcare grounds alone. The question should not be "can we afford universal healthcare?" The question should be "can we afford not to have universal healthcare when the cost of not having it is reduced military readiness, reduced economic productivity, and reduced global competitiveness?"

Congress won't ask this question because the answer terrifies their donors.

THE MILITARY HEALTH COMPLEX VS. THE CIVILIAN HEALTH CRISIS

The military spends approximately $60 billion annually on healthcare for active-duty service members, their families, and retirees through the Department of Defense and TRICARE system.[(208)] This represents approximately 7 percent of total defense spending dedicated to keeping military personnel healthy.

The principle is clear: the military recognizes that healthy service members are more capable, suffer fewer injuries, perform better, and have higher retention. The military invests in prevention through fitness programs, nutrition standards, and mental health services. Active-duty service members have access to comprehensive healthcare. Military retirees receive healthcare for life. Military families receive dependent healthcare coverage.

This is expensive. This is also clearly justified. When the military calculates costs, it recognizes that health investment produces military capability. The military does not debate whether fitness programs are "sustainable." The military does not ask whether mental health counseling is "affordable." The military recognizes these as force multipliers that increase capability.

Yet for the civilian population, Congress applies entirely different logic. When healthcare is proposed for civilians, Congress demands proof of fiscal sustainability. Congress weighs costs against budgets. Congress treats healthcare as a discretionary expense rather than a force multiplier.

This is backwards. Civilian health is more strategically important than military health precisely because a civilian population that is unfit, mentally ill, and substance-dependent cannot sustain a military. The military's health investment only matters if it defends a healthy, productive population.

The hypocrisy is staggering. Congress appropriates $60 billion yearly to keep 2.9 million service members healthy.[(209)] That's approximately $20,690 per person. Congress refuses to appropriate equivalent funding to keep 330 million civilians healthy. The per-capita spending would actually be lower because economies of scale would reduce costs. VA spends approximately $12,000 per veteran annually (U.S. Department of Veterans Affairs, 2024)[160]. Extending that model to all Americans would cost approximately $4 trillion annually—less than current healthcare spending of $4.8 trillion.

The math works. The policy works. The VA proves it works. Congress refuses because insurance companies and pharmaceutical firms demand they refuse.

The Department of Defense's healthcare spending should be framed differently. It should not be evaluated in isolation as "military spending." It should be reframed as "national health defense spending." Once reframed, the absurdity of denying equivalent spending on civilian health becomes obvious.

If the military justifies $60 billion annually to keep service members healthy, the United States must justify universal healthcare to keep civilians healthy. Anything less is strategic negligence bordering on treason.

CONGRESS FUNDS WARS BUT NOT HEALTH

Congress appropriated $2.3 trillion for wars in Iraq and Afghanistan between 2001 and 2022.[(210)] No debate about affordability. No concerns about deficits. No questions about fiscal sustainability. Congress wrote the checks because wars demand immediate action.

Those wars killed approximately 7,000 American service members and wounded 53,000 more.[(211)] Tragic losses. Worthy of remembrance and compensation through VA healthcare.

Preventable disease kills 900,000 Americans annually.[(212)] Heart disease: 700,000 deaths yearly. Cancer: 600,000 deaths yearly. Diabetes: 100,000 deaths yearly. Many of these deaths are preventable through early screening, treatment, and lifestyle interventions that universal healthcare would provide. Over 20 years, preventable disease killed 18 million Americans—2,571 times more than Iraq and Afghanistan combined.

Congress spent $2.3 trillion to prevent 7,000 combat deaths. Congress refuses to spend equivalent amounts to prevent 900,000 yearly deaths from preventable disease. This is not policy. This is sociopathy.

The calculation is clear: preventing combat deaths costs approximately $328 million per death prevented ($2.3 trillion divided by 7,000 deaths). Preventing disease deaths through universal healthcare would cost substantially less per death prevented because the intervention is medical care rather than military deployment.

Congress knows this math. They choose war spending over health spending because defense contractors donate more than patients do. Because insurance companies demand preservation of the current system. Because pharmaceutical firms profit from disease rather than prevention.

The result is a nation that treats military casualties as sacred while treating civilian casualties from preventable disease as acceptable. A nation that honors soldiers killed by enemy bullets while ignoring civilians killed by insurance company denials. A nation that builds monuments to war dead while allowing 68,000 Americans to die annually from lack of health insurance (American Journal of Public Health, 2009)[82].

This is not patriotism. This is betrayal.

FAMILY SUPPORT AS NATIONAL DEFENSE

National security depends ultimately on family stability. Families that are economically secure, healthy, and stable produce children who grow into productive citizens. Families devastated by medical bankruptcy, untreated illness, and healthcare insecurity produce children who are less capable of contributing to national strength.

The logic is straightforward yet absent from national security discussions: every family that avoids medical bankruptcy is a family with economic capacity to invest in children's education. Every child with preventive healthcare access is a child more likely to graduate high school and serve productively whether militarily or civilly. Every parent with mental health treatment is a parent more likely to be employed and capable of supporting family. Every family with healthcare security is a family more likely to remain stable and productive.

Medical bankruptcy affects 530,000 families annually (Himmelstein et al., 2019)[64]. Each bankruptcy represents a family pushed into economic crisis by healthcare costs. Children in these families face reduced educational opportunity, increased stress, and decreased economic mobility. These children become adults less capable of military service, less capable of economic productivity, less capable of supporting national objectives.

Medical debt affects 100 million Americans.[(213)] Eighteen percent of Americans have medical debt in collections (Consumer Financial Protection Bureau, 2022)[65]. This debt destroys credit scores, prevents homeownership, limits economic opportunity, and creates multi-generational poverty. Each person carrying medical debt is a person whose economic capacity is diminished, whose family stability is threatened, whose contribution to national strength is reduced.

Yet the United States treats family healthcare security as a consumer good to be purchased individually rather than a national asset to be invested in collectively. Healthcare insecurity cascades through families, producing children who inherit medical debt, reduced educational opportunity, and decreased capacity for national contribution.

Congress watches this happen. They do nothing. Medical bankruptcies continue. Medical debt accumulates. Families collapse. And Congress appropriates another $858 billion for defense while refusing to defend families against healthcare costs.

A strategic reframing of family healthcare as family security, and family security as national security, would justify healthcare investment on grounds that currently justify military spending. If the nation spends $858 billion annually to defend against external threats, the nation must spend resources to defend families against internal healthcare threats.

Congress won't reframe because doing so would expose their priorities. They value defense contractors over families. They value insurance company profits over family stability. They value pharmaceutical revenues over children's futures.

The result is a nation that spends trillions defending families from foreign enemies while allowing domestic healthcare costs to destroy those same families from within.

THE RECRUITMENT CRISIS CONGRESS CREATED

The Army missed its recruiting goal by 15,000 soldiers in 2022.[(214)] The Army missed its goal by 10,000 in 2023. The Navy, Air Force, and Marine Corps face similar shortfalls. Every service branch struggles to find qualified recruits.

The primary disqualifier: health conditions. Seventy-seven percent of military-age Americans fail to meet entrance standards (DOD, 2020)[203]. Obesity, mental health conditions, substance abuse, and chronic disease eliminate the vast majority of potential recruits before they reach a recruiter's office.

This is a crisis Congress created through healthcare policy neglect. Every young person disqualified for obesity is a person who lacked access to preventive care, nutrition education, and early intervention. Every young person disqualified for mental health is a person who lacked access to counseling and treatment. Every young person disqualified for substance abuse is a person who lacked access to addiction services.

Universal healthcare would reduce these disqualifications substantially. Primary care access would catch obesity early. Mental health services would treat depression and anxiety before they become disqualifying. Substance abuse treatment would prevent addiction from becoming permanent disqualification.

The cost of providing this care is substantially less than the cost of failing to recruit. The Army spends approximately $22,000 per recruit on recruitment and training.(215) Missing recruitment goals by 15,000 soldiers represents $330 million in wasted recruitment capacity. Preventing the health conditions that cause disqualifications would cost far less per person than recruiting replacements.

Congress knows this. The Department of Defense produces reports on recruitment challenges. The Government Accountability Office analyzes military readiness. Congressional Research Service briefs members on healthcare's impact on recruitment. All the information exists. Congress ignores it because acting on it would require confronting healthcare industry donors.

The result is a military that cannot recruit enough healthy Americans to maintain force strength. A military that lowers standards to fill ranks. A military that deploys soldiers who are less physically capable, less mentally resilient, and less able to meet combat demands than previous generations.

This is what happens when Congress values insurance company profits over national defense. This is what happens when pharmaceutical donations matter more than military readiness. This is what happens when healthcare policy is written by industry lobbyists instead of strategic planners.

The recruiting crisis will worsen. Obesity rates continue rising. Mental health conditions continue spreading. Substance abuse continues accelerating. Each year, the pool of qualified recruits shrinks further. Each year, the military becomes weaker. Each year, national security deteriorates.

Congress created this crisis. Only Congress can fix it. They won't because their donors won't let them.

THE PATHWAY FORWARD: NATIONAL SERVICE AND NATIONAL HEALTH

A comprehensive solution requires integrating national service with national healthcare. Every young American should serve the nation for two years after high school. Military service for those capable and willing. Healthcare service for those interested in medicine. Infrastructure service for those focused on building. Environmental service for those concerned about conservation.

The principle: all citizens owe service to the nation, with choices about how to serve.

A healthcare service option would attract many young people who want to avoid combat but value public service. Some would become healthcare providers or pursue medical education. Others would serve as healthcare workers, supporting clinical staff in hospitals and clinics. This would accomplish multiple objectives simultaneously: provide national service experience, build healthcare infrastructure, and create pathways into healthcare careers.

Such service would be structured around the VA system or an expanded American Hospital System. Participants would serve in VA facilities or public hospitals, learning healthcare systems while delivering care. Upon completion of service, participants would have access to education benefits including medical school funding or loan forgiveness, exactly as military service members receive.

This model accomplishes several strategic objectives:

Builds healthcare workforce capacity, reducing dependency on fragmented private healthcare labor markets.

Creates service pathways for people without military aptitude, expanding national service beyond military recruitment.

Ensures healthcare facilities are adequately staffed across rural and urban areas through service distribution requirements.

Integrates young people across socioeconomic status through shared service experience, building social cohesion.

Creates healthcare workers oriented toward public service rather than private profit.

Ensures veterans understand healthcare systems before they depend upon them.

Builds healthcare literacy across entire population through exposure during service years.

Germany operates such a system.(216) Israel integrates healthcare and military service.(217) Switzerland's civil service includes healthcare delivery options.(218) These are proven models that work.

Congress could enact this tomorrow. The legal authority exists. The administrative capacity exists. The facilities exist. The need exists.

Congress won't do it because insurance companies and hospital chains would lose control over healthcare labor markets. Because pharmaceutical firms would lose captive customers. Because healthcare industry donors demand preservation of the current fragmented system.

So young Americans enter adulthood without service experience, without healthcare skills, without understanding of public systems. They remain dependent on private insurance that denies claims. They work for hospital chains that maximize profits. They pay pharmaceutical companies whatever prices are demanded.

This serves corporate interests. It undermines national interests. It weakens national security. And Congress allows it because their donors profit from it.

THE CHOICE CONGRESS REFUSES TO MAKE

The choice is clear: invest in population health or accept military decline.

Invest in universal healthcare and produce a generation of recruits who meet physical and mental standards. Refuse to invest and watch recruitment fail as chronic disease spreads.

Invest in preventive care and reduce healthcare costs that drain economic capacity for defense spending. Refuse to invest and watch healthcare inflation consume resources needed for military modernization.

Invest in family healthcare security and strengthen the social foundation that supports military capability. Refuse to invest and watch medical bankruptcy destroy families whose children should be serving.

Congress chooses decline. They choose corporate profits over national strength. They choose insurance company revenues over military readiness. They choose pharmaceutical donations over population health.

This is treason by another name. Treason is betraying your country to foreign enemies. What do you call betraying your country to domestic corporations? What do you call sacrificing national security for campaign donations? What do you call allowing population health to deteriorate while defense contractors prosper?

You call it Congress. You call it the current system. You call it what happens when lobbying money determines national policy.

The military cannot defend a nation too sick to sustain it. The economy cannot support defense spending when healthcare inflation consumes resources. Families cannot produce capable citizens when medical bankruptcy destroys economic security.

Every metric of national strength depends on population health. Every strategic calculation requires healthy civilians to succeed. Every military plan assumes an economically productive population to fund it.

Congress ignores these connections because acknowledging them would require choosing between donors and country. They consistently choose donors. The evidence is overwhelming. The health sector spent over $739 million lobbying Congress in 2024 (OpenSecrets, 2025)[1]. Pharmaceutical companies contributed $89 million to campaigns (OpenSecrets, 2025)[2]. Those donations buy silence on proposals that would strengthen national security through improved population health.

The result is a nation with the strongest military in the world defending a population growing progressively weaker. A nation that spends more on defense than the next ten nations combined while its recruiting pool shrinks from preventable disease. A nation that projects power globally while collapsing internally from healthcare failures.

This cannot continue. The math doesn't work. The strategy doesn't work. The current system weakens America every single day.

The solution exists. The VA proves it works. Expanding the VA model to all Americans would improve population health, reduce healthcare costs, strengthen military recruitment, enhance economic productivity, and secure families against medical bankruptcy.

Congress knows this. They choose not to act because their donors profit from the current system. Insurance companies profit from denial. Pharmaceutical firms profit from high prices. Hospital chains profit from consolidation. All of them donate to Congress. All of them demand preservation of the current system.

So Americans die from preventable disease while Congress debates insurance subsidies. Families collapse under medical debt while Congress appropriates billions for defense contractors. Military recruitment fails while chronic disease spreads through the population.

This is what betrayal looks like. Not foreign enemies breaching borders. Domestic corporations purchasing Congress and using it to extract wealth from sick Americans while national security deteriorates.

A nation that cannot ensure its population is healthy cannot ensure its population is strong. A nation that cannot ensure its population is strong cannot ensure it will remain free.

Congress refuses to learn this lesson. Americans will pay the price. The bill comes due when recruiting fails. When economic capacity to fund defense collapses. When families destroyed by medical costs cannot produce capable citizens. When population health deteriorates so far that no amount of military spending compensates.

The choice is healthcare or decline. Congress chooses decline because that's what their donors pay them to choose. Every day they make that choice, America grows weaker. Every dollar diverted to insurance profits is a dollar not invested in population health. Every family destroyed by medical bankruptcy is a family that cannot contribute to national strength.

This is not policy failure. This is policy success—for the corporations buying Congress. For Americans, it's catastrophic. For national security, it's suicidal.

CHAPTER 11

IDEOLOGICAL AND POLICY OBJECTIONS: ANSWERED ONE BY ONE

Congress does not reject the American Hospital System proposal because it is economically unsound. Congress rejects it because accepting it would require acknowledging a fundamental truth: the private healthcare industry has captured Congress, and Congress has chosen corporate profit over citizen welfare.

Yet objections persist. Some are sincere. Most are not. All are answerable. This chapter addresses every major objection systematically, with data, with citations, with acknowledgment of legitimate concerns and clear refutation of rhetorical smokescreens.

The objections follow a predictable pattern. Opponents raise one concern. When that concern is answered with evidence, they shift to another. When that objection falls, they cycle back to earlier arguments as if the previous refutation never occurred. This is not an honest debate. This is rhetorical obstruction designed to delay until political will exhausts itself.

This chapter ends that pattern. Every objection gets a complete answer. Once answered here, further repetition of these objections should be recognized for what it is: bad faith obstruction dressed as policy concern.

A. "THE ACA HAS HIGH DEDUCTIBLES AND UNAFFORDABLE COST-SHARING"

The objection states itself clearly. ACA marketplace plans carry high deductibles. Even with subsidies, many people cannot afford to use their insurance. Cost-sharing remains a barrier to care. Therefore, expanding the ACA model is pointless.

The objection is factually accurate. It is also irrelevant to the proposal at hand.

The Deductible Problem Is Real But Not Unique to the ACA

Current ACA marketplace plans vary significantly in their cost-sharing structures. Bronze plans typically carry individual deductibles around $7,000 (Kaiser Family Foundation, 2024)[31]. Silver plans range lower. Gold plans lower still. Even Silver plans, the most popular tier, often leave people with substantial out-of-pocket exposure before insurance begins paying.

A person with a $4,000 deductible and a family income of $35,000 faces a genuine problem. That deductible represents over 11 percent of annual income. It functions as a barrier to care. People skip medical visits. They delay treatment. They pay out of pocket rather than satisfy deductibles. This is documented reality.

But here is what opponents never mention: employer-sponsored insurance carries identical or worse deductibles. The average employer-sponsored family plan carries a deductible of $1,735 (Kaiser Family Foundation, 2024)[33]. Since 2010, average employer-sponsored deductibles have increased 123 percent while wages increased only 27 percent. A worker with employer insurance faces the same problem as an ACA enrollee. Yet this fact never surfaces in objections to the ACA.

The American Hospital System proposal directly addresses this problem in ways private markets cannot.

How the American Hospital System Solves High Deductibles

The proposal contemplates direct federal employment of clinicians, unified provider networks, and streamlined administrative structures. These operational characteristics dramatically reduce costs per patient. Lower costs per patient translate to lower deductibles or elimination of deductibles entirely.

The VA operates without deductibles for most services. VA patients pay modest copayments: typically $10 for primary care, $15 for specialty care, $5 for prescriptions, with annual caps on out-of-pocket spending. A veteran with a chronic condition requiring monthly specialist visits and regular prescriptions faces $60-80 in annual out-of-pocket costs plus copayments, not thousands in deductible obligations.

This is not theoretical. The VA achieves this structure at lower cost per beneficiary than any comparator system. The VA spends approximately $12,000 per veteran annually (U.S. Department of Veterans Affairs, 2024)[160]. Medicare spends $15,000 per beneficiary. Employer insurance spends $22,500 per enrollee. The American Hospital System, operating at VA cost levels, could structure benefits to eliminate or substantially reduce deductibles while remaining fiscally sound.

The private sector cannot replicate this because profit extraction is not optional. Insurers require margins. Hospital systems require return on invested capital. Pharmaceutical manufacturers require pricing power. These institutional facts mean private systems cannot achieve VA cost structures. The American Hospital System, operating as a public enterprise, can.

Deductibles Are Not Consumer Protection; They Are Cost Shifting

The argument is sometimes made that high deductibles serve a valuable function: they make consumers more price-conscious, they encourage appropriate utilization, they create "skin in the game" that deters unnecessary care. This theory has been tested extensively. The evidence is clear: high deductibles do not accomplish these goals. They accomplish something else entirely: they reduce care utilization, including necessary care.

A landmark study tracked high-deductible plan enrollees over multiple years, comparing their utilization patterns to lower-deductible plans (Wharam et al., 2023)[35]. The research found that high deductibles reduced preventive care utilization by 15 to 20 percent without reducing overall healthcare spending. People did not become more efficient consumers. They became less healthy consumers. They skipped screening colonoscopies. They delayed mammograms. They postponed blood pressure checks. Then they incurred expensive emergency care for untreated conditions.

A 2024 Commonwealth Fund study found that 41 percent of American adults with health insurance reported difficulty affording care in the past year (Commonwealth Fund, 2024)[32]. Among those with ACA marketplace coverage, 39 percent reported cost-related barriers to care. These are not people making rational economic choices. These are people rationing necessary care because they cannot afford deductibles and copayments.

The American Hospital System proposal eliminates this problem not through altruism but through structural design. When a health system operates on principles of coverage rather than profit, cost-sharing barriers become unnecessary. Prevention becomes economically rational because the system captures the benefit of prevented disease. A person who receives a colonoscopy early catches polyps before they become cancer; the system saves money on cancer treatment. A person who gets blood pressure screening and medication avoids strokes; the system saves money on stroke management. In systems designed to maximize population health rather than extract maximum revenue, cost-sharing barriers work against the system's financial interests.

The Dishonesty of the Deductible Objection

Opposition to the American Hospital System on deductible grounds is dishonest if it does not simultaneously oppose employer-sponsored insurance for identical deductible structures. It is dishonest if it does not oppose Medicare Advantage plans, which increasingly impose high deductibles and narrow networks comparable to ACA plans (Kaiser Family Foundation, 2019)[167].

The deductible objection is selective criticism designed to attack the public option while leaving untouched the private sector's identical problems. It is argument in bad faith. It should be recognized as such.

The honest version of the deductible objection would state: "All private insurance plans carry unaffordably high deductibles. This is a systemic problem across the entire private insurance market that should be regulated regardless of whether insurance is public or private." But that objection would require attacking the private sector. Instead, opponents focus exclusively on deductibles in the ACA while ignoring deductibles in employer plans.

This selective criticism reveals the true motivation: not healthcare affordability, but protection of existing private sector arrangements.

B. "PEOPLE NEED SKIN IN THE GAME"

The argument states that consumers must bear some financial responsibility for healthcare decisions, or they will demand excessive services, driving costs upward. Without deductibles, copayments, or coinsurance, people would visit doctors too frequently, demand unnecessary tests, take expensive medications when cheaper alternatives exist. "Skin in the game" creates financial discipline that protects cost containment.

The phrase sounds reasonable. It appeals to common sense about economic incentives. People do respond to prices. Markets do work through price signals. Therefore, healthcare must incorporate consumer price exposure or costs will spiral.

This argument fails empirically, theoretically, and logically.

Empirical Failure: Cost Containment in Systems Without "Skin in the Game"

Every major developed nation operates healthcare systems with minimal patient cost-sharing for primary care, specialists, and medications. These systems achieve lower per-capita costs than the United States while delivering superior health outcomes.

Germany, for example, imposes patient copayments of €10 per visit for primary care and €10 per hospital day, capped at 2 percent of household income annually.[(219)] But these copayments are minimal compared to United States patient cost-sharing. Germans face no deductibles. They face no annual out-of-pocket maximums that leave patients bankrupt after catastrophic illness. The German healthcare system spends 12.2 percent of GDP on healthcare and covers the entire population (OECD, 2024)[17]. The United States spends 17.3 percent of GDP and leaves 25 million people uninsured (CDC, 2024)[21].

Canada imposes even lower patient cost-sharing. Primary care visits, specialist visits, and hospital care are free at point of service. Prescriptions carry modest copayments, but these vary by province and income. Canada spends 10.7 percent of GDP on healthcare, covers everyone, and achieves health outcomes superior to the United States.

The United Kingdom's National Health Service charges no patient cost-sharing for any care: no deductibles, no copayments, no coinsurance. It is free at point of service for all residents (National Health Service Act, 1946)[18]. The NHS spends 11.3 percent of GDP, covers everyone universally, and achieves health outcomes superior to the United States.

If "skin in the game" is necessary for cost containment, these systems would be collapsing under uncontrolled utilization. Instead, they control costs while maintaining access. The claim that patient cost-sharing is necessary for cost containment is contradicted by the entire developed world.

Theoretical Failure: The "Skin in the Game" Theory Misunderstands Healthcare Economics

The "skin in the game" argument assumes that healthcare operates like retail markets. In retail markets, price signals work efficiently. Higher prices signal scarcity; lower prices signal abundance. Consumers respond by adjusting purchasing decisions. This process coordinates supply and demand without central planning.

Healthcare is not a retail market. Healthcare involves decisions about medical necessity, not preferences for discretionary consumption. A person does not choose whether to have a heart attack any more than they choose whether to have a stroke. A person with diabetes does not choose whether to take insulin based on price; they take insulin because they will die without it. A person does not comparison-shop between colonoscopy providers based on cost; if their doctor recommends colonoscopy for cancer screening, medical necessity drives the decision.

Patient cost-sharing cannot function as a price signal in a market where consumers lack medical expertise, demand is driven by clinical need rather than preference, and information asymmetry is profound. A patient cannot determine whether an MRI is medically necessary. A patient cannot evaluate whether a particular surgical approach is appropriate. A patient cannot assess whether medication X is more cost-effective than medication Y. Patients depend entirely on providers for these determinations.

When a patient faces a high deductible, they do not become a more efficient consumer. They become a rationing consumer. They skip necessary care. They delay treatment. They ask their doctor to do less, not to choose better. "Skin in the game" does not improve decision-making in healthcare. It substitutes financial burden for medical judgment.

Logical Failure: If "Skin in the Game" Controls Costs, Why Are U.S. Costs So High?

The United States has the highest patient cost-sharing among developed nations. Americans face the highest deductibles, highest copayments, highest coinsurance rates, and highest out-of-pocket maximums. If "skin in the game" controls costs, American healthcare should be the least expensive on earth. Instead, it is the most expensive.

The United States spends more than double per capita what Germany, Canada, and the United Kingdom spend. Yet Americans bear far more financial burden per encounter. This inverts the theoretical prediction entirely. The nation with the most "skin in the game" has the highest costs. The nations with minimal patient cost-sharing have the lowest costs. The theory predicts the opposite pattern. The theory is wrong.

The actual drivers of cost are not consumer utilization patterns. The actual drivers are prices set by monopolistic hospitals (Cooper et al., 2019)[150], pharmaceutical pricing power held by PBMs, administrative overhead that consumes 25-30 percent of healthcare spending in private systems (Health Affairs, 2023)[81], and profit extraction by insurance companies, pharmaceutical manufacturers (Wouters et al., 2020)[3], and healthcare corporations. Patient cost-sharing does not address any of these drivers. It only shifts costs from payers to patients.

What "Skin in the Game" Actually Accomplishes

"Skin in the game" does not control costs. "Skin in the game" controls utilization by deterring care. It prevents poor and sick people from seeking care. It redistributes costs from insurers to individuals. It accomplishes political theater: the appearance of consumer responsibility while doing nothing about underlying cost drivers.

A 2023 study published in Health Affairs tracked patients with high-deductible plans over two years following a serious diagnosis.[(220)] Among patients with diabetes, high-deductible plans led to 14 percent reduction in medication adherence compared to lower-deductible plans. Patients were not becoming more efficient consumers. They were abandoning necessary medications because they could not afford deductibles and copayments. The result was increased hospitalizations, increased emergency department visits, and ultimately higher total costs for the system.

This is the hidden function of "skin in the game": it appears to control costs while actually shifting costs from insurers to individuals, increasing total system spending by forcing emergency care that could have been prevented through affordable primary care.

The American Hospital System Rejects "Skin in the Game" Logic

The American Hospital System proposal eliminates the "skin in the game" framework entirely. It replaces it with a different economic model: cost containment through monopoly prevention, price negotiation, administrative streamlining, and prevention-focused care design.

Under this model, the system captures the economic benefit of prevention. When a person receives screenings, receives medication for chronic conditions, receives preventive procedures, the system benefits by reducing emergency care costs. There is no financial incentive to deter care. There is every financial incentive to promote care because the system captures the cost savings from prevented disease.

This is not theoretical. The VA operates this way. The VA provides low-cost preventive care, subsidizes chronic disease management, and captures the benefit through reduced emergency care costs and better outcomes (Kerr et al., 2004)[169]. The system thrives financially through prevention, not through deterrence.

Citizens do not need "skin in the game." Citizens need a health system designed around their health, not around profit extraction.

C. "GOVERNMENT KILLS INNOVATION"

The objection states that government-operated healthcare will stifle medical innovation. Private sector profit incentives drive investment in new drugs, new devices, new procedures. Government healthcare, operated on nonprofit principles with no opportunity for extraordinary returns, would reduce research investment. Innovation would slow. Patients would lose access to breakthrough treatments.

This is the most theoretically sophisticated objection to public healthcare. It contains a kernel of truth wrapped in a structure of half-truths and omissions. The empirical record reveals the truth beneath the appearance.

The Empirical Record: Where Does Medical Innovation Actually Come From?

Medical innovation originates from multiple sources: pharmaceutical companies, device manufacturers, hospitals, and universities. Tracking the funding sources reveals a striking pattern: federal funding plays a substantially larger role than private sector funding in driving fundamental innovation.

A comprehensive analysis by the NIH found that of the 262 drugs approved by the FDA from 2010 through 2016, 210 (80 percent) were supported by federally funded research conducted at NIH, universities, or other public institutions.[(221)] Federal funding did not conduct the final commercialization testing—private pharmaceutical companies conducted Phase III trials and brought drugs to market. But the fundamental research that identified drug targets, established mechanisms of action, and demonstrated basic safety was overwhelmingly funded by the federal government.

For cancer drugs specifically, an analysis examined 36 cancer drugs approved by the FDA between 2010 and 2016.[(222)] Of these, 35 (97 percent) involved research funded by the National Institutes of Health, National Cancer Institute, or other federal agencies. Again, private pharmaceutical companies conducted later-stage testing and commercialization. But the discovery science that enabled these drugs came from federal research funding.

Similarly, a 2017 study analyzing the sources of funding for major biomedical innovations found that federal funding through NIH accounted for approximately 75 percent of all "transformative" biomedical innovations—innovations that fundamentally changed medical practice—between 2002 and 2012.[(223)] Private sector funding focused overwhelmingly on incremental innovations: slight variations on existing drugs, modifications of existing devices, incremental improvements rather than transformative breakthroughs.

The role of federal funding in driving innovation is not disputed by serious researchers. It is acknowledged, sometimes grudgingly, by industry analysts. Congress knows this. They choose to ignore it because pharmaceutical companies pay them to ignore it.

Why Federal Funding Drives Discovery Innovation While Private Funding Focuses on Commercialization

The distinction between discovery and commercialization is critical. Discovery research—understanding disease mechanisms, identifying drug targets, establishing basic safety—is high-risk, long-timeline research with uncertain payoff. A researcher might spend five years investigating a protein target only to discover the approach is unviable. Private companies cannot absorb this failure rate. Their investors demand acceptable returns within reasonable timeframes.

Federal funding through NIH, NSF, and DoD explicitly subsidizes high-risk, long-timeline research. Public funding assumes some failures will occur. Public funding does not require positive return on every project. Public funding can support decades-long research programs investigating disease mechanisms that may or may not yield commercial products.

Private companies focus on later-stage development: taking a drug or device that has shown promise and bringing it to market. This requires enormous capital investment. Companies will not make this investment unless the discovery phase has de-risked the approach sufficiently to justify commercialization costs. Federal funding provides this de-risking. Private companies then capitalize on federally-funded discoveries by conducting late-stage testing and commercialization.

This division of labor is efficient. It is not evidence that private funding drives innovation. It is evidence that private funding commercializes innovations discovered through public funding.

The VA as an Innovation Engine

The Veterans Health Administration provides a direct counterexample to the claim that government healthcare stifles innovation. The VA has pioneered innovations now standard throughout American medicine:

Cognitive processing therapy and prolonged exposure therapy for PTSD were developed and refined at VA facilities (Resick et al.,

2015)[179]. These evidence-based treatments are now the gold standard for trauma therapy, taught in graduate psychology programs nationwide. Private providers later adopted what VA researchers developed.

The VA developed VistA, one of the most advanced integrated electronic health records in American healthcare (Brown et al., 2003)[183]. VistA was revolutionary in its unified architecture, allowing seamless information sharing across an entire national system. Private healthcare systems attempted to replicate this architecture for decades without success. Many private EHR systems remain fragmented, incapable of the information integration VA achieves.

The VA pioneered prosthetics innovation, developing advanced prosthetics including the DEKA arm (Resnik et al., 2014)[193]. The VA's commitment to serving veterans with complex limb loss drove innovation that private markets would not have pursued because the population served was too small to justify private sector R&D investment.

The VA pioneered telehealth implementation on a national scale, beginning in 2003 and continuously expanding telehealth access for rural veterans (Darkins et al., 2008)[198]. When COVID-19 forced private healthcare systems to scramble implementing telehealth in 2020, the VA already had a mature infrastructure and trained workforce (Heyworth et al., 2020)[199]. The VA's decade of telehealth development positioned it to expand access rapidly while private systems struggled with basic implementation.

The VA developed the Whole Health approach, integrating conventional medicine with evidence-based complementary therapies (Kligler et al., 2022)[197]. This integrated model treats the person holistically rather than fragmenting care across multiple providers. Private health systems are now attempting to replicate this model, but the VA developed it first.

These innovations did not emerge from profit incentives. They emerged from a health system committed to serving a specific patient population with complex medical needs. When government healthcare is focused on population health and unlimited by profit extraction, innovation flourishes.

Congress knows government drives innovation. They pretend

otherwise because admitting the truth would undermine pharmaceutical industry talking points.

Why Private Healthcare Innovation Focuses on High-Margin Products

Private pharmaceutical companies invest overwhelmingly in drugs for conditions affecting wealthy populations in wealthy nations. They invest minimally in drugs for conditions affecting poor populations or diseases prevalent in low-income nations. This is not malice; it is mathematics. A drug for erectile dysfunction or age-related wrinkles affects millions of wealthy men willing to pay premium prices. A drug for malaria or tuberculosis affects millions of poor people in low-income nations unwilling or unable to pay premium prices.

Private innovation follows profit, not need. This means private innovation generates many incremental variations on existing drugs—countless statins of different half-lives, antidepressants of different formulations—while neglecting genuine public health needs. Public funding generates innovation oriented to medical need regardless of profitability.

A public healthcare system operating the American Hospital System model would maintain substantial research investment. Federal funding through NIH, NSF, VA research programs, and direct research conducted within American Hospital System facilities would continue. But research investment would be oriented toward reducing costs, improving outcomes, and addressing health disparities—outcomes the private system ignores because they are not profitable.

The False Trade-off: Innovation Versus Affordability

The objection implies a trade-off: accept high drug prices to fund innovation; reject affordable drugs because innovation requires profit extraction. This trade-off does not exist. Evidence demonstrates that affordable pricing and innovation are compatible. Generic drugs, biosimilars, and price-regulated drugs in other developed nations do not stifle innovation because innovation continues to be federally funded.

Germany regulates pharmaceutical prices substantially. German drug prices are 50-70 percent lower than United States prices for identical drugs.[224] Yet pharmaceutical innovation continues in Germany. German pharmaceutical companies remain global innovators. Regulated pricing did not eliminate innovation; it eliminated excess profit.

The American Hospital System would maintain federal funding for research while eliminating profit extraction. Research would continue. Innovation would continue. Prices would fall to affordable levels. The false trade-off between innovation and affordability would be resolved by restructuring the system to separate discovery funding from commercialization profit.

Congress perpetuates the innovation myth because pharmaceutical companies demand they perpetuate it. Every member of Congress who repeats this objection has taken pharmaceutical industry money. Every single one.

D. "THIS IS SOCIALISM"

The objection raises the word socialism as if it ends the conversation. Socialism is un-American. Socialism fails. Socialism oppresses freedom. Therefore, any government-run healthcare system is socialist and should be rejected.

The objection requires examination of what socialism actually is, what socialism the American system already contains, and why the label—whatever its accuracy—should not determine policy.

What Socialism Actually Is

Socialism is an economic system in which the means of production are owned collectively rather than privately, and goods are distributed according to need rather than purchased according to ability to pay. Classic socialism envisions state ownership of factories, farms, transportation, and all productive capacity. The state manages production and distribution to serve collective interests rather than generate private profit.

An American Hospital System is not socialism under this definition. The American Hospital System retains private ownership of most productive capacity. Private pharmaceutical companies continue existing. Private medical device manufacturers continue existing. Private hospital chains continue existing. Private practices continue existing. The American Hospital System operates as a new option alongside existing private healthcare, not as replacement of all private healthcare.

A person could choose American Hospital System coverage or private insurance. A person could work for a private hospital or a public hospital. A person could invest in private healthcare corporations or decline investment. Productive capacity remains substantially private. The system is not socialist; it is a mixed economy with public and private sectors coexisting.

What "Socialism" Actually Exists in the United States Already

The United States operates numerous public systems providing services on socialist principles: distribution according to need rather than ability to pay, collective ownership of productive capacity, nonprofit operation:

Military healthcare: The Department of Defense operates military hospitals and employs military physicians.[(225)] Veterans' dependents receive care through military providers without paying for care. Care is provided according to need, not payment. Military healthcare is a public, collectively-owned system distributed according to need. It is socialism, if socialism is defined as collective ownership and distribution according to need.

Veterans healthcare (VA): The Veterans Health Administration operates 1,380 medical facilities and employs 482,831 people (U.S. Office of Personnel Management, 2024)[201]. Veterans receive care according to need without individual purchasing decisions determining access. The VA is a public system owned collectively and distributed according to need. It is socialism.

Medicare: Medicare operates a single-payer system covering 65 million elderly and disabled Americans.[(226)] Medicare is publicly owned. Medicare is distributed according to clinical need regardless of ability to pay. Medicare is socialism.

Medicaid: Medicaid operates a public program covering low-income Americans. Medicaid is collectively owned and distributed according to need. Medicaid is socialism.

Public health departments: Local, state, and federal public health departments provide disease surveillance, vaccination programs, and disease prevention according to need regardless of payment ability. Public health is collectively owned and need-distributed. It is socialism.

Police: Police services are publicly owned, collectively funded through taxation, and distributed equally to all residents regardless of payment ability. Police are socialism.

Fire services: Fire departments are publicly owned, funded through taxation, and provided according to need without individual purchasing. Fire services are socialism.

Public education: Public schools are collectively owned, funded through taxation, and distributed according to need regardless of family wealth. Public education is socialism.

Social Security: Social Security is a collectively funded insurance program distributing retirement income and disability income according to need and contribution history (Social Security Administration, 2024)[62]. Social Security is socialism.

The United States is already a mixed economy containing substantial socialist elements. The objection that the American Hospital System is "socialism" is objectively accurate but politically dishonest. The United States already operates multiple large-scale socialist systems. If socialism were inherently un-American, police, fire, military healthcare, VA, Medicare, Medicaid, public schools, and Social Security would all be un-American. They are not un-American. They are quintessentially American institutions, created by American legislation, operated by American public agencies, funded by American taxpayers, serving American citizens.

The Real Objection Is Not the Label But the Scope

The true objection to the American Hospital System is not that it is "socialism." The true objection is that it expands the scope of public provision beyond the currently accepted boundaries. Americans accept public police. Americans accept public fire departments. Americans accept public education. Americans accept Medicare, Medicaid, VA, and military healthcare. What Americans do not accept—or what certain political factions do not accept—is expansion of public healthcare beyond these existing programs to cover everyone.

This is not an objection to socialism as a principle. It is an objection to expanding public provision beyond currently normalized boundaries. The political difficulty is not philosophical but incremental: where should the boundary between public and private provision be drawn?

This question deserves honest debate. It deserves examination of evidence about which provision model works better. It deserves comparison of outcomes, costs, access, and quality between public and private systems. It does not deserve dismissal through rhetorical attachment of a politically loaded label.

The American Hospital System is not socialism in the ideological sense that it eliminates private enterprise or centralizes all productive capacity. It is public provision of healthcare, the same way public education provides education, public fire departments provide fire services, and public police provide law enforcement. The United States already operates extensive public provision of essential services. The question is whether healthcare should join this list.

That question should be answered on empirical grounds, not terminological grounds. The evidence suggests healthcare should join this list because public provision achieves better outcomes at lower cost than private provision. That evidence should drive policy, not fear of labels.

Congress screams "socialism" because their donors demand they scream it. Healthcare executives and pharmaceutical CEOs donate millions to keep Congress screaming. It works. Americans hear "socialism" and stop thinking critically about evidence.

E. "THE GOVERNMENT CAN'T RUN HEALTHCARE"

The objection states flatly: government is inherently incompetent at running complex systems. Healthcare is the most complex system conceivable. Therefore, government healthcare would fail.

This objection confronts a simple empirical problem: the government is already running healthcare, successfully, at unprecedented scale.

The VA Operates the World's Largest Integrated Healthcare System

The Veterans Health Administration operates 1,380 healthcare facilities serving 9.1 million enrolled veterans.[(227)] The VA operates in all 50 states and U.S. territories. The VA employs 482,831 people, making it the second-largest federal employer (U.S. Office of Personnel Management, 2024)[201]. The VA operates on an annual budget of approximately $87 billion for direct healthcare provision (U.S. Department of Veterans Affairs, 2024)[160].

The VA is larger than Kaiser Permanente, the largest integrated healthcare delivery system in the private sector. Kaiser operates in eight states and Washington D.C., serving 12.7 million members.[(228)] The VA serves comparable population size across all 50 states plus territories.

The VA is larger than UnitedHealth Group, the largest health insurer in America. UnitedHealth provides insurance to 85 million individuals but does not operate integrated delivery systems comparable to VA's scope.[(229)]

If government cannot run healthcare, the VA would be collapsing under management incompetence. Instead, the VA operates successfully, serving a patient population more complex than the general population, achieving outcomes superior to private healthcare on multiple metrics, spending less per patient than any comparator system.

Medicare Operates a Single-Payer System Covering 65 Million People

Medicare operates a publicly administered health insurance system covering 65 million Americans: all citizens 65 and older, younger people with disabilities, and people with end-stage renal disease.[(230)] Medicare is one of the largest government programs, with annual spending exceeding $848 billion (Centers for Medicare & Medicaid Services, 2024)[63].

Medicare enrollment grew from 9.3 million in 1966 to 65 million today. Despite covering an increasing proportion of the population as the elderly population grew, Medicare administratively maintained itself through program evolution, payment model adaptation, and integration of new benefits. Medicare did not collapse. Medicare did not become incompetent. Medicare adapted to changing circumstances.

Medicare has lower administrative costs than private insurance—just 2 percent of spending compared to 7-8 percent for private plans (Health Affairs, 2023)[81]. Medicare achieves this efficiency while managing more complex beneficiary populations: elderly and disabled individuals with multiple chronic conditions requiring intensive management.

If government cannot run healthcare, Medicare would demonstrate this through administrative failure. Instead, Medicare demonstrates successful long-term management of a large health system.

The Military Operates Integrated Healthcare Delivery for Military Personnel

The Department of Defense operates the Military Health System, providing integrated healthcare to active-duty service members, retirees, and their families.[(231)] The Military Health System operates 77 military medical centers and 363 military clinics across the United States and worldwide. The Military Health System serves approximately 9.3 million beneficiaries (U.S. Department of Defense, 2024)[209].

The Military Health System operates successfully despite serving a geographically dispersed population across multiple countries, managing complex injuries and conditions specific to military service, and maintaining continuous availability during military operations. The Military Health System adapted to changes in military deployment patterns, medical technology, and troop composition.

If government cannot manage healthcare, the Military Health System would demonstrate this. Instead, military healthcare functions effectively, maintaining readiness of active-duty personnel and providing healthcare to retired service members.

The Actual Problem: Political Sabotage, Not Governmental Incompetence

The VA does not face management challenges because VA is managed incompetently. The VA faces challenges because Congress, controlled by healthcare industry interests, deliberately starves VA funding, deliberately refuses to expand VA infrastructure proportional to veteran population growth, and uses VA budget as political leverage in healthcare industry battles.

After 2014, when the VA faced genuine wait time problems (Government Accountability Office, 2015)[161], Congress addressed the problem by demanding VA hire more providers, expand facilities, and improve scheduling—actions Congress would not have demanded if Congress believed government was inherently incompetent. Congress proved it believed government could manage healthcare; Congress just chose to limit government's budget and authority while healthcare industry interests lobbied Congress to restrict VA expansion.

Similarly, Medicare faces challenges not from administrative incompetence but from political restrictions: the 1965 legislation that created Medicare (Social Security Amendments, 1965)[59] explicitly prohibited Medicare from negotiating drug prices. This prohibition was inserted at pharmaceutical industry insistence. When Medicare attempted to negotiate drug prices, Congress restricted Medicare's authority. When Medicare finally gained limited negotiation authority in 2022 (Congressional Budget Office, 2022)[12], it immediately negotiated lower prices.

The "government can't run healthcare" objection mistakes political restriction for institutional incompetence. Government healthcare has not failed. Government healthcare has been deliberately constrained by political forces hostile to public provision.

Congress sabotages government healthcare, then points to the sabotage as evidence government cannot work. This is not policy analysis. This is corporate-funded propaganda.

F. "WE SHOULD USE PRIVATE MARKETS"

The objection states that private markets provide the best healthcare outcomes. Competition drives innovation. Price signals align supply and demand. Consumer choice drives providers to improve quality. Therefore, policy should strengthen private markets rather than create government alternatives.

The objection mistakes ideology for evidence. The evidence overwhelmingly demonstrates that private markets in healthcare have failed and continue failing Americans.

Private Markets Dominate Healthcare Now: Outcomes Are Worst Among Developed Nations

The United States relies on private markets more extensively than any other developed nation. Private insurance covers 160 million Americans through employers.(232) Private out-of-pocket payments exceed $460 billion annually.(233) Private hospital systems operate the vast majority of hospital beds. Private pharmaceutical companies price drugs without government negotiation (until very recently, with severely limited scope).

If private markets work well, American healthcare should deliver superior outcomes at affordable costs. The evidence shows the opposite:

Cost: The United States spends 17.3 percent of GDP on healthcare, the highest percentage among developed nations (Centers for Medicare & Medicaid Services, 2024)[73]. Germany spends 12.2 percent (OECD, 2024)[17]. Canada spends 10.7 percent. The United Kingdom spends 11.3 percent (National Health Service Act, 1946)[18]. Despite spending vastly more per capita, the United States delivers inferior outcomes.

Access: The United States leaves 25 million people uninsured (CDC, 2024)[21]. Germany, Canada, and the United Kingdom provide universal coverage. The United States is the only major developed nation that does not.

Outcomes: Life expectancy in the United States is 76.1 years, lower than Canada (82.9 years), Germany (82.2 years), and the United Kingdom (81.3 years).[(234)] Infant mortality in the United States is 5.5 per 1,000 live births, higher than Canada (4.6), Germany (3.4), and the United Kingdom (3.8).[(235)] Maternal mortality in the United States is 32.9 deaths per 100,000 live births, higher than Canada (16.3), Germany (7.3), and the United Kingdom (7.2).[(236)]

The United States has privatized healthcare to a greater degree than any other developed nation. American healthcare outcomes are worse than comparable nations. American healthcare costs more than comparable nations. This is not a mystery. This is expected outcome of a system designed around profit extraction rather than population health.

Private Markets in Healthcare Do Not Function as Theory Predicts

Market theory assumes numerous competitors, perfect information, free entry and exit, and that consumers make rational purchasing decisions. Healthcare markets satisfy none of these conditions:

Monopoly concentration: In 47 states, the top two insurers control more than 50 percent of the market (American Medical Association, 2024)[18]. In 14 states, a single insurer controls more than 75 percent. In 90 percent of metropolitan hospital markets, the top two hospital systems control 70-90 percent of inpatient capacity (Cooper et al., 2019)[150]. Three pharmacy benefit managers control 80 percent of all prescription drug negotiations.[(237)] This is not competition. This is concentrated monopoly.

Information asymmetry: Consumers lack medical expertise to evaluate treatment necessity or quality. Consumers cannot comparison-shop between providers effectively because networks restrict access. Providers hold overwhelming information advantage. Consumers make purchasing decisions under duress (acute illness), with incomplete information, unable to comparison-shop. These conditions eliminate the rational consumer assumption underlying market theory.

Barriers to entry: New healthcare entrants face prohibitive barriers: regulatory licensing, capital requirements, network access restrictions. New insurers cannot enter markets because existing insurers control provider networks. New hospitals cannot enter markets because existing systems control supply. Competition cannot emerge to correct existing monopolies.

Profit-driven care decisions: Because providers profit from high volume, high-price services, financial incentives align toward overutilization of profitable services and underutilization of unprofitable services. A hospital profits by performing more surgeries even if surgery is not medically necessary. A PBM profits when drug prices are high because rebate base increases. Financial incentives corrupt care decisions away from medical optimality toward profit maximization.

Private healthcare markets do not function as market theory predicts because healthcare markets lack the conditions necessary for market function. Applying market ideology to healthcare and expecting market outcomes is analytically naïve.

Congress knows this. They pretend markets work because pretending protects their donors' profits.

Price Deregulation in Drug Markets Demonstrates Private Market Failure

A natural experiment demonstrates private market failure in pharmaceutical pricing. When Medicare Part D launched in 2003, Congress explicitly prohibited Medicare from negotiating drug prices. This provision, demanded by pharmaceutical industry interests, left price-setting entirely to private markets: manufacturers set prices; PBMs negotiated rebates; insurers passed costs to consumers.

The result: pharmaceutical prices skyrocketed. Brand-name drug prices increased 82 percent between 2010 and 2021, far exceeding inflation.(238) Insulin prices tripled (Medbelle, 2021)[20]. Specialty drugs pricing soared. Patients rationed medications or abandoned treatment because of cost.

In contrast, countries that empowered government to negotiate drug prices achieved vastly lower prices. Germany regulates pharmaceutical prices. German drug prices are 50-70 percent lower than U.S. prices. The United Kingdom negotiates drug prices through NICE. U.K. drug prices are 60-70 percent lower than U.S. prices. When government negotiated limited numbers of drugs through Medicare negotiation starting in 2024, prices fell immediately (Congressional Budget Office, 2022)[12]. The first 10 negotiated drugs achieved 22 percent average price reduction.

Private market pricing failed to control drug costs. Government negotiation worked immediately. The evidence is clear. Markets do not control pharmaceutical pricing. Monopoly power controls pricing. Government negotiation controls pricing.

Congress refuses to negotiate because pharmaceutical companies pay them to refuse. Every member who voted against drug price negotiation took pharmaceutical money. The correlation is perfect.

The Private Market Objection Is Ideological, Not Empirical

The objection that "we should use private markets" is not based on evidence. American healthcare is already dominated by private markets. American healthcare delivers inferior outcomes at highest cost among developed nations. This is the empirical result of private market dominance.

The objection persists not because evidence supports it but because it serves ideological commitments: belief in market superiority independent of evidence, commitment to private enterprise independent of performance, and financial interest in maintaining private healthcare's profit extraction.

Honest evaluation of evidence suggests private markets have failed in healthcare. Government negotiation, public provision, and price regulation should replace market ideology with evidence-based policy.

G. "REPUBLICANS HAVE A BETTER PLAN"

The objection suggests that while private markets may need some reform, Republicans have developed alternative healthcare reforms superior to the American Hospital System proposal. These alternatives should be considered before embracing government healthcare.

The objection deserves examination: Do Republicans have a healthcare plan? What does the plan contain? How would the plan perform compared to alternatives?

Republicans Have Had 13+ Years to Produce a Comprehensive Healthcare Plan

Republicans have controlled the House of Representatives for portions of this period. Republicans have controlled the Senate for portions of this period. Republicans have controlled the presidency for portions of this period. Republican healthcare experts have published extensively on healthcare reform. Conservative think tanks have developed healthcare proposals.

Despite these opportunities and resources, Republicans have not produced a comprehensive healthcare plan that would provide universal coverage, contain costs, and improve outcomes. This is not coincidental. It reflects the political difficulty of maintaining private market dominance while expanding coverage to currently uninsured populations.

The Republican Healthcare Platform: Tax Breaks for the Rich

The primary Republican healthcare reform proposal relies on mechanisms that benefit wealthy people while abandoning everyone else:

Health Savings Accounts (HSAs): HSAs allow people with high-deductible plans to deposit pre-tax money into accounts for healthcare expenses. Account contributions accumulate, generating tax-deferred savings. Theoretically, this incentivizes people to save for healthcare expenses.

High-deductible plans: These plans minimize premium costs through high deductibles, shifting cost-sharing to patients. With an HSA, patients can draw from accumulated savings to pay deductibles.

Reduced regulation: Removing requirements that insurance plans cover specific services, allowing plans to vary in coverage, permitting consumers greater flexibility in plan design.

Medicaid block grants: Converting Medicaid from an open-ended entitlement to fixed federal block grants, allowing states to reduce coverage or eligibility rather than maintaining current scope.

Why Republican Proposals Are Garbage

HSAs solve no healthcare problem. HSAs provide tax benefits to wealthy people while leaving uninsured and underinsured populations without solutions.

HSAs benefit people with sufficient income to save. A person earning $200,000 can fund an HSA, accumulate savings, and use those savings to cover healthcare costs. A person earning $35,000 cannot save enough to cover high-deductible costs. The person lives paycheck to paycheck. An HSA is meaningless.

A 2024 analysis found that approximately 80 percent of HSA contributions are made by people with household income exceeding $100,000. Among people with household income below $50,000, HSA participation is negligible. HSAs function as tax benefits for wealthy people, not healthcare reform for uninsured populations.

High-deductible plans shift costs to patients. Patients already bear too much cost-sharing. Policies that increase cost-sharing deepen the problem rather than solving it (Wharam et al., 2023)[35].

Medicaid block grants would convert Medicaid from a guarantor of coverage to a state-managed program with fixed federal funding. States would face choices: expand coverage at state expense, or restrict coverage to fit within federal block grants. Block grants create incentive for states to restrict Medicaid eligibility and benefits.

Block grant proposals consistently include projections showing coverage would decrease. Analysis from multiple organizations consistently finds that block grants would result in millions losing coverage.

Why Republicans Have Not Produced Comprehensive Reform

Republicans have not produced comprehensive healthcare reform because comprehensive reform requires either accepting the status quo (leaving 25 million uninsured) or accepting that government must expand healthcare access. Accepting status quo is politically untenable. Accepting government expansion contradicts Republican ideology.

The result is a fundamental contradiction in Republican healthcare proposals: they promise to expand coverage without requiring mandates, without raising taxes, without government expansion. This promise is mathematically impossible. Markets cannot expand coverage to currently uninsured populations without either mandating purchase or subsidizing coverage.

Republican proposals do not address fundamental problems: too many uninsured, costs too high, outcomes worse than comparator nations. American Hospital System proposal does.

Congress Republicans have no plan because their donors don't want a plan. Insurance companies profit from the current chaos. Pharmaceutical firms profit from the current chaos. Hospital chains profit from the current chaos. Republican proposals protect corporate profits while pretending to care about healthcare access.

THE IDEOLOGICAL ROOT: PROFIT VS. HEALTH

Objections to public healthcare ultimately reduce to a single conflict: whether healthcare should be organized around profit extraction or population health. Every objection examined in this chapter reflects this underlying tension.

High deductibles extract costs from patients, benefiting insurers. Skin-in-the-game logic justifies cost-shifting. Innovation funding objections protect pharmaceutical profit (Wouters et al., 2020)[3]. Socialism objections protect private enterprise. Government incompetence objections protect private management. Private market objections protect private profiteering. Republican plan objections protect existing corporate arrangements.

All objections share a common thread: they prioritize private sector profit over public health. They assume profit-driven healthcare is preferable to need-driven healthcare despite evidence to the contrary.

The American Hospital System explicitly prioritizes population health over profit extraction. Universal coverage replaces selective coverage. Need-based access replaces ability-to-pay access. Cost containment replaces profit maximization. Innovation serving health needs replaces innovation serving profitable conditions.

This is not ideologically neutral. This is a choice to reject profit as organizing principle and embrace health as organizing principle. That choice is not uniquely "socialist." That choice is uniquely American—it aligns with the principle that government exists to promote general welfare, not to enable private profit.

Answering objections to public healthcare requires understanding that objections do not rest on evidence or logic. Objections rest on commitment to private enterprise regardless of consequences. Refuting evidence requires moving debate from whether public healthcare works—evidence is overwhelming—to whether government should provide healthcare even if it works better.

That debate deserves honest engagement. Congress has not provided it. Congress has chosen instead to obscure the debate through rhetorical objections based on ideology disguised as analysis.

This chapter provides the analysis. This chapter demonstrates objections fail on empirical grounds, theoretical grounds, and logical grounds. What remains is political will. Congress must choose: does healthcare serve health, or does healthcare serve profit?

Everything else flows from that choice.

Congress has already chosen. They chose profit. They chose their donors over their constituents. They chose corporate wealth over public health. They chose campaign contributions over American lives.

The evidence is overwhelming. The objections are lies. The corruption is complete. What remains is whether Americans will force Congress to choose differently.

CHAPTER 12
CONGRESS—THE STRUCTURAL FAILURE AT THE HEART OF THE CRISIS

THE FUNDAMENTAL TRUTH

Congress is not failing healthcare policy. Congress is failing the people who elected them.

This is not metaphor. This is structural reality documented in campaign finance records, lobbying disclosures, employment trajectories, and legislative outcomes. Congress has been captured by the industries it is supposed to regulate. The people's representatives have become industry agents. Democracy, in healthcare policy, has ceased to function.

Everything preceding this chapter traces back to one root cause. Congress refuses to act. Congress actively protects the industries causing the crisis. Congress legislates for donors, not constituents.

The crisis is not that our healthcare system is broken. The crisis is that our political system is broken. Until Congress changes, nothing else will.

LOBBYING: THE VOICE OF INDUSTRY DROWNING OUT THE PEOPLE

Money flows through Washington. Healthcare corporations pour hundreds of millions into lobbying because lobbying works. It translates directly into legislative outcomes favorable to the industries funding it. Members of Congress respond to these financial pressures with legislation that protects corporate profits while millions of Americans spiral into medical debt.

The Scale of Healthcare Industry Lobbying

The health sector spent $739 million on federal lobbying in 2024 (OpenSecrets, 2025)[1], making it the single largest lobbying presence in Washington by sector. This is not marginal influence. This is dominance. Healthcare corporations employ more lobbyists, spend more money, and generate more political access than any other sector of the American economy.

When the health sector wants Congress to act, Congress acts. When the health sector wants Congress to block reform, Congress blocks it. The people's interests are secondary.

The pharmaceutical and health products industry alone spent $294 million on lobbying in 2024.[(239)] The American Hospital Association spent $24 million.[(240)] Insurance companies, pharmacy benefit managers, medical device manufacturers, and diagnostic testing companies each spent millions more.

Over time, this spending has accelerated at critical policy moments. PhRMA increased spending from $27 million in 2023 to $31 million in 2024, with $7.6 million spent in the fourth quarter alone as Congress negotiated year-end healthcare provisions.[(241)] The Pharmaceutical Care Management Association nearly doubled its lobbying expenditure from $9 million in 2022 to $18 million in 2024 as lawmakers considered PBM reform legislation.[(242)]

Notice the pattern. When legislation threatens corporate interests, lobbying spending spikes. Money appears at critical moments. Members of Congress receive calls from industry representatives.

Industry lawyers draft talking points. Congressional staff are reminded of campaign contributions. Bills die in committee or are gutted of meaningful provisions.

This is not speculation. This is how Washington operates. Every member of Congress knows this. Every staff member knows this. Every lobbyist knows this. The question is not whether this happens. The question is why Americans tolerate it.

Lobbying Spending Does Not Buy Publicity. It Buys Access and Power.

When healthcare corporations spend $739 million on federal lobbying, they are not buying newspaper ads or television commercials. They are buying access. They are buying influence. They are buying the ability to shape legislation behind closed doors where ordinary citizens cannot see it.

A pharmaceutical company that spends $31 million on lobbying in a single year is not trying to persuade the general public. The general public does not read lobbying filings. The pharmaceutical company is trying to persuade one specific audience: members of Congress and their staff.

That money buys meetings. It buys email access. It buys phone calls returned promptly. It buys the ability to have industry lawyers sit at the table when legislation is being drafted. It buys the ability to influence the terms of debate before the public ever hears about it.

Consider a concrete example. When Congress considers legislation to regulate pharmacy benefit managers, representatives from CVS Caremark, Express Scripts, and Optum do not sit passively in their offices hoping Congress will see reason. They deploy teams of lobbyists. They arrange meetings with key committee members. They provide "technical assistance" to Congressional staff drafting the legislation. They outline which provisions are "problematic" from an operational standpoint. They suggest "alternative approaches" that achieve the stated policy goals while protecting their profit margins.

A Congressional staffer, faced with complex technical questions about how PBMs work, often turns to industry experts for guidance.

The industry expert happens to be a highly paid lobbyist employed by the company being regulated. Is it surprising that the lobbyist's "technical assistance" always results in language that protects industry interests? Of course not.

This is the mechanism of capture. Not overt bribery. Not explicit quid pro quo. Rather the subtle, normalized, structural reality that industry has permanent presence in Washington while the public does not. Industry has resources to hire armies of lawyers and lobbyists. The public has citizens who work other jobs, pay taxes, and hope their representatives will act in the public interest.

The imbalance is not accidental. It is structural. It is the inevitable result of allowing unlimited money into political campaigns and allowing the industries being regulated to employ unlimited lobbyists.

The Revolving Door: Where Loyalty Gets Purchased After Leaving Congress

The most insidious aspect of healthcare lobbying is not the money spent while someone is in Congress. It is the money offered after someone leaves Congress. Former members of Congress know how the system works. They know which buttons to push. They know which staff members to call. They know which committees drive policy. They know the informal relationships that determine which bills advance and which die.

Healthcare corporations desperately want former members of Congress as employees. Not because they expect those former members to perform specific tasks. Because those former members have something money alone cannot buy: relationships built over years of service, credibility as former elected officials, and the ability to open doors that ordinary lobbyists cannot.

Research on revolving door dynamics found that 32 percent of HHS appointees exited to private industry positions after their government service, compared to only 15 percent who came from industry before their appointments (Jain et al., 2022)[170]. At the Centers for Disease Control and Prevention, 54 percent of appointees departed for industry jobs.

The pattern is consistent across healthcare agencies. The offices with the most power over healthcare corporations see the highest rates of industry exit. The revolving door spins fastest at the CDC, CMS, the FDA, and the Office of the Deputy Secretary. These are precisely the agencies with the most regulatory authority over healthcare industries.

Former FDA Commissioner Scott Gottlieb joined Pfizer's Board of Directors within four months of resigning as FDA commissioner in 2019.(243) During his tenure at the FDA, Gottlieb promoted biosimilar policies that directly affected Pfizer's business interests. The timeline is too convenient to ignore. Gottlieb shaped policy at the agency. Pfizer rewarded him with a board position worth hundreds of thousands of dollars annually.

This creates obvious incentive structures. A pharmaceutical executive at the FDA knows that their decisions on drug pricing, approval timelines, and regulatory enforcement will affect their post-government earning potential. Companies like Pfizer, Eli Lilly, and Merck are watching how FDA officials treat their industry. Officials who are hostile to pharmaceutical company interests may find that job offers are scarce when they leave government. Officials who are friendly to pharmaceutical company interests may find lucrative board positions and consulting arrangements waiting for them.

Research on Department of Health and Human Services appointees between 2004 and 2020 found that a standard deviation increase in former staff connections predicts an 18 percent increase in lobbying revenue during a lobbyist's first year after leaving Capitol Hill.(244)

The numbers reveal the financial magnitude. A Congressional staffer earning $60,000-$100,000 annually leaves government and immediately commands $300,000-$500,000 annually as a healthcare industry lobbyist or consultant. The difference is transformative. For someone carrying student loans, with a family to support, or with retirement concerns, the financial incentive to maintain friendly relationships with healthcare corporations while in government is enormous.

Nobody needs to explicitly tell a Congressional staffer that their career prospects depend on being nice to pharmaceutical companies. The incentive structure creates the behavior automatically. A staffer who consistently blocks pharmaceutical industry interests knows that the lobbying world will be closed to them. A staffer who finds ways to accommodate industry concerns while technically doing their job knows that lucrative opportunities await after government service.

This is why the revolving door is so pernicious. It operates through incentive structures rather than explicit corruption. It does not require direct bribery or conscious betrayal. It simply creates financial pressure toward industry-friendly behavior.

Congressional Committee Capture: Where Healthcare Policy Gets Made

Most Americans believe Congress debates legislation on the House or Senate floor, where all members participate equally and the best arguments prevail. This is fairy tale. Most legislation never reaches the floor. Most legislative work happens in committees. Committees are where bills are drafted, negotiated, modified, and either advanced or killed.

Committee members hold disproportionate power. A member of the House Ways and Means Committee, which has jurisdiction over healthcare policy and taxation, exercises far more power over healthcare legislation than a member who serves on committees unrelated to healthcare. Committee chairs exercise even more power. The Chair of the Health Subcommittee has more power over healthcare policy than 430 other members of Congress combined.

Healthcare corporations know this. They know which committee members have jurisdiction over their industries. They cultivate relationships with those members specifically. They provide campaign contributions to those members specifically. They arrange meetings specifically with those members and their staff.

The result is committee capture. Members who have jurisdiction over healthcare policy receive disproportionate campaign funding from healthcare corporations. These same members, unsurprisingly, tend to vote in ways favorable to healthcare corporations. Their legislative proposals tend to protect healthcare industry interests. Their statements, when discussing healthcare policy, tend to echo industry talking points.

This is not unique to healthcare. It is how Congress works across all policy domains. Industries with concentrated interests lobby the committees that have jurisdiction over them. Those committees become captured by industry. The public interest, diffused across 330 million Americans who each want affordable healthcare but lack organized lobbying infrastructure, loses.

Consider a specific example. The House Ways and Means Committee writes tax policy. It has jurisdiction over the healthcare tax code. Pharmaceutical companies have decades-long relationships with this committee. Pharmaceutical industry representatives meet regularly with Ways and Means members and staff. When pharmaceutical companies need favorable tax treatment or want to prevent unfavorable tax treatment, they go to Ways and Means.

A pharmaceutical company that employs 20,000 people in a Congressional district has leverage. The member representing that district knows that pharmaceutical companies are major employers and major campaign donors. When the pharmaceutical industry's tax position becomes an issue, the member faces pressure to vote in the industry's favor. The member is told that voting against pharmaceutical interests might affect campaign funding. The member is told that pharmaceutical companies might reduce investment in the district if healthcare policy becomes hostile.

This is not unique to one member or one district. This pattern repeats across Congress. Industries with concentrated financial interests exercise disproportionate influence on the members of Congress who have jurisdiction over them.

CAMPAIGN FINANCE: BUYING VOTES DIRECTLY

If lobbying is the subtle art of access and influence, campaign finance is the blunt instrument of direct financial incentive. Healthcare corporations and their employees donate hundreds of millions of dollars to political campaigns. Members of Congress who vote for industry interests receive substantial campaign funding. Members who vote against industry interests face well-funded primary opponents.

The Scale of Healthcare Industry Campaign Contributions

During the 2023-2024 election cycle, the pharmaceutical and health products industry contributed tens of millions to candidates. Between 2012 and 2020, pharmaceutical industry contributions to federal candidates jumped 170 percent, reaching $89 million in the 2020 cycle (OpenSecrets, 2025)[2].

These numbers represent campaign contributions from pharmaceutical industry employees, pharmaceutical company political action committees, and pharmaceutical industry trade associations. The money flows explicitly to candidates and campaigns. Every contribution is documented in Federal Election Commission filings. Yet the donations continue, year after year, with minimal public scrutiny.

Individual members receive substantial amounts. Multiple senators received over $200,000 each from pharmaceutical and health products industry sources during recent election cycles.[245] Newly elected senators received over $100,000 each from pharmaceutical industry sources during their campaigns.

These are not hypothetical contributions made by anonymous corporations. Pharmaceutical company employees make individual contributions. They bundle contributions from multiple employees and forward them to candidates' campaigns. The contributions come with implicit understanding: the candidate receiving hundreds of thousands of dollars from pharmaceutical industry sources will vote in ways favorable to pharmaceutical industry interests.

The Mechanism: How Campaign Contributions Shape Votes

Campaign contributions do not need to be explicit quid pro quo arrangements to shape voting behavior. The mechanism operates through straightforward financial incentive.

Assume a member of Congress faces re-election. Re-election campaigns are expensive. Television advertising costs money. Digital advertising costs money. Direct mail costs money. Phone banking costs money. Building and maintaining campaign infrastructure costs money. A competitive re-election campaign costs millions of dollars.

Where does a member of Congress get millions of dollars? From donors. And who are the largest donors? Industries with concentrated financial interests that depend on favorable government policy. Healthcare corporations are among the largest donors.

A member of Congress considering a vote on pharmaceutical pricing knows that voting for price controls will anger pharmaceutical companies. That member knows that pharmaceutical companies donate to his or her campaign. That member knows that voting against pharmaceutical interests might result in pharmaceutical companies redirecting their donations to a primary opponent.

A primary opponent funded by pharmaceutical industry money runs substantial advertising against the incumbent member. The primary opponent messages that the incumbent member wants to "hurt pharmaceutical innovation" or "drive pharmaceutical jobs out of the district." The primary opponent saturates the district with mailers, television ads, and digital advertising. The incumbent member, facing a well-funded primary opponent funded by healthcare industry money, faces a difficult choice.

This is not theoretical. This happens regularly. Members who consistently vote against healthcare industry interests face well-funded primary opponents. Members who consistently vote for healthcare industry interests receive strong campaign support and face no primary challenges.

Research has found that campaign contributions buy not just access but favorable policy outcomes: members voting for healthcare industry interests receive substantially more campaign funding than members voting against industry interests, and this funding differential predicts future voting behavior (Wouters et al., 2020)[3].

The system is self-reinforcing. Members who want to run for re-election need money. Healthcare corporations have money. Healthcare corporations expect access and favorable votes. Members who want to run for higher office need even more money. Healthcare corporations control enormous resources and donate based on voting records. The incentive structure pushes every ambitious member of Congress toward voting for healthcare industry interests.

Super PACs: Unlimited Money, Unlimited Power

The Citizens United decision of 2010 opened floodgates that have never been closed. Super PACs—political action committees that raise and spend unlimited money on elections—now dominate campaign finance. Super PACs spend unlimited amounts on advertising attacking or supporting candidates based on their voting records.

Healthcare corporations, through Super PACs, spend unlimited money supporting candidates who vote for healthcare industry interests. The same Super PACs spend unlimited money attacking candidates who vote against healthcare industry interests.

The political calculation is simple. A member of Congress considering a vote that would harm healthcare industry interests knows that Super PACs funded by healthcare corporations will spend millions attacking that member in the next election. A Super PAC runs television ads calling the member "anti-innovation" or "hostile to jobs." A Super PAC funds digital advertising attacking the member's character or integrity.

Conversely, a member voting for healthcare industry interests knows that those same Super PACs will support the member's re-election. They will run positive ads supporting the member. They will fund voter contact to support the member. They will provide resources for the member's campaign.

The incentive structure is overwhelming. Few members of Congress have the courage or conviction to vote against healthcare industry interests when doing so means facing unlimited spending against them in the next election. The political cost is too high. The financial disadvantage is too great.

REVOLVING DOOR POLITICS: CAREERS PURCHASED BEFORE SERVICE ENDS

The most direct form of political capture occurs through the revolving door. Members of Congress leave office and immediately obtain lucrative positions with the industries they previously regulated. Healthcare lobbyists, consultants, and executives are often former members of Congress or former Congressional staff.

These individuals are valuable not for any unique skill or expertise, but simply because they know how Congress works and have relationships with current members. Healthcare corporations pay hundreds of thousands or millions of dollars for access to these relationships.

The Financial Incentive: Post-Congressional Employment Opportunities

A member of Congress earns $174,000 annually. This is substantial income, but in Washington D.C., it is not extraordinary wealth. A long-term member might accumulate $5-10 million in net worth by the time they leave office, but they are not wealthy by the standards of corporate executives or successful private attorneys.

When a member of Congress leaves office, they suddenly face a dramatic financial choice. They become a private attorney or consultant and attempt to build a successful law or consulting practice. This requires developing a client base, establishing a reputation, and working for years before accumulating substantial wealth. Or they leverage their Congressional experience and relationships to obtain immediate high-paying positions.

Healthcare corporations eagerly hire former Congressional staff and former members. A former staff member from the House Ways and Means Committee commands $300,000-$500,000 annually as a healthcare industry lobbyist or consultant. A former member of Congress commands $500,000-$2,000,000 annually or more on a corporate board or as a lobbying firm partner.

The financial incentive is transformative. A Congressional staffer earning $80,000 annually leaves office and immediately earns four to six times that salary. The difference is life-changing. For someone with student loans, with family obligations, or with the normal financial concerns facing middle-income Americans, this financial opportunity is irresistible.

The calculation faced by a young Congressional staff member is clear. Spend five to ten years in Congressional office earning $60,000-$150,000 annually while helping craft legislative deals favorable to healthcare corporations. Upon leaving office, leverage those relationships to obtain a lucrative position earning $400,000+ annually. Or take principled stands against healthcare industry interests and risk finding the lobbying world closed when you leave office.

The incentive structure creates the behavior automatically. Nobody needs to explicitly tell a staff member that voting against pharmaceutical interests will cost them post-government employment opportunities. The staff member simply observes that colleagues who maintained friendly relationships with pharmaceutical companies find lucrative opportunities waiting for them after government service. Colleagues who voted against pharmaceutical interests find fewer opportunities.

Historical Precedent: How the Revolving Door Operates

The healthcare revolving door has functioned for decades. Former members of Congress from both parties regularly appear as healthcare industry lobbyists, consultants, and executives. This has become so normalized that it barely generates comment.

A member of Congress serves a district for ten to twenty years, developing relationships with healthcare organizations in that district. The member reaches the end of their Congressional career and leaves office. Weeks later, that former member announces a position with a healthcare corporation or healthcare lobbying firm. The former member's primary value is access and relationships. The former member calls other members of Congress and arranges meetings. The former member explains how the legislative process works. The former member advises on political strategy.

Healthcare corporations pay enormous sums for these services precisely because they are effective. A former member calling a current member with a request for a meeting will usually get that meeting. A former member providing political advice is credible in a way that outside consultants are not. A former member's presence in a lobbying firm signals that the firm has serious connections inside Congress.

The system works as intended. Former members obtain lucrative positions. Healthcare corporations obtain access and influence. Congress becomes populated by members who understand that voting against healthcare industry interests will close doors when they leave office.

The Consequence: Voting Behavior Shaped by Future Employment Prospects

The long-term consequence of the revolving door is that Congressional voting behavior becomes predictable based on healthcare industry interests. Members who might otherwise be skeptical of pharmaceutical pricing practices, hospitable to antitrust enforcement, or supportive of Medicare drug negotiation face subtle pressure to reconsider their positions. The pressure comes not from explicit threats, but from knowledge that voting against healthcare industry interests will affect post-government employment prospects.

This is why regulatory agencies like the FDA see the highest rates of industry exit. Members of Congress and staffers working on healthcare issues understand that their decisions affect healthcare industry profitability. They understand that healthcare corporations are watching their voting records. They understand that voting against industry interests will affect which healthcare corporations hire them after government service.

The revolving door thus creates a form of implicit corruption. Not explicit bribery. Not direct quid pro quo. Rather the structural reality that post-government employment prospects depend on maintaining friendly relationships with regulated industries.

Specific Examples: The Door Swings Both Ways

The revolving door does not operate in one direction only. It swings both ways. Industry employees move into government positions. Government employees move into industry positions. The result is that government agencies become staffed by former industry employees who retain sympathy for industry interests.

Consider the FDA's approval process for new drugs. The FDA employs scientists and physicians who evaluate drug safety and efficacy. These employees earn $100,000-$200,000 annually. After several years at the FDA, these employees leave government and obtain positions with pharmaceutical companies earning $200,000-$400,000 annually, plus stock options and bonuses worth hundreds of thousands more.

The incentive structure is obvious. An FDA reviewer who is sympathetic to pharmaceutical companies' interests knows that faster drug approvals, more generous interpretations of data, and fewer questions about safety records will make that reviewer attractive to pharmaceutical companies. An FDA reviewer who is skeptical of pharmaceutical claims and demands rigorous evidence before approving drugs may find that job offers from pharmaceutical companies are scarce.

This does not require conscious corruption. An FDA reviewer simply needs to be aware that pharmaceutical companies are watching their work. The reviewer's future depends partly on their decisions at the FDA. Industry-friendly decisions improve prospects. Industry-skeptical decisions harm prospects. The incentive structure creates the behavior.

Similarly, industry employees move into government positions. A pharmaceutical company executive leaves the industry and joins the FDA's regulatory division. That person spent twenty years in industry. That person has relationships throughout the pharmaceutical industry. That person understands industry's perspective intimately. Is it surprising that this person's regulatory decisions tend to be friendly to pharmaceutical interests? Of course not.

The revolving door thus creates a permanent blending of government and industry interests. The line between government regulator and industry participant becomes blurred. Government agencies become captured by the industries they regulate because they are staffed by industry loyalists.

LEGISLATIVE STAGNATION: CONGRESS REFUSES TO ACT

The combined effect of lobbying, campaign finance, and the revolving door is Congressional stagnation on healthcare reform. Congress refuses to act on problems that are obvious to everyone. Congress refuses to enforce existing law. Congress refuses to pass new legislation addressing the healthcare crisis.

What Congress Will Not Do: The Litmus Test of Industry Capture

Congress will not break up healthcare monopolies. The Sherman Antitrust Act (1890)[83] exists. Federal agencies have authority to enforce it. Courts are willing to hear cases. Yet Congress tolerates insurer concentration, hospital consolidation, and PBM dominance that would trigger immediate federal action in any other sector. Congress is not incapable of enforcing antitrust law. Congress is unwilling to enforce it in healthcare because healthcare corporations have captured Congress.

Congress will not regulate pharmacy benefit managers. The abusive practices of CVS Caremark, Express Scripts, and Optum are documented and undeniable. These companies manipulate rebates, exclude drugs from formularies for financial reasons, and extract billions in value from the healthcare system while harming patients. Congress could pass legislation requiring transparent rebate accounting, limiting formulary exclusions, or separating PBMs from insurance companies. Congress refuses. Healthcare corporations employ teams of lobbyists opposing any regulation. Congress listens.

Congress will not extend ACA subsidies permanently. The ACA reduced the uninsured rate from 16 percent to 8.2 percent (CDC, 2024)[21]. The subsidies cost approximately 1.8 percent of the federal budget. The subsidies would cost approximately $35 billion annually to extend permanently (CBO, 2024)[14]. This is trivial relative to federal spending. Congress should extend them. Congress refuses. Insurance corporations prefer the uncertainty of expiring subsidies because uncertainty depresses enrollment and increases premiums, protecting insurance industry profits.

Congress will not meaningfully regulate drug prices. Medicare was explicitly prohibited from negotiating drug prices through the "non-interference" clause in the Medicare Modernization Act. This prohibition was not accidental. It was written by pharmaceutical industry lobbyists. The Inflation Reduction Act (CBO, 2022)[12] partially reversed this prohibition but with numerous carve-outs protecting pharmaceutical industry interests. Congress should fully enable Medicare to negotiate drug prices like every other developed nation does. Congress refuses, limiting drug negotiations to a small number of drugs and protecting pharmaceutical company pricing power.

Congress will not address rural hospital closures. 166 rural hospitals have closed since 2010 (University of North Carolina, 2023)[42]. Rural communities have lost emergency departments, obstetric services, and primary care access. Congress could purchase struggling rural hospitals and convert them to public facilities. Congress could subsidize critical access hospitals to ensure viability. Congress refuses. Hospital corporations lobby against intervention and Congress listens.

Congress will not enforce existing antitrust law against healthcare monopolies. The Federal Trade Commission and Department of Justice possess full authority to bring cases against anticompetitive healthcare mergers, monopolistic pricing practices, and other violations of antitrust law. Congress could direct these agencies to prioritize healthcare cases. Congress could provide adequate funding for healthcare antitrust enforcement. Congress refuses. Healthcare corporations oppose antitrust enforcement and Congress protects industry interests.

What Congress Will Do: The Proof of Industry Capture

If Congress actually opposed healthcare industry interests, Congress would pass legislation addressing these problems. Congress does not pass such legislation. Congress instead passes legislation protecting healthcare industry interests.

Congress actively protects the tax exemption for employer-sponsored insurance despite knowing that this tax break worth $310 billion annually (Joint Committee on Taxation, 2024)[53] perpetuates the employment-based system and creates instability. Congress could eliminate this tax break and use the revenue to fund universal healthcare. Congress refuses. Insurance corporations depend on this tax break and Congress protects it.

Congress permits continued consolidation in healthcare despite documented price increases resulting from mergers (Cooper et al., 2019)[150]. When the Federal Trade Commission challenges hospital mergers, Congress does not support the agency. Congress defunds antitrust enforcement. Congressional members pressure the FTC to accept mergers that the agency believes are anticompetitive. Healthcare corporations want consolidation. Congress delivers it.

Congress passes legislation benefiting pharmaceutical companies at the expense of consumers. Congress extends patent protections for drugs. Congress permits pay-to-delay arrangements where generic manufacturers are paid to delay market entry. Congress permits "evergreening" where pharmaceutical companies make trivial modifications to drugs and claim patent extension. These are not natural market phenomena. These are deliberate legislative choices made by Congress to benefit pharmaceutical companies at the expense of consumers and taxpayers.

Congress blocks attempts at transparency. When states or advocacy organizations propose legislation requiring disclosure of PBM rebates, Congress does not support such measures. When patient advocates propose legislation limiting pharmaceutical company direct-to-consumer advertising, Congress blocks it. When organizations propose legislation requiring transparency in hospital pricing, Congress permits industry to lobby against it.

Congress protects pharmaceutical company profits through patent law. Congress passed the Hatch-Waxman Act, creating mechanisms allowing pharmaceutical companies to extend patent protections. Congress passed the Biologics Price Competition and Innovation Act, creating 12-year exclusivity periods for biologic drugs. These are Congressional choices. Congress could shorten exclusivity periods. Congress could restrict brand-name drug advertising. Congress could enable generic competition. Congress refuses. Pharmaceutical companies benefit and Congress protects them.

The pattern is consistent. When healthcare industry interests and public interests conflict, Congress chooses healthcare industry interests. Congress is not protecting the public. Congress is protecting the industries that fund its campaigns and offer post-government employment.

THE STRUCTURAL REALITY: HOW DEMOCRACY FAILS

Understanding how democracy fails in healthcare requires understanding that failure is not accidental. It is structural. It emerges from the normal operation of a political system where money determines access and influence.

Money Determines Access and Influence

A healthcare corporation with $50 million to spend on lobbying deploys armies of lawyers, policy experts, and political strategists to influence Congress. These resources are not available to patients, consumer advocates, or public health organizations. The imbalance is not close. Healthcare corporations have thousands of employees dedicated to political and regulatory affairs. Consumer advocacy organizations have dozens, if any.

When a healthcare corporation wants Congress to act or block action, the corporation has resources to make its position heard. Congress receives calls from industry representatives. Industry lawyers draft legislative language. Industry consultants brief Congressional staff. Industry executives donate to campaigns. The resources devoted to industry influence are overwhelming.

When patients want Congress to act on healthcare, what resources do they have? Patients contact their representatives. But Congressional offices receive thousands of constituent contacts daily. An email from a constituent carries almost no weight compared to a call from a pharmaceutical industry lobbyist. Patients organize politically. But organizing requires resources: money for advertising, staff to coordinate efforts, time for volunteer work. Most patients lack these resources.

The structural imbalance is not surprising. It is the inevitable result of allowing unlimited money into politics and allowing industries to employ unlimited lobbyists. Healthcare industry interests dominate because healthcare industry interests have vastly more resources than opposing interests.

Congress Becomes an Industry Protection Racket

The combined effect of lobbying, campaign finance, and the revolving door is that Congress transforms from a body representing constituents into a body protecting the industries that fund its members' campaigns and offer post-government employment.

This is not corruption in the traditional sense. Traditional corruption involves explicit quid pro quo. "Vote for my bill and I will donate to your campaign." Traditional corruption is prosecutable. Members of Congress prosecuted for corruption are convicted because the quid pro quo is explicit.

The healthcare system operates through structural corruption that is legal because the quid pro quo is never explicit. Pharmaceutical companies donate to campaigns without explicitly saying "we expect you to vote for our interests." Yet the expectation exists. Pharmaceutical companies offer post-government employment without explicitly saying "vote for our interests and we will hire you." Yet the incentive exists.

Congress operates as a protection racket on behalf of healthcare corporations. Congress protects healthcare industry interests. Congress blocks reform. Congress maintains the status quo. Congress does this not because members believe it is right policy. Congress does this because Congressional members depend on healthcare industry money for re-election and post-government employment.

Members of Congress understand this. Lobbyists understand this.

Industry executives understand this. The general public, having limited access to information about lobbying spending and campaign finance, often does not understand this. But inside Washington, everyone understands that Congress exists to protect industry interests, not public interests.

The Result: A Political System That Protects Corporate Interests, Not Public Interests

The inevitable result is that healthcare policy becomes healthcare industry policy. Legislation is written by industry lawyers. Legislation protects industry interests. Reform efforts fail because Congress blocks them. Change does not happen because Congress, captured by industry, refuses to permit change.

This is not unique to healthcare. This pattern repeats throughout Congress. Industries dominating particular policy domains shape policy in those domains. Agricultural policy is shaped by agricultural corporations. Energy policy is shaped by energy corporations. Financial policy is shaped by financial corporations. Banking regulations are written by bankers.

In each domain, the public interest loses to industry interests because industry interests have vastly more political resources. The public's desire for affordable housing does not overcome real estate industry lobbying. The public's desire for clean energy does not overcome fossil fuel industry lobbying. The public's desire for strong financial regulations does not overcome banking industry lobbying.

This is how democracy fails. Not through overt authoritarian takeover. Not through abandonment of elections or constitutional forms. Democracy fails through the slow capture of legislative institutions by organized private interests. Democracy fails when the people's representatives become industry agents. Democracy fails when Congress systematically protects corporate profits over human welfare.

COMPARING HEALTHCARE TO OTHER SECTORS: THE ANTITRUST DOUBLE STANDARD

To understand how completely Congress has abandoned its responsibility to enforce antitrust law in healthcare, consider how Congress treats monopolies in other sectors.

What Congress Has Done in Other Sectors

When Standard Oil controlled 90 percent of oil refining in 1911, Congress supported the Justice Department's antitrust case. The Supreme Court ordered Standard Oil's breakup (Standard Oil Co. v. United States, 1911)[86] into 34 independent companies. Prices fell. Competition increased. Innovation accelerated. Congress treated monopoly as unacceptable.

When AT&T controlled 80 percent of telecommunications through the Bell System, Congress supported antitrust enforcement. The company was broken up (United States v. AT&T, 1982)[90] into seven independent regional phone companies. Long-distance service became affordable. Mobile technologies emerged. Innovation accelerated. Congress treated monopoly as unacceptable.

When Microsoft attempted to monopolize web browsers in the 1990s, Congress was aware of the Justice Department's antitrust case (United States v. Microsoft Corp., 2001)[92]. While the government ultimately settled rather than winning a complete victory, the case established that antitrust enforcement in technology was appropriate and necessary. Congress did not block this enforcement. Congress accepted that antitrust law applies to technology companies.

Today, Congress supports antitrust enforcement in technology, energy, finance, and agriculture. The government actively investigates Google's search monopoly (U.S. Department of Justice, 2023)[97]. The government challenges Amazon's marketplace practices (Federal Trade Commission, 2023)[101]. The government pursues antitrust cases against Meta (Federal Trade Commission, 2020)[102] and Apple (U.S. Department of Justice, 2024)[100]. Congress appropriates funds for antitrust enforcement. Congressional members support these enforcement actions.

Yet in healthcare, Congress does nothing while three companies control 80 percent of pharmacy benefit management. Congress does nothing while single insurers control 75-80 percent of entire state insurance markets (American Medical Association, 2024)[18]. Congress does nothing while hospital consolidation eliminates local competition across the nation. Congress actively blocks antitrust enforcement when it threatens healthcare industry interests.

The Explanation: Healthcare Industry Lobbying Dominates Congress

The difference is not that healthcare monopolies are somehow legally defensible under antitrust law while technology or energy monopolies are not. All of these monopolies would violate the Sherman Act if the government chose to enforce it. The difference is that healthcare corporations have captured Congress while other industries have not captured Congress to the same degree.

Healthcare industry lobbying ($739 million in 2024) exceeds technology industry lobbying and energy industry lobbying. Healthcare corporation campaign contributions to Congress exceed contributions from most other sectors. Healthcare corporations offer lucrative post-government employment to departing members and staff at rates exceeding most other industries.

Congress responds by protecting healthcare industry monopolies while pursuing antitrust enforcement in other sectors. This is not neutral application of law. This is selective enforcement driven by political capture.

WHAT WOULD REAL REFORM LOOK LIKE?

If Congress acted in the public interest rather than healthcare industry interest, what would healthcare policy look like?

Antitrust Enforcement

Congress would fully enforce the Sherman Antitrust Act in healthcare. The Department of Justice and Federal Trade Commission would aggressively challenge healthcare mergers that reduce competition. Dominant insurers would be broken up. Hospital consolidation would be prevented. Pharmacy benefit manager monopolies would be dismantled. Competition would discipline prices. Healthcare corporations would compete on quality and efficiency rather than on financial engineering and market dominance.

This is not radical. This is how Congress treats every other sector. If three companies controlled 80 percent of the oil refining market, Congress would demand action. If three companies controlled 80 percent of telecommunications, Congress would demand action. Three companies controlling 80 percent of pharmaceutical distribution should trigger the same response.

Congress could pass legislation explicitly directing the Department of Justice and FTC to prioritize healthcare antitrust cases. Congress could provide increased funding for antitrust enforcement. Congress could pass legislation reducing barriers to antitrust enforcement in healthcare by lowering proof standards or streamlining litigation.

Drug Price Negotiation

Congress would eliminate restrictions on Medicare drug price negotiation. Medicare would negotiate drug prices directly with pharmaceutical companies, just as the VA does. Medicare would achieve the same 50 percent price reductions the VA achieves. Pharmaceutical companies would remain profitable but at lower prices. Americans would pay the same as patients in Canada, Britain, Germany, and other developed nations (OECD, 2024)[17].

This is not price control. This is market negotiation. The VA proves that government negotiation works. Pharmaceutical companies complain that Medicare negotiation will reduce innovation. This is false. The VA negotiates lower prices and pharmaceutical companies still develop drugs (Cleary et al., 2018)[221]. The public demand for innovation is satisfied. Pharmaceutical company profit margins are reduced, but profit remains.

Congress should repeal the Medicare Modernization Act's non-interference clause entirely rather than merely permitting limited negotiation of a small number of drugs. Congress should extend Medicare drug negotiation authority to all drugs covered under Medicare Part D. Congress should extend similar negotiation authority to Medicaid.

Regulation of Pharmacy Benefit Managers

Congress would regulate pharmacy benefit managers directly. Rebate structures would be transparent. PBMs would be prohibited from excluding drugs from formularies for financial reasons unrelated to clinical value. PBMs would be prohibited from negotiating better prices for themselves while forcing higher prices on patients. PBM ownership of insurance companies would be prohibited to eliminate conflicts of interest.

This is not burdensome regulation. This is basic conflict-of-interest prevention. A company should not be able to negotiate rebates for itself while representing an insurer. A company should not be able to use insurance company market power to drive manufacturer rebates that the PBM captures for itself.

Congress should pass legislation requiring PBM transparency in rebate accounting. Congress should require that rebates be passed through to consumers or employers rather than captured by PBMs. Congress should prohibit vertical integration between PBMs and insurance companies, requiring divestiture of existing integrated arrangements.

Hospital Merger Prevention

Congress would prevent further hospital consolidation. The Federal Trade Commission would block mergers that reduce competition. The FTC would break up existing monopolistic hospital systems. Competition would return to healthcare markets. Prices would fall. Rural hospitals would remain viable because they would face competition rather than consolidation pressures.

This is not unprecedented. Congress and the courts have broken up monopolies throughout American history. Monopolies in healthcare should be treated the same as monopolies in other sectors.

Congress should pass legislation strengthening the FTC's authority to challenge hospital mergers. Congress should pass legislation making clear that hospital consolidation presumptively violates antitrust law when it reduces competition below certain thresholds. Congress should support the FTC's current enforcement actions against hospital consolidation.

Campaign Finance Reform

Congress would pass campaign finance reform eliminating unlimited money in politics. Contribution limits would be restored. Super PACs would be prohibited. The revolving door would be closed through strict cooling-off periods preventing former members and staff from immediately becoming lobbyists for industries they previously regulated.

This would not prevent healthcare corporations from donating to campaigns. It would level the playing field so that patient advocates and public health organizations could compete for political influence. It would reduce the financial pressure on members of Congress to vote for industry interests.

Congress should pass legislation requiring disclosure of lobbying meetings and lobbying contacts with Congressional staff. Congress should pass legislation prohibiting gifts from lobbyists to Congressional members and staff. Congress should pass legislation requiring lobbyists to disclose which industries fund their work.

Enforcement of Existing Law

Congress would direct federal agencies to enforce existing laws. The Sherman Antitrust Act exists. The FTC Act exists. The ACA's provisions against unfair practices exist. Congress would direct the Department of Justice and Federal Trade Commission to enforce these laws aggressively in healthcare. Congress would provide adequate funding for enforcement. Congress would support agency action rather than pressuring agencies to accept anticompetitive behavior.

Congress should appropriate sufficient funds for FTC and DOJ enforcement. Congress should pass legislation protecting agency independence from political pressure. Congress should pass legislation requiring annual reports on antitrust enforcement in healthcare.

THE FUNDAMENTAL QUESTION: WILL CONGRESS CHANGE?

The fundamental question facing the nation is whether Congress will change. Will members of Congress stop depending on healthcare industry donations? Will the revolving door close? Will Congress remember that it exists to serve the public, not to protect corporate profits?

The answer depends on the people. The answer depends on whether Americans will organize, mobilize, and demand that Congress remember whom it serves. The answer depends on whether voters will hold members accountable for voting with healthcare industry interests against public interests.

This has happened before. The civil rights movement forced Congress to pass civil rights legislation despite Southern opposition. The environmental movement forced Congress to pass clean air and water legislation despite industry opposition. The labor movement forced Congress to pass labor protections despite business opposition.

The healthcare movement can force Congress to pass healthcare reform. But only if Americans demand it. Only if voters make clear that voting for healthcare industry interests will cost members their seats. Only if the political price of industry capture exceeds the financial benefit of industry donations.

CONCLUSION: CONGRESS IS THE CRISIS

Everything in this book traces back to one fundamental truth: Congress is the crisis. Congress refuses to break up healthcare monopolies. Congress refuses to regulate pharmacy benefit managers. Congress refuses to extend ACA subsidies. Congress refuses to negotiate drug prices. Congress refuses to prevent hospital consolidation. Congress refuses to reform its own campaign finance system.

Congress does not refuse these reforms because the reforms are impractical or impossible. Every developed nation has addressed these problems successfully. Congress refuses because healthcare corporations have captured Congress. Healthcare corporations donate to campaigns (OpenSecrets, 2025)[1],[2]. Healthcare corporations employ lobbyists (Wouters et al., 2020)[3]. Healthcare corporations offer post-government employment to departing members and staff (Jain et al., 2022)[170]. Congress responds by protecting healthcare industry interests.

Democracy dies not from revolution or invasion. Democracy dies from capture. Democracy dies when the people's representatives stop representing the people and start representing the industries that fund them. This is where America is now. This is the crisis.

The healthcare crisis will end only when Congress changes. When members of Congress stop depending on healthcare industry donations. When the revolving door closes. When Congress remembers that it exists to serve the public, not to protect corporate profits. Until Congress changes, nothing else will.

The question is whether Americans will demand this change. The question is whether the people will reclaim their democracy from the corporations that have captured it. The question is whether Congress can be forced to act in the public interest despite the financial pressure to protect industry interests.

The answer depends on political will. The law is ready. The tools exist. The solutions are proven. What is missing is the power of the people demanding that Congress remember whom it serves.

CHAPTER 13
THE ROADMAP CONGRESS REFUSES TO FOLLOW

Congress knows exactly what needs to happen. The legislative pathway exists. The funding mechanisms are clear. The implementation timeline is feasible. The legal authority is unambiguous.

Congress refuses to act.

This chapter documents the precise steps Congress must take to fix American healthcare. Every statute that requires amendment. Every funding mechanism that must be established. Every executive action that can proceed immediately. Every timeline that determines when Americans get relief.

Congress will not follow this roadmap. Not because it is impractical. Not because it is unconstitutional. Not because it is unaffordable. Congress will refuse because healthcare corporations pay Congress to refuse.

The roadmap exists anyway. When voters finally force Congress to act, when political pressure overwhelms corporate money, when democracy briefly reasserts itself over plutocracy, this chapter provides the blueprint Congress will follow.

A. ANTITRUST ENFORCEMENT: THE LAWS CONGRESS REFUSES TO ENFORCE

The Sherman Antitrust Act has been federal law since 1890 (Sherman Antitrust Act, 1890)[83]. Congress has not repealed it. Courts have not invalidated it. The statute remains fully enforceable against healthcare monopolies.

Congress simply refuses to enforce it.

1. Breaking Up Insurance Monopolies: The Action DOJ Refuses to Take

The Department of Justice possesses complete authority under 15 U.S.C. § 2 to prosecute health insurers maintaining illegal monopolies.[(246)] The statute prohibits any person from monopolizing interstate commerce.[(247)] No new legislation required. No constitutional amendment needed. Pure executive function that requires only political will.

Healthcare insurance markets satisfy every element of illegal monopoly. UnitedHealth controls 40 percent of Wisconsin's insurance market.[(248)] Anthem controls 30 percent. Two companies control 70 percent of an entire state's population. Markets with Herfindahl-Hirschman Index above 2,500 are "highly concentrated" under DOJ guidelines (U.S. Department of Justice, 2010)[106]. Most state insurance markets exceed HHI of 5,000 (American Medical Association, 2024)[18].

Congress knows this. DOJ knows this. Everyone knows this.

Nobody acts because insurance corporations donate millions to Congressional campaigns and offer lucrative post-government employment to DOJ officials who look the other way.

What DOJ should do:

File Section 2 Sherman Act complaints against dominant insurers in every state where single insurers control 75+ percent of markets or where top two insurers control 80+ percent. Alabama, where Blue Cross controls 86 percent. North Dakota, where single insurers control 80+ percent. Michigan, where two insurers control 70 percent (American Medical Association, 2024)[18].

Seek structural relief requiring divestiture. UnitedHealth must divest OptumRx and Optum Health, separating insurance from pharmacy benefit management and physician practices. CVS Aetna must divest Caremark. Anthem must divest its PBM operations.

Seek conduct remedies prohibiting exclusive contracts that prevent competing insurers from accessing hospital networks or employer groups.

File preliminary injunctions immediately to prevent further consolidation during litigation.

Timeline if DOJ acted: Complaints filed within 60-90 days. Preliminary injunctions within 30 days of filing. Discovery and litigation 2-4 years. But cases would proceed immediately while healthcare corporations scramble to negotiate consent decrees.

Why DOJ won't act: Attorney General answers to President. President answers to donors. Healthcare industry donates hundreds of millions. UnitedHealth employs former DOJ officials as lobbyists and consultants. The revolving door ensures that current DOJ officials know lucrative private sector jobs await them if they don't rock the boat.

This is corruption. Legal corruption. Structural corruption. But corruption nonetheless.

2. Blocking Hospital Mergers: The Enforcement FTC Abandons

The Clayton Act Section 7 prohibits mergers whose effect "may be substantially to lessen competition."[(249)] The Federal Trade Commission possesses authority to challenge hospital mergers under this provision.

The FTC occasionally challenges mergers. Sanford/Essentia in Minnesota. A handful of others. But most hospital consolidation proceeds with minimal opposition while the FTC watches prices rise 5-30 percent post-merger (Cooper et al., 2019)[150].

What FTC should do:

Establish blanket enforcement policy challenging all hospital mergers where resulting HHI exceeds 2,500 or where merger increases HHI by 200+ points (U.S. Department of Justice, 2010)[106]. No exceptions. No negotiated settlements preserving partial mergers. Complete prohibition.

Challenge vertical mergers between insurers and hospitals. CVS Aetna acquiring hospitals creates insurer controlling both sides of negotiation. Challenge immediately.

Challenge private equity acquisitions of multiple hospital systems in same region. Cerberus Capital, KKR, and other PE firms consolidating hospitals face antitrust litigation.

Timeline if FTC acted: Policy statement issued within 30 days. Preliminary injunctions filed against pending mergers within 60 days. Merger challenges proceed immediately.

Why FTC won't act: FTC Commissioners are Presidential appointments requiring Senate confirmation. Healthcare corporations lobby Senate aggressively during confirmation hearings. Nominees who promise aggressive antitrust enforcement don't get confirmed. Nominees who get confirmed know what is expected: look tough, file occasional high-profile cases, but let most consolidation proceed.

Hospital systems donate to Senate campaigns. Hospital executives bundle contributions for key Senators. The message is clear: confirm friendly commissioners or lose campaign funding.

3. Prosecuting PBM Collusion: The Criminal Case DOJ Ignores

Three pharmacy benefit managers control 80+ percent of prescription drug negotiations (Fein, 2023)[105]. CVS Caremark, Express Scripts, Optum Rx. This concentration enables collusive pricing satisfying Sherman Act Section 1 prohibition on conspiracy in restraint of trade.

Evidence of coordination exists. Identical formulary decisions across competing PBMs. Market-wide rebate structure changes timed identically despite supposedly independent negotiations. Industry-wide price increases during periods when all three PBMs allegedly negotiated separately.

What DOJ should do:

Impanel federal grand juries investigating PBM rebate structures and formulary coordination. Subpoena internal communications, pricing emails, strategy documents. Criminal prosecution under 15 U.S.C. § 1 carries penalties up to ten years imprisonment and fines up to $1 million per day for per se violations.[(250)]

Alternatively, civil enforcement seeking structural remedies. Force divestiture of PBMs from vertically integrated insurers. Prohibit coordinated pricing strategies.

Timeline if DOJ acted: Grand jury investigations begin within 60 days. Subpoenas issued immediately. Evidence gathering 6-18 months. Criminal indictments or civil complaints follow.

Why DOJ won't act: PBM executives donate to campaigns. PBM lobbying budgets exceed $18 million annually for single organizations (OpenSecrets, 2024)[242]. PBMs employ former DOJ prosecutors as defense counsel and lobbyists. Current DOJ prosecutors know that aggressive investigation of PBMs closes doors to lucrative private sector employment after government service.

Congress could direct DOJ to investigate. Congress refuses. Healthcare corporations pay Congress to refuse.

B. FUNDING THE SOLUTION CONGRESS WON'T FINANCE

An American Hospital System requires dedicated revenue. The funding mechanisms are straightforward. The numbers work. The fiscal projections are sound.

Congress refuses to appropriate the money because doing so would require taxing the wealthy or regulating corporations. Congress serves the wealthy and protects corporations. The people's healthcare needs are secondary.

1. Premium-Based Revenue: The Model Congress Abandons

The ACA Marketplace operates on premium revenue. Federal subsidies lower premiums for low-income enrollees. Higher-income individuals pay market rates. The model works. An American Hospital System replicates this structure.

Revenue mechanism:

Enrollees earning 100-200 percent of federal poverty level pay $0-50 monthly premiums (ASPE, 2025)[26]. Federal government subsidizes remainder.

Enrollees earning 200-400 percent pay premiums covering 30-50 percent of costs. Federal subsidy covers remainder.

Enrollees above 400 percent pay full actuarial rates, approximately $800-1,200 monthly for family coverage (Kaiser Family Foundation, 2024)[33].

Revenue projection:

50 million enrollees, approximately 15 percent of population. Average monthly premium $400 across all income groups generates $240 billion annual premium revenue.

Assuming 40 percent are low-income paying minimal premiums:

- 20 million low-income × $20 average monthly = $4.8 billion
- 30 million higher-income × $600 average monthly = $216 billion
- Total premium revenue = $220.8 billion

Federal subsidy requirement assuming $400 billion total annual cost: $400 billion minus $220.8 billion = $179.2 billion annual federal subsidy.

This is substantially less than current federal spending on Medicare ($848 billion), Medicaid ($616 billion), and ACA marketplace subsidies ($125-130 billion) (Centers for Medicare & Medicaid Services, 2024)[63].

Legislative action required:

Congress enacts American Hospital System Act establishing separate program with dedicated premium revenue authority and appropriations capped at $180 billion annually during initial phase. Legislation explicitly states funding does not reduce Medicare or Medicaid appropriations.

Why Congress won't act: $180 billion appropriation requires offsetting revenue or deficit spending. Offsetting revenue requires taxing someone. Congress refuses to tax wealthy individuals or corporations because wealthy individuals and corporations fund Congressional campaigns. Deficit spending faces opposition from deficit hawks who suddenly discover fiscal responsibility when spending benefits ordinary Americans rather than defense contractors or corporate tax cuts.

2. Employer Mandate: The Tax Congress Protects Corporations From Paying

Employers currently spend approximately $22,500 per employee on health insurance premiums (Kaiser Family Foundation, 2024)[159]. An employer mandate requires employers to provide coverage or pay equivalent tax into American Hospital System.

Tax structure:

Employers with 50+ employees must either offer health insurance meeting minimum standards OR pay employer health tax of $600 monthly per employee (~$7,200 annually) into American Hospital System fund.

Employers under 50 employees exempt but may voluntarily participate.

Revenue projection:

Approximately 150 million Americans have employer-sponsored coverage (Kaiser Family Foundation, 2024)[232]. If 25 percent of employers covering 37.5 million employees elect to pay tax rather than maintain private insurance:

37.5 million employees × $7,200 annually = $270 billion

Combined with premium revenue, federal subsidy falls below $100 billion annually if employer participation reaches 25-30 percent.

Legislative action required:

Congress enacts employer health tax through Internal Revenue Code amendment. Tax is revenue-neutral to employers, replacing current insurance premiums but redirecting funds through federal system rather than private insurers.

Why Congress won't act: Employer mandate means corporate taxes. Every major corporation lobbies against mandate. Business groups threaten primary challenges against members supporting mandate. Corporate PACs redirect donations to opponents. Chamber of Commerce runs attack ads.

Congress hears corporations loud and clear. Congress ignores workers who would benefit from stable public insurance replacing employer-based coverage vulnerable to job loss.

3. Drug Pricing Savings: The Money Congress Gives Pharmaceutical Companies

Applying VA drug pricing to all federal healthcare programs saves $60-70 billion annually.[(251)] Congress should dedicate these savings to American Hospital System, creating cycle where cost control funds expansion.

Mechanism:

Authorize Medicare and American Hospital System to negotiate drug prices collectively, extending VA's 54 percent discount to broader population.

Estimated savings: $50-60 billion annually.

Dedicate 50 percent ($25-30 billion) to American Hospital System fund. Remainder flows to deficit reduction.

Legislative action required:

Expand Inflation Reduction Act provisions (Congressional Budget Office, 2022)[12] to all government healthcare programs. Grant American Hospital System negotiating authority alongside Medicare.

Establish drug savings fund dedicated to American Hospital System.

Why Congress won't act: Pharmaceutical companies contributed $89 million to federal candidates in 2020 cycle (OpenSecrets, 2025)[2]. Drug negotiation reduces pharmaceutical profits. Pharmaceutical companies oppose negotiation aggressively. Congress listens to pharmaceutical companies because pharmaceutical companies pay Congress.

Every senator who blocks expanded drug negotiation has taken pharmaceutical money. Every representative who votes against negotiation receives pharmaceutical campaign contributions. The corruption is documented in Federal Election Commission filings.

4. Progressive Income Tax Surcharge: The Tax on Wealth Congress Refuses

Dedicated healthcare surcharge on high incomes funds American Hospital System while maintaining progressive tax structure.

Tax structure:

3 percent surcharge on taxable income above $250,000 individuals, $500,000 couples, dedicated entirely to American Hospital System.

Revenue projection:

Approximately 2 million high-income filers subject to surcharge. Average taxable income above thresholds approximately $500,000.

$500,000 × 3 percent × 2 million filers = $30 billion annual revenue.

Legislative action required:

Enact healthcare surcharge through Internal Revenue Code Section 1 amendment establishing new bracket. Earmark revenue through reconciliation for American Hospital System.

Why Congress won't act: Tax increase on wealthy individuals. Wealthy individuals donate most campaign money. Wealthy individuals fund Super PACs. Wealthy individuals employ lobbyists. Congress represents wealthy individuals, not the 98 percent of Americans earning under $250,000 who would pay nothing.

Members of Congress are themselves wealthy. Senate millionaires vote on tax increases affecting themselves. Predictably, Senate millionaires vote against tax increases.

5. Carbon Tax: The Climate Solution Congress Kills

Carbon tax ($50 per metric ton CO_2) generates $75-100 billion annually while incentivizing emissions reduction.[252] Dedicate 30-40 percent ($25-30 billion) to American Hospital System. Environmental and health objectives align.

Why Congress won't act: Fossil fuel industry opposes carbon tax. Fossil fuel companies donate millions to Congressional campaigns. Oil executives bundle contributions. Koch network funds opposition ads. Congress protects fossil fuel profits over climate stability and healthcare funding.

6. Financial Transaction Tax: Wall Street's Money Congress Won't Touch

Financial transaction tax (0.1 percent on stock trades, 0.01 percent on derivatives) generates $50-70 billion annually.(253) Dedicate 50 percent ($25-35 billion) to American Hospital System.

Why Congress won't act: Financial industry opposes transaction tax. Wall Street firms donate heavily to both parties. Securities Industry and Financial Markets Association employs armies of lobbyists. High-frequency trading firms threaten to relocate operations. Congress caves immediately.

Financial sector profits $100+ billion annually from transactions that produce zero social value. Congress refuses to tax these transactions because Wall Street owns Congress.

C. IMPLEMENTATION TIMELINE CONGRESS WILL DELAY INDEFINITELY

A phasea rollout manages operational complexity and builds political constituency. Pilot in five states. Expand to 15 states. Roll out nationally. Simple. Feasible. Proven approach.

Congress will delay every phase, sabotage every pilot, underfund every expansion.

Phase 1: Pilot Program Congress Will Strangle (Years 1-2)

What should happen:

American Hospital System launches in five pilot states. California, New York, Texas, Minnesota, Florida. Geographic diversity. Underutilized VA facilities. High uninsured rates. Political viability.

Year 1: Legislation passed. VA facilities expanded. Provider networks established. Premium rates calculated. Marketing launched.

Year 2: Open enrollment. Initial enrollees transition. Claims processing activated. Performance metrics established.

Enrollment target: 2-3 million across five states.

Budget authorization: $15-20 billion annual appropriation.

What Congress will do:

Underfund the pilot. Authorize $15 billion but appropriate $8 billion. Force program to launch undercapitalized.

Select hostile states. Instead of California and New York where infrastructure exists, mandate pilots in states with Republican governors committed to sabotaging program. Texas Governor refuses state cooperation. Florida rejects federal coordination.

Impose impossible requirements. Demand program achieve Medicare-equivalent outcomes within six months. Require balanced budget from day one despite knowing startup costs always exceed initial revenue. Set performance thresholds designed for failure.

Schedule inadequate evaluation periods. Demand Congressional review after 12 months when program needs 24-36 months to demonstrate results. Declare pilot "failed" before program fully operational.

Why Congress will sabotage: Insurance corporations want pilot to fail. Hospital systems want pilot to fail. Pharmaceutical companies want pilot to fail. All donate to Congress. Congress delivers what donors demand.

Republican members oppose public healthcare ideologically and protect corporate interests financially. Democratic members face pressure from healthcare industry donors and lack courage to fight corporate opposition. Pilot gets sabotaged from both sides.

Phase 2: Regional Expansion Congress Will Block (Years 3-4)

What should happen:

Based on successful pilot, expand to 10-15 additional states. Target states with hospital consolidation, rural healthcare deserts, high uninsured rates, demonstrated pilot support.

Enrollment target: 10-15 million cumulative.

Budget authorization: $50-75 billion.

What Congress will do:

Declare pilot unsuccessful based on manipulated metrics. Insurance industry-funded think tanks produce reports claiming pilot "cost overruns" and "quality concerns." Congress cites these reports to block expansion authorization.

If expansion somehow proceeds, Congress underfunds it catastrophically. Authorize $50 billion, appropriate $20 billion. Program cannot scale under these constraints.

Impose new restrictions. Prohibit expansion to states with functioning marketplaces. Limit enrollment to unemployed adults. Exclude families. Every restriction designed to minimize enrollment and guarantee failure.

Phase 3: National Rollout Congress Will Never Allow (Years 5-10)

What should happen:

American Hospital System available nationwide. 50-75 million enrolled. Market share sufficient to constrain private insurance premiums through competition. Budget authorization $150-200 billion stabilizing at sustainable level.

What will actually happen:

Congress will never authorize national expansion. Program will remain perpetually "experimental." Enrollment capped. Funding limited. Private insurance protected from competition.

Or Congress kills program entirely. Claims program "unsustainable" despite evidence otherwise. Phases out enrollment. Transfers remaining beneficiaries to private insurers. Declares experiment concluded.

Healthcare corporations win. American people lose. Congress pockets campaign contributions and moves to next corporate priority.

D. EXECUTIVE ACTIONS PRESIDENT WON'T TAKE, CONGRESS WON'T SUPPORT

Presidents possess authority to act immediately on healthcare. VA expansion, antitrust enforcement, drug price negotiation, rural hospital acquisition. All executable through executive action without Congressional approval.

Presidents refuse to act because healthcare corporations fund Presidential campaigns and employ former administration officials.

1. VA Eligibility Expansion: The Authority President Won't Use

VA Secretary possesses authority under 38 U.S.C. § 1701 to expand eligibility beyond veterans.[(254)] Secretary issues regulatory guidance expanding eligibility to "veterans and other individuals whose medical needs can be served by VA infrastructure without reducing veteran access."

Veterans retain priority access. Non-veterans pay actuarial rates. Non-veteran revenue supports VA infrastructure expansion benefiting veterans.

Timeline: Guidance issued within 30-60 days. Implementation begins immediately.

Why President won't act: Insurance corporations lobby White House directly. Insurance executives meet with Chief of Staff. Insurance industry threatens opposition to President's legislative agenda. President caves.

Even if President initially supports expansion, healthcare industry funding of opposition in next election ensures reversal. New President reverses executive order day one. VA expansion dies.

2. Antitrust Enforcement: The Authority DOJ Won't Exercise

Attorney General directs Antitrust Division to initiate healthcare monopoly enforcement without Congressional action. Issue policy statement. Impanel grand juries. File preliminary injunctions. Announce criminal investigations.

Timeline: 60-90 days to launch enforcement initiative.

Why Attorney General won't act: Same revolving door dynamics. Same campaign contributions. Same corporate pressure. DOJ Antitrust Division becomes career graveyard for aggressive prosecutors. Ambitious prosecutors who want federal judgeship appointments or private sector partnerships learn to avoid controversial cases.

3. Drug Price Negotiation: The Authority HHS Won't Use

HHS Secretary possesses authority to negotiate drug prices under Medicare statute. Inflation Reduction Act expanded authority (Congressional Budget Office, 2022)[12]. HHS extends negotiation to American Hospital System immediately, securing VA-equivalent pricing.

Why HHS won't act: Pharmaceutical industry lobbying. PhRMA meets with HHS Secretary monthly. Pharmaceutical executives sit on HHS advisory boards. Agency capture is complete.

4. Rural Hospital Acquisition: The Authority VA Won't Exercise

VA Secretary clarifies authority to acquire distressed hospitals under 38 U.S.C. § 8110.[(255)] Announces acquisition program targeting financially distressed rural and urban community hospitals.

Why VA won't act: Hospital industry opposes federal acquisition. American Hospital Association lobbies against. Private equity firms acquiring distressed hospitals at discount prices don't want federal competition. VA receives message through Congressional appropriators threatening budget cuts.

E. CONGRESSIONAL LEGISLATION THAT WILL NEVER PASS

Four priority bills would transform American healthcare. All are feasible. All are constitutional. All are affordable. None will pass because Congress is owned by the industries these bills regulate.

1. The American Hospital System Act: Dead on Arrival

Omnibus legislation establishing legal framework.

What bill should contain:

Title I: VA eligibility expansion to citizens lacking affordable coverage. Veterans retain 90 percent capacity priority.

Title II: Funding authorization of $15-20 billion annually during pilot. Separate accounting from VA, Medicare, Medicaid.

Title III: Drug price negotiation authority. Formulary exclusion power. VA-style rebate collection.

Title IV: Provider network standards. Direct contracts with hospitals and physicians.

Title V: Quality and transparency requirements. Public reporting of outcomes, satisfaction, financial performance.

Title VI: Pilot phase in five states. Evaluation within 24 months before expansion.

Legislative timeline if Congress acted: 120 days from introduction to signature.

What actually happens:

Bill introduced with fanfare. Immediately assigned to hostile committee. Chairman schedules no hearings. Bill dies in committee. Never reaches floor vote. Sponsor faces primary challenge funded by healthcare industry. Loses.

Even if bill somehow reaches floor, amendments gut it. Private insurance protections added. Enrollment caps imposed. Funding slashed. What remains is unrecognizable shell accomplishing nothing.

2. The Antitrust Enforcement Act: Industry Protection Disguised as Reform

Strengthens healthcare antitrust enforcement.

What bill should contain:

Presumption that healthcare markets with HHI above 2,500 are concentrated. Mergers increasing HHI by 200+ points presumptively illegal.

FTC and DOJ authority for preliminary injunctions halting mergers.

Criminal prosecution of PBM collusion. Minimum penalties for healthcare antitrust violations.

Hospital acquisition disclosure requirements.

What actually happens:

Bill introduced. Healthcare industry lobbyists descend. "Concerns" raised about "overreach." Amendments added creating loopholes. Final version requires extensive proof of harm, making enforcement harder than current law. Bill praised as "reform" while accomplishing nothing.

3. The Healthcare Employer Contribution Act: Corporate Tax Congress Won't Pass

Employer mandate requiring coverage or tax payment.

What bill should contain:

Employers 50+ must offer qualified coverage or pay $600 monthly per employee into American Hospital System fund.

Qualified coverage defined: preventive care, emergency services, mental health, prescription drugs.

Employers offering private insurance deduct premiums paid up to $400 monthly.

Revenue flows to American Hospital System.

What actually happens:

Business groups mobilize opposition. Chamber of Commerce calls it "job killer." NFIB claims small business devastation despite small business exemption. Republicans unanimously oppose. Democrats split. Bill dies.

4. The Drug Price Negotiation Act: Pharmaceutical Protection Act

Expands drug price negotiation across federal programs.

What bill should contain:

Complete repeal of Medicare Part D "non-interference" clause.

Medicare, Medicaid, VA, American Hospital System negotiate collectively.

Formulary exclusion permitted for unreasonable pricing.

Rebate fund capturing savings for program funding.

What actually happens:

Pharmaceutical industry launches massive lobbying campaign. PhRMA spends $31 million in single quarter (OpenSecrets, 2024)[241]. Industry-funded patient advocacy groups testify against bill claiming negotiation threatens "innovation." Congress believes pharmaceutical industry propaganda over evidence.

Bill fails or passes only with amendments protecting pharmaceutical profits. "Negotiation" limited to handful of drugs. Price reductions capped. Pharmaceutical companies declare victory.

F. BUDGET RECONCILIATION: THE PROCEDURAL TRICK CONGRESS WON'T USE

Budget reconciliation requires only 50 Senate votes plus Vice President rather than 60-vote supermajority.[(256)] Healthcare reform is reconciliation-eligible because it involves federal spending and revenue.

What should happen:

Senate passes budget resolution with reconciliation instructions. 15 days.

Reconciliation bill drafted incorporating American Hospital System Act, employer mandate, drug negotiation. 30-45 days.

Floor debate and passage. 20-30 days.

Total: 65-90 days.

What actually happens:

Reconciliation requires unified party control. Even with party control, moderate senators demand concessions. Healthcare industry targets moderates with advertising and campaign threats. Moderates fold.

Bill gets watered down during negotiations. Enrollment caps added. Funding reduced. Provisions stripped. What passes bears no resemblance to original proposal.

Or bill fails entirely. Single moderate senator threatens opposition. Leadership caves to demands. Bill dies without vote.

G. STATE-LEVEL COOPERATION GOVERNORS WILL REFUSE

States should enact enabling legislation facilitating federal expansion. Authorize VA facility operations. Coordinate Medicaid integration. Permit hospital acquisitions. Expand workforce training.

What happens instead:

Republican governors refuse cooperation. Declare American Hospital System "federal overreach." File lawsuits blocking implementation. Request preliminary injunctions preventing VA expansion in their states.

Democratic governors express support but face legislative opposition. State legislatures controlled by Republicans block enabling legislation. Blue state governors must fight hostile legislatures.

Healthcare industry lobbies state capitols. State-level hospital associations oppose federal competition. State medical societies express "concerns." Insurance companies fund opposition campaigns.

Result: Federal program launches in handful of states while most states block participation. Program denied critical mass necessary for success.

H. THE REAL IMPLEMENTATION TIMELINE

Here is what actually happens if reformers somehow gain power:

Year 1: Political battle to pass legislation. Healthcare industry spends $500+ million on lobbying and advertising opposing reform. Floor fight in Congress. Narrow passage through reconciliation after gutting compromises.

Year 2: Regulatory warfare. Healthcare industry sues claiming legislation unconstitutional. Requests preliminary injunctions blocking implementation. Sympathetic federal judges in Texas issue nationwide injunctions. Years of litigation follow.

Year 3-5: Limited pilot programs in friendly states only. Enrollment far below projections due to state opposition, inadequate funding, regulatory uncertainty. Healthcare industry declares pilot "failure" and demands termination.

Year 6-10: Political backlash. Republicans retake Congress or Presidency. Immediately move to defund and dismantle program. Democrats lack votes to prevent cuts. Program withers through starvation.

Year 10+: American Hospital System exists as small, underfunded program serving fraction of intended population. Hailed as "compromise" between public and private healthcare. Actually represents complete victory for healthcare industry and total defeat for reform.

I. COST PROJECTIONS CONGRESS WILL IGNORE

Implementation costs: $5.5-8.6 billion one-time investment.

Operating costs at full implementation: $300-348 billion annually.

Revenue sources: $320-345 billion annually from premiums, employer contributions, drug savings, tax surcharge.

Federal subsidy requirement: $0-25 billion annually. Cost-neutral to slight revenue positive.

These numbers demonstrate American Hospital System is affordable. Total federal healthcare spending currently: Medicare $848 billion, Medicaid $616 billion, VA $301 billion, ACA subsidies $125-130 billion, federal employee benefits $50-60 billion (Centers for Medicare & Medicaid Services, 2024)[63].

American Hospital System represents rationalization of existing spending into more efficient structure, not new spending explosion.

Congress doesn't care: Cost-effectiveness is irrelevant when campaign contributions determine votes. Insurance corporations opposing reform don't care that reform saves money. Hospital systems opposing competition don't care that system reduces costs. Pharmaceutical companies opposing negotiation don't care that negotiation is fiscally responsible.

Congress votes for corporate profits, not fiscal responsibility.

CONCLUSION: THE ROADMAP CONGRESS WILL NEVER FOLLOW

Every word in this chapter is true. Every citation is accurate. Every projection is grounded in evidence. Every legislative provision is constitutionally sound. Every funding mechanism is fiscally responsible. Every timeline is realistic.

None of it matters.

Congress will not pass this legislation because Congress does not represent the American people. Congress represents the healthcare corporations that fund Congressional campaigns and employ former members as lobbyists.

The roadmap exists for the moment when crisis overwhelms corporate power. When enough Americans demand change that political calculation shifts. When electoral consequences of inaction exceed benefits of corporate donations. When democracy briefly reasserts itself.

That moment will come. Healthcare costs will continue rising. Medical bankruptcies will continue destroying families. Americans will continue dying from lack of insurance. Eventually the human cost exceeds what voters tolerate.

When that moment arrives, this chapter provides the blueprint. Congress will have no excuse. The pathway will be documented. The funding will be identified. The timeline will be clear.

Congress will implement reform or voters will replace Congress with representatives willing to act.

The choice is simple. The consequences are clear. What remains is whether Congress remembers whom it serves before voters force the issue through primary challenges and general election defeats.

This roadmap is achievable. The question is whether Congress possesses the courage to follow it or whether voters must first replace Congress entirely.

The pathway forward exists. Whether Congress takes it determines whether American democracy survives corporate capture.

CHAPTER 14
CONCLUSION: POWER, RESPONSIBILITY, AND THE FUTURE OF AMERICAN HEALTH

America does not lack money, knowledge, or institutional capacity. America lacks political will. That is the through-line of this white paper.

The chapters preceding this one have established a simple but uncomfortable truth: the crisis in American healthcare is not primarily technical, fiscal, or constitutional. It is political. It is the predictable result of a Congress that has chosen to protect corporate revenue streams over public health, and to weaponize budget rhetoric rather than use the tools it already possesses.

The Affordable Care Act is not the villain in this story. It is one of the few federal instruments that actually works inside the constraints Congress itself created. The American Hospital System proposed in this white paper is not a radical departure from American tradition. It is a disciplined extension of what the federal government already does for veterans, seniors, and federal employees—scaled, rationalized, and opened to the broader public.

What remains is to state the argument plainly:

- America can solve this.
- The ACA is not the burden—Congressional inaction is.

- Good government equals healthy people.
- Healthy people create a strong economy and a strong military.
- This path is achievable, moral, constitutional, and urgent.

The rest of this chapter will tie those claims together and place responsibility where it belongs.

America Can Solve This

The United States has already done harder things than guaranteeing affordable healthcare. It has fought global wars, rebuilt shattered economies, constructed interstate highways, electrified rural America, landed humans on the moon, and eradicated diseases that once terrorized entire continents. None of those achievements were free. All of them required federal leadership, taxation, regulation, and long-term planning.

Healthcare reform is modest by comparison. The federal government already spends roughly $1.94 trillion annually on Medicare, Medicaid, the VA, ACA marketplace subsidies, and federal employee health benefits. Those funds are not theoretical. They are already appropriated, already taxed, already moving through the system.

What this white paper has shown is that Congress could reorganize a portion of that existing spending into a more coherent structure—the American Hospital System—without meaningfully increasing total healthcare costs. It could extend the logic of the VA and Medicare to a broader civilian population, introduce real competition where markets have consolidated into local monopolies, and use federal purchasing power to discipline prices.

There is no economic law that requires the United States to spend 17.3 percent of GDP on healthcare while leaving millions uninsured, when peer nations cover their entire populations with better outcomes at 10–12.5 percent of GDP. There is no constitutional clause that forbids Congress from regulating healthcare prices, enforcing antitrust law against hospital and insurer cartels, or establishing a national public option grounded in its taxing and spending powers.

America's healthcare crisis is not proof of impossibility. It is proof of neglect.

The ACA Is Not the Burden—Congressional Inaction Is

Throughout this paper, one claim has surfaced repeatedly: the ACA is not the problem. Congress is.

The evidence is straightforward:

- The shortcomings critics attribute to the ACA—high deductibles, narrow networks, limited provider choice, rural access problems—exist across the entire private insurance landscape: employer plans, off-market individual plans, Medicare Advantage, and non-ACA products.
- Rural insurer scarcity predated the ACA by decades; the marketplaces merely revealed an already existing gap.
- When Congress refuses to adjust subsidies or regulate deductibles, it is not exposing a flaw in the ACA's design; it is choosing to leave systemic problems untouched and then blaming the one program that made coverage possible for 40+ million people.

The pattern is clear. Congress invokes "fiscal responsibility" to justify cutting or failing to renew ACA subsidies while simultaneously approving far larger, unpaid-for tax cuts, corporate subsidies, and defense spending increases. This is not neutral budgeting. It is ideological preference disguised as arithmetic.

If Congress were genuinely concerned about deductibles, it would regulate them across all plans. If it were genuinely concerned about narrow networks, it would enforce robust network standards system-wide. If it were genuinely concerned about rural access, it would subsidize coverage in those markets instead of using rural scarcity as a pretext to dismantle the marketplaces entirely.

The ACA is not the burden. The burden is a Congress that will not use its own tools. The burden is a political class that refuses to confront provider monopolies, drug-price exploitation, and private-insurer administrative bloat—then presents cuts to working families' coverage as the only responsible option.

Good Government Equals Healthy People

A government is not judged by how little it spends, but by what its spending accomplishes. "Small government" and "big government" are distractions. The meaningful distinction is between good government and bad government.

Good government ensures clean water, safe food, reliable infrastructure, functioning courts, and predictable rules for commerce. No serious person argues that these functions are "socialist" when they benefit their own community. Healthcare belongs in that same category of basic public infrastructure.

A government that allows preventable disease to spread, treats mental health as an afterthought, and tolerates vast disparities in life expectancy across income and race is not fiscally cautious. It is failing its core purpose. A government that spends more on bureaucratic friction—billing codes, denials, redundant networks—than on actual care is not prudent. It is captured.

This white paper has shown that federal healthcare investment is economically rational: healthier workers are more productive, earn higher incomes, and pay more taxes; healthier communities experience less crime, less dependency, and more stable growth; healthier populations lower long-term costs by preventing catastrophic illness instead of repeatedly paying to treat it at its most expensive stages.

Good government, in a rich nation, is government that treats health as a public good—not a speculative commodity whose value is determined by shareholders and lobbyists.

Healthy People, Strong Economy, Strong Military

American political rhetoric often treats healthcare, the economy, and national security as separate silos: one committee for health, another for budget, another for defense. In reality, they are the same conversation.

This white paper has argued that healthcare is economic infrastructure. A sick workforce cannot sustain a competitive economy. Every day of work lost to preventable disease, every worker disabled by untreated conditions, every premature death reduces GDP and erodes the tax base that funds everything else.

The national security implications are equally stark. A sick population cannot defend itself. Chronic disease erodes the capacity to fund defense. Untreated mental illness destabilizes communities. Substance abuse and preventable illness weaken both the civilian economy and the recruitment pool for the armed forces.

As documented in Chapter 11, the Department of Defense already confronts a recruiting crisis in which roughly three-quarters of Americans aged 17–24 do not meet military standards without waivers, with obesity, mental health conditions, and substance use as leading disqualifiers. This is not an accidental by-product of an otherwise healthy society; it is the predictable outcome of decades of fragmented, unequal, and expensive healthcare access.

From a budgetary perspective, the inefficiency of the current system is a direct tax on military capacity. If the United States spent a share of GDP on healthcare comparable to other high-income nations, while covering everyone, it could free hundreds of billions annually for defense modernization, infrastructure, education, or deficit reduction.

Healthy people generate strong economies. Strong economies support capable militaries. There is no plausible path to long-term American security that does not run through universal, efficient, affordable healthcare.

This Path Is Achievable, Moral, Constitutional, and Urgent

Achievable.

The American Hospital System outlined in this white paper does not require dismantling existing programs or inventing unprecedented legal authority. It consolidates parts of current federal spending, leverages existing administrative capacity (especially within the VA), and introduces a national public option that competes with, rather than abolishes, private insurance. At full implementation, projected revenues closely match operating costs, with only modest or potentially zero net federal subsidy required.

Constitutional.

Congress has every tool it needs: the power to tax and spend for the general welfare, the power to regulate interstate commerce, and the authority to condition federal funds on compliance with quality and access standards. No amendment is required. No emergency exception is needed. Congress simply must use powers it has repeatedly used for Social Security, Medicare, Medicaid, veterans' benefits, and civil rights enforcement.

Moral.

In a nation that spends trillions annually on healthcare and defense, allowing millions to remain uninsured or underinsured is not an accident; it is a choice. The moral claim here is not abstract. Every preventable death from lack of coverage, every bankruptcy from medical bills, every young person disqualified from service due to treatable conditions is a foreseeable consequence of policy. When foreseeable harms are left unaddressed despite clear remedies, they become moral failures, not unfortunate outcomes.

The United States already recognizes a duty to care for veterans who risked their lives for the country. The same logic extends outward: the state also has an obligation not to treat the health of civilians as collateral damage in ideological battles about the size of government.

Urgent.

Delay is not neutral. While Congress holds hearings, defers votes, and recycles talking points, chronic disease advances, life expectancy stagnates, hospital consolidation accelerates, and out-of-pocket burdens grow. The longer the current structure persists, the more entrenched provider monopolies and corporate insurers become, and the more expensive reform will be to implement.

Urgency is not panic. It is recognition that time is now an active variable in the equation. Every year of inaction compounds the economic, social, and security costs of a dysfunctional system.

Where Responsibility Now Rests

This white paper has done what it can do. It has:

- Corrected the record on what the ACA is and is not.
- Demonstrated that the ACA's perceived flaws are systemic private-insurance problems, not unique failures of the marketplaces.
- Documented the capture of federal healthcare policy by corporate interests.
- Framed healthcare as economic infrastructure and national security policy, not merely a welfare program.
- Proposed a concrete, costed, constitutionally grounded roadmap for a national public option rooted in existing institutions.

What remains cannot be accomplished by paper. It must be accomplished by people.

Responsibility now rests in three places:

1. **Congress.** Members of Congress cannot claim ignorance. The data are clear. The legal authority is established. The design options are available. When Congress chooses not to extend ACA subsidies, not to enforce antitrust in healthcare markets, and not to move forward with a national public option, it is not constrained by law. It is constrained by fear of donors, lobbyists, and short-term political backlash.

2. **The Executive Branch.**Presidents and their administrations have significant authority to enforce existing antitrust law, regulate prices within public programs, expand pilots modeled on the VA, and use rulemaking to strengthen the

ACA marketplaces. They cannot do everything without Congress, but they can do far more than they have.

3. **The Public.** Ultimately, elected officials move when the risk of inaction exceeds the risk of action. That inflection point is determined by voters, advocates, health professionals, employers, and civic leaders who decide whether healthcare policy is an afterthought or a first-order priority.

If constituents treat healthcare as a peripheral issue—secondary to party identity, cultural grievances, or short-term tax cuts—Congress will continue to behave as it has. If, instead, voters evaluate their representatives explicitly on whether they protect coverage, discipline prices, and advance a coherent plan for universal access, the incentive structure will change.

A Final Statement of the Case

The thesis of this white paper can be condensed to a single claim:

A wealthy democracy that refuses to provide affordable healthcare to its people is not saving money; it is sacrificing its own future.

The United States has the resources, the institutional experience, and the legal authority to build a healthcare system that is more rational, more just, and more efficient than the one it currently tolerates. The ACA has already proven that federal intervention can expand coverage, strengthen economic productivity, and stabilize families without collapsing markets or bankrupting the Treasury.

The American Hospital System outlined in these pages demonstrates that a national public option, rooted in the VA model and financed largely through existing streams of federal spending, is not utopian. It is a policy choice among many, fully compatible with constitutional principles and capitalist markets.

The open question is not **whether** America can solve this. It can. The open question is **who** will accept responsibility for doing so, and **when**.

If Congress acts—using the tools already in its hands—American healthcare can become what it should have been all along: a foundation for prosperity, security, and human dignity, rather than a source of preventable suffering and economic drag. If Congress refuses, the costs of inaction will grow until they can no longer be disguised as prudence.

Good government equals healthy people. Healthy people sustain strong economies and strong militaries. Strong, healthy societies endure.

The choice now belongs to the people and to those who claim to represent them.

DID YOU ENJOY THIS BOOK?

I sure hope so!

Please join our family and write a review. Reviews are the "tip jar" of the book publishing industry. New readers weigh reviews heavily in deciding to make a purchase. You being so generous as to share your experience is the lifeblood of the success of "The Affordable Care Act" To do this please scan the QR code below

I appreciate you!
Eric Lawrence Frazier

BECOME A MEMBER TODAY

Why Become a Member of The Power Is Now Media?

Unlock exclusive access to the most powerful real estate, mortgage, credit, and wealth-building content in the industry.

For a limited time, become a member for only $10/month or $60/year. Your membership delivers undeniable value, insider access, and proven tools to help you buy, sell, invest, and build wealth with confidence.

Membership Benefits

Exclusive Streaming & Shows

- Unlimited access to The Power Is Now TV Network library of hundreds of shows, podcasts, and webinars.
- Daily programming on homeownership, real estate investing, mortgages, credit, and financial literacy (Federal Reserve, 2024)[1].

- Member-only live streams and roundtable discussions with top industry leaders.

Free Digital Resources

- Real estate eBooks, guides, and reports on buying, selling, investing, and credit strategies (Consumer Financial Protection Bureau, 2023)[7].
- Buyer & Seller Guides, HUD Homes Guide, and Foreclosure Market Reports, updated quarterly (U.S. Department of Housing and Urban Development, 2025)[55].
- Access to The Power Is Now Media Resource Library of downloadable content.

Magazines & Newsletters

- Complimentary subscription to The Power Is Now National Real Estate Magazine.
- Complimentary subscription to The Power Is Now HUD Homes for Sale Magazine.
- Complimentary subscription to The Power Is Now TV Guide Magazine.
- Complimentary subscription to Faith, Family & Finance Magazine.
- Weekly newsletters with videos, infographics, and market insights (Federal Reserve Bank of New York, 2023)[9].

Member Engagement

- Invitations to attend and participate in live recordings of the Real Estate Roundtable and Business Roundtable.
- Networking opportunities with agents, lenders, investors, and entrepreneurs nationwide.
- Priority access to quarterly webinars for first-time

homebuyers, investors, and asset managers (U.S. Department of Housing and Urban Development, 2025)[55].
- Monthly group coaching sessions on Personal Finance, Real Estate, Mortgage, and Media (Federal Reserve, 2024)[1].

Discounts & Savings

- Member-only discounts on media services (podcast hosting, YouTube TV production, private-label magazines, website redesigns, social media management).
- Exclusive pricing on advertising, sponsorships, and coaching programs.

Community & Recognition

- Become part of a national network of professionals and consumers committed to real estate wealth-building.
- Opportunities to feature your story, listings, or business on The Power Is Now TV Network.

Special Membership Offer

Join now at www.thepowerisnow.com

Special Launch Price: $10/month or $60/year (limited-time offer through year-end).

Regular Price: $50/month or $325/year.

Don't wait—membership pays for itself many times over.

For over 16 years, The Power Is Now has been dedicated to educating and empowering people in real estate, mortgage, credit, and wealth-building (Consumer Financial Protection Bureau, 2023)[7]. Now, through our membership program, you can unlock exclusive access to everything we offer.

For only $10 a month or $60 a year, you'll get unlimited access to hundreds of shows on The Power Is Now TV Network, free eBooks and real estate guides, four magazine subscriptions, weekly newsletters, and live roundtable access with industry leaders. You'll also enjoy discounts on media services, group coaching, and the chance to network with professionals across the country.

But here's the best part—you'll be part of a movement. A national community committed to real estate wealth-building, financial literacy, and creating generational wealth (Federal Reserve, 2024)[1].

So go to www.thepowerisnow.com today and become a member. This special pricing is only available until the end of the year. Join us, and let's build wealth together.

SCAN ME

ABOUT THE POWER IS NOW

The Power Is Now Media is an online multimedia company founded in 2009 by Eric L. Frazier MBA, headquartered in Riverside, California. We are advocates for homeownership, wealth building, and financial literacy. We create and publish original educational content about real estate through nationally syndicated Radio, Podcasts, Magazines, TV, Social Media, Streaming platforms, and special online seminars and webinars. We are an online platform and resource for everyone to learn about homeownership, housing, loan programs, and down payment assistance to achieve financial literacy and the American dream of homeownership. We are supported by housing finance agencies, real estate associations, and civic, religious, and community organizations. We help them amplify their voice about the services and programs they offer in lending, housing, and homeownership. Visit us at www.thepowerisnow.com

The Mission of the Power is Now Media is to inspire and educate consumers and real estate professionals to build wealth through the acquisition, management, and sale of real estate with information and support we provide via our website, live and on-demand TV, and social media platforms that empower everyone to own real estate now and achieve the American dream of homeownership. Our company slogan is "We are leading the conversation about real homeownership."

The Power Is Now Media corporate office is located at 3739 6th Street, Riverside, CA 92501. Telephone/Fax: 800-401-8994. Eric Lawrence Frazier MBA is a California Licensed Loan Originator (NMLS License #461807) and Real Estate Broker (License #O1148434).

ABOUT THE AUTHOR

Mr. Eric Lawrence Frazier, MBA, is the President and CEO of The Power Is Now Media, a national multimedia company dedicated to real estate education, empowerment, and thought leadership. Through its expansive platform—comprising the Power Is Now website (www.thepowerisnow.com), national podcast networks, social media channels, and live-stream television platforms—the company delivers timely, authoritative content on real estate, lending, economics, and government policy.

In addition to leading the media network, Mr. Frazier serves as the Publisher and Editor-in-Chief of The Power Is Now Publishing, which produces books and magazines dedicated to real estate, financial literacy, and wealth building. Since its founding, the publishing division has created a wide range of educational materials, including The Power Is Now Magazines, a suite of online real estate publications launched in 2013 that feature market insights, national news, and educational resources for both homebuyers and professionals.

Mr. Frazier is a graduate of the University of Redlands in Redlands, California, where he earned a Master of Business Administration (MBA) with an emphasis in Finance as well as a Bachelor of Science in Business Administration and Management. He has lectured on the U.S. mortgage crisis at the University of California, Riverside, addressing international business leaders from India, and has served as an adjunct professor.

With nearly four decades of expertise in mortgage banking, Mr.

Frazier is nationally recognized for his leadership in origination, underwriting, operations, management, and marketing. He has also built a distinguished career in real estate sales and brokerage, holding a California real estate license for over thirty years and a broker's license (#01143484) for more than twenty-eight years. Together with his wife, he founded Frazier Group Realty (www.fraziergrouprealty.com), a full-service, family-owned real estate company based in Riverside, California.

Mr. Frazier's professional leadership extends into numerous industry associations. He is the former President of the Orange County Realtist chapter of the National Association of Real Estate Brokers (NAREB) and a former Director of the California Association of Real Estate Brokers. He has also served as Vice President of the Orange County chapter of the National Association of Hispanic Real Estate Professionals (NAHREP) and as an Advisory Board Member of the Orange County chapter of the Asian Real Estate Association of America (AREAA). He has served on the Board of Directors of the Riverside Fair Housing Council, was a past member of the Pacific West Association of Realtors, and is currently a member of the Inland Valley Association of Realtors (IVAR).

Beyond real estate, Mr. Frazier is deeply engaged in civic and community leadership. He has served on the Board of Directors of Project Tomorrow (www.tomorrow.org), a national nonprofit organization dedicated to education. He is an active member of the 100 Black Men of America, the NAACP, and the National Association of Mortgage Brokers. He is also the past President and Director of the State of California African American Museum (www.caamuseum.org).

His spiritual leadership is rooted in the church. Mr. Frazier is a pastor and leads The Power Is Now Ministries, a ministry of the North Fontana Church, a 501(c)(non-profit) organization, where he continues to serve through teaching, outreach, and mentorship.

A man of diverse talents, Mr. Frazier is also an author, blogger, poet, singer, songwriter, motivational speaker, business consultant, and coach to both for-profit and nonprofit organizations, as well as a personal financial coach. He is the published author of six books spanning poetry, African American wealth, credit, and business. His personal interests include golf, running, and jazz music.

Mr. Frazier is especially committed to mentorship, striving to be a role model for African American men and dedicating time to coaching young people and adults. His greatest joy, however, is found in family. He has been married to the love of his life, Ruby, for over forty years, and together they have raised four accomplished daughters. His three eldest daughters hold master's degrees in management and business, while his youngest has earned a bachelor's degree in apparel merchandising and management.

All of Mr. Frazier's professional accomplishments, affiliations, and ongoing work can be found at **www.linkedin.com/in/ericfrazier**.

FOLLOW ME ON SOCIAL MEDIA

Lets Connect

LET'S CONNECT ON LINKEDIN

REFERENCES

REFERENCES - CHAPTER I

1. OpenSecrets. (2025). *Health sector lobbying spending, 2024*. Center for Responsive Politics. https://www.opensecrets.org/federal-lobbying/sectors/summary?id=H

2. OpenSecrets. (2025). *Pharmaceuticals/health products: Long-term contribution trends*. Center for Responsive Politics. https://www.opensecrets.org/industries/totals.php?cycle=2024&ind=H04

3. Wouters, O.J., Berenbeim, D.M., & Gu, J. (2020). Lobbying expenditures and economic outcomes in the pharmaceutical industry. *JAMA Internal Medicine*, 180(4), 499-506. https://jamanetwork.com/journals/jamainternalmedicine/fullarticle/2762509

4. OpenSecrets. (2023). *Bob Menendez - Career summary*. Center for Responsive Politics. https://www.opensecrets.org/

members-of-congress/bob-menendez/summary?cid=N00009638

5. OpenSecrets. (2023). *Kyrsten Sinema - Career summary*. Center for Responsive Politics. https://www.opensecrets.org/members-of-congress/kyrsten-sinema/summary?cid=N00033983

6. OpenSecrets. (2023). *Scott Peters - Career summary*. Center for Responsive Politics. https://www.opensecrets.org/members-of-congress/scott-peters/summary?cid=N00033591

7. OpenSecrets. (2023). *Kurt Schrader - Career summary*. Center for Responsive Politics. https://www.opensecrets.org/members-of-congress/kurt-schrader/summary?cid=N00031233

8. OpenSecrets. (2023). *Richard Burr - Career summary*. Center for Responsive Politics. https://www.opensecrets.org/members-of-congress/richard-burr/summary?cid=N00002221

9. Public Citizen. (2019). *From Capitol Hill to K Street: The revolving door in the pharmaceutical industry*. https://www.citizen.org/article/from-capitol-hill-to-k-street/

10. Congressional Budget Office. (2019). *H.R. 3, Elijah E. Cummings Lower Drug Costs Now Act: Cost estimate*. https://www.cbo.gov/publication/55936

11. OpenSecrets. (2021). *Mitch McConnell - Career summary*. Center for Responsive Politics. https://www.opensecrets.org/members-of-congress/mitch-mcconnell/summary?cid=N00003389

12. Congressional Budget Office. (2022). *Estimated budgetary effects of Public Law 117-169, the Inflation Reduction Act of 2022.* https://www.cbo.gov/publication/58455

13. OpenSecrets. (2022). *Pharmaceutical manufacturing: Contributions to candidates and parties, 2022 cycle.* https://www.opensecrets.org/industries/contrib.php?ind=H4300&cycle=2022

14. Congressional Budget Office. (2024). *Federal subsidies for health insurance coverage for people under 65: Tables.* https://www.cbo.gov/publication/60106

15. Committee for a Responsible Federal Budget. (2017). *Tax Cuts and Jobs Act: Final conference report.* https://www.crfb.org/blogs/tax-cuts-and-jobs-act-final-conference-report

16. U.S. Department of Defense. (2024). *Defense budget overview: Fiscal year 2025.* https://comptroller.defense.gov/Budget-Materials/

17. Centers for Medicare & Medicaid Services. (2025). *2025 Marketplace open enrollment period report.* https://www.cms.gov/newsroom/fact-sheets/2025-marketplace-open-enrollment-period-report

18. American Medical Association. (2024). *Competition in health insurance: A comprehensive study of U.S. markets, 2024 update.* https://www.ama-assn.org/system/files/ama-competition-health-insurance-2024.pdf

19. Beaulieu, N.D., Dafny, L.S., Landon, B.E., Dalton, J.B., Kuye, I., & McWilliams, J.M. (2020). Changes in quality of care after hospital mergers and acquisitions. *Journal of the American Medical Association*, 382(1), 51-59. https://jamanetwork.com/journals/jama/fullarticle/2759569

20. Medbelle. (2021). *Insulin prices: A global comparison.* https://www.medbelle.com/insulin-prices/

21. Centers for Disease Control and Prevention. (2024). *Health insurance coverage: Early release of estimates from the National Health Interview Survey, 2023.* National Center for Health Statistics. https://www.cdc.gov/nchs/data/nhis/earlyrelease/insur202405.pdf

REFERENCES - CHAPTER II

1. Kaiser Family Foundation. (2024). *Medicaid expansion enrollment.* https://www.kff.org/medicaid/issue-brief/status-of-state-medicaid-expansion-decisions-interactive-map/

2. Kaiser Family Foundation. (2025). *Marketplace enrollment by employment status.* https://www.kff.org/private-insurance/issue-brief/who-enrolls-in-the-aca-marketplaces/

3. Kaiser Family Foundation. (2025). *Age distribution of marketplace enrollees above 400% FPL.* https://www.kff.org/private-insurance/issue-brief/marketplace-enrollment-by-age-and-income/

4. Kaiser Family Foundation. (2025). *Gig economy workers and ACA coverage.* https://www.kff.org/private-insurance/issue-brief/gig-workers-and-health-insurance/

5. ASPE. (2025). *HHS poverty guidelines for 2025.* U.S. Department of Health and Human Services. https://aspe.hhs.gov/topics/poverty-economic-mobility/poverty-guidelines

6. Kaiser Family Foundation. (2025). *Premium contributions under enhanced subsidies.* https://www.kff.org/health-

reform/issue-brief/how-the-american-rescue-plan-act-affects-subsidies/

7. Kaiser Family Foundation. (2024). *Eliminating the subsidy cliff: Coverage above 400% FPL.* https://www.kff.org/health-reform/issue-brief/eliminating-the-aca-subsidy-cliff/

8. Centers for Medicare & Medicaid Services. (2025). *State-based marketplace platforms.* https://www.cms.gov/marketplace/about/overview/state-marketplaces

9. Internal Revenue Service. (2024). *Premium tax credit: Applicable percentage table.* https://www.irs.gov/affordable-care-act/individuals-and-families/premium-tax-credit-claiming-the-credit-and-reconciling-advance-credit-payments

10. Commonwealth Fund. (2025). *Average marketplace subsidy amounts, 2025.* https://www.commonwealthfund.org/publications/issue-briefs/2025/marketplace-subsidy-savings

11. Commonwealth Fund. (2025). *Enhanced premium tax credit impact on monthly savings.* https://www.commonwealthfund.org/publications/issue-briefs/2024/enhanced-subsidies-impact

12. Commonwealth Fund. (2025). *Low-cost plan availability on HealthCare.gov.* https://www.commonwealthfund.org/publications/issue-briefs/2024/low-premium-plans-marketplace

13. Commonwealth Fund. (2025). *Pre-enhancement subsidy eligibility for low-cost plans.* https://www.commonwealthfund.org/publications/issue-briefs/2023/marketplace-affordability-pre-american-rescue-plan

14. Center on Budget and Policy Priorities. (2024). *Family premium costs under enhanced ACA subsidies.* https://www.cbpp.org/research/health/enhanced-aca-subsidies-make-coverage-more-affordable

15. Centers for Medicare & Medicaid Services. (2025). *Bronze plan actuarial value and deductibles.* https://www.cms.gov/marketplace/about/plans/metal-tiers

16. Centers for Medicare & Medicaid Services. (2025). *Silver plan enrollment and cost-sharing reductions.* https://www.cms.gov/marketplace/about/plans/silver-plans-csr

17. Centers for Medicare & Medicaid Services. (2025). *Gold plan actuarial value and cost-sharing.* https://www.cms.gov/marketplace/about/plans/gold-plans

18. Centers for Medicare & Medicaid Services. (2025). *Platinum plan enrollment statistics.* https://www.cms.gov/marketplace/about/plans/platinum-plans

19. Centers for Medicare & Medicaid Services. (2025). *Maximum out-of-pocket limits for 2025.* https://www.cms.gov/marketplace/about/plans/out-of-pocket-maximum

20. Center on Budget and Policy Priorities. (2025). *Cost-sharing reduction impacts by income level.* https://www.cbpp.org/research/health/understanding-cost-sharing-reductions

21. Kaiser Family Foundation. (2024). *Pre-ACA insurance market conditions and uninsured rates.* https://www.kff.org/uninsured/report/the-uninsured-a-primer-key-facts-about-health-insurance-and-the-uninsured/

22. Commonwealth Fund. (2024). *Health outcomes among newly insured ACA enrollees.* https://www.commonwealthfund.

org / publications / issue-briefs / 2024 / aca-coverage-health-outcomes

23. MoneyGeek. (2025). *Health insurance claim denial rates by insurer*. https: / / www.moneygeek.com / insurance / health / analysis / claim-denial-rates /

REFERENCES - CHAPTER III

1. Kaiser Family Foundation. (2024). *Average deductibles for bronze and silver marketplace plans*. https: / / www.kff.org / health-costs / issue-brief / 2024-marketplace-average-deductibles /

2. Commonwealth Fund. (2024). *Affordability challenges among insured adults*. https: / / www.commonwealthfund.org / publications / surveys / 2024 / affordability-health-insurance-coverage

3. Kaiser Family Foundation. (2024). *Employer health benefits annual survey: Deductibles*. https: / / www.kff.org / health-costs / report / 2024-employer-health-benefits-survey /

4. America's Health Insurance Plans. (2024). *High-deductible health plan enrollment trends*. https: / / www.ahip.org / resources / high-deductible-health-plan-trends-2024

5. Wharam, J.F., Zhang, F., Wallace, J., et al. (2023). Vulnerable and less vulnerable women in high-deductible health plans experienced delayed breast cancer care. *Health Affairs*, 42(5), 644-652. https: / / www.healthaffairs.org / doi / 10.1377 / hlthaff.2022.01434

6. Avalere Health. (2023). *Analysis of provider network adequacy in ACA marketplace plans*. https: / / avalere.com / insights / analysis-of-aca-marketplace-network-adequacy

7. Kaiser Family Foundation. (2023). *Hospital network adequacy in marketplace plans*. https://www.kff.org/private-insurance/issue-brief/provider-network-adequacy-in-marketplace-plans/

8. National Association of Insurance Commissioners. (2024). *Network adequacy standards: Employer-sponsored plans*. https://content.naic.org/sites/default/files/inline-files/network-adequacy-2024.pdf

9. Kaiser Family Foundation. (2024). *Insurer participation on ACA marketplaces, 2024*. https://www.kff.org/private-insurance/issue-brief/insurer-participation-aca-marketplaces-2024/

10. Robert Wood Johnson Foundation. (2022). *Rural health insurance market competition before and after the ACA*. https://www.rwjf.org/en/insights/our-research/2022/06/rural-health-insurance-markets.html

11. Centers for Disease Control and Prevention. (2023). *Rural health disparities*. https://www.cdc.gov/rural-health/php/data-research/index.html

12. University of North Carolina. (2023). *Rural hospital closures: 2010-2023*. Cecil G. Sheps Center for Health Services Research. https://www.shepscenter.unc.edu/programs-projects/rural-health/rural-hospital-closures/

13. Patient Advocate Foundation. (2023). *Health insurance claim appeal rates and outcomes*. https://www.patientadvocate.org/explore-our-resources/health-insurance-appeals/

14. U.S. Department of Health and Human Services. (2023). *Medicare Advantage prior authorization and claim denials*. Office

of Inspector General. https://oig.hhs.gov/oei/reports/OEI-09-18-00260.asp

15. Mental Health America. (2024). *Access to mental health care in private insurance.* https://mhanational.org/issues/2024/mental-health-america-access-care

16. National Association of Dental Plans. (2024). *Dental benefits coverage: Individual market analysis.* https://www.nadp.org/Dental_Benefits_Basics/Dental_Coverage_Facts.aspx

17. American Psychological Association. (2024). *Mental health provider network adequacy in private insurance.* https://www.apa.org/topics/mental-health/insurance-network-adequacy

18. Center on Budget and Policy Priorities. (2024). *Regulating cost-sharing in health insurance: Policy options.* https://www.cbpp.org/research/health/regulating-cost-sharing-comprehensive-approach

REFERENCES - CHAPTER IV

1. National War Labor Board. (1942). *General Order No. 1: Wage stabilization.* https://fraser.stlouisfed.org/title/national-war-labor-board-449/general-order-1-8086

2. Blumberg, L.J., & Holahan, J. (2019). *The origins of employer-sponsored health insurance.* Urban Institute. https://www.urban.org/research/publication/origins-employer-sponsored-health-insurance

3. Thomasson, M.A. (2003). The importance of group coverage: How tax policy shaped U.S. health insurance. *American Economic Review*, 93(4), 1373-1384. https://www.aeaweb.org/articles?id=10.1257/000282803769206359

4. Internal Revenue Service. (1943). *Revenue Ruling 43-88: Employer health insurance contributions*. https://www.irs.gov/pub/irs-drop/rr-43-88.pdf

5. Joint Committee on Taxation. (2024). *Estimates of federal tax expenditures for fiscal years 2024-2028*. https://www.jct.gov/publications/2024/jcx-1-24/

6. Tax Policy Center. (2023). *Distribution of the tax exclusion for employer-sponsored health insurance by income*. https://www.taxpolicycenter.org/model-estimates/tax-benefit-employer-sponsored-health-insurance

7. Employee Retirement Income Security Act. (1974). *Public Law 93-406*. https://www.dol.gov/general/topic/health-plans/erisa

8. Jacobson, P.D., & Parmet, W.E. (2007). A new era of unenforced mandates: The health insurance portability and accountability act. *American Journal of Public Health*, 97(3), 399-403. https://ajph.aphapublications.org/doi/10.2105/AJPH.2005.076026

9. Truman, H.S. (1945). *Special message to Congress recommending a comprehensive health program*. https://www.trumanlibrary.gov/library/public-papers/192/special-message-congress-recommending-comprehensive-health-program

10. Starr, P. (1982). *The social transformation of American medicine*. Basic Books. https://www.basicbooks.com/titles/paul-starr/the-social-transformation-of-american-medicine/9780465079353/

11. Social Security Amendments. (1965). *Public Law 89-97: Medicare and Medicaid*. https://www.ssa.gov/history/1965amend.html

12. Marmor, T.R. (2000). *The politics of Medicare* (2nd ed.). Aldine de Gruyter. https://www.degruyter.com/document/doi/10.4324/9780203791868/politics-medicare-theodore-marmor

13. Health Security Act. (1993). *H.R. 3600: American Health Security Act of 1993*. https://www.congress.gov/bill/103rd-congress/house-bill/3600

14. Johnson, H., & Broder, D.S. (1996). *The system: The American way of politics at the breaking point*. Little, Brown and Company. https://www.hachettebookgroup.com/titles/haynes-johnson/the-system/9780316469418/

15. Patient Protection and Affordable Care Act. (2010). *Public Law 111-148*. https://www.congress.gov/bill/111th-congress/house-bill/3590

16. Canadian Medicare. (1966). *Medical Care Act of 1966*. https://www.canada.ca/en/health-canada/services/health-care-system/reports-publications/health-care-system/canada.html

17. Organisation for Economic Co-operation and Development. (2024). *Health spending (indicator)*. https://data.oecd.org/healthres/health-spending.htm

18. National Health Service Act. (1946). *9 & 10 Geo. 6 c. 81*. https://www.legislation.gov.uk/ukpga/Geo6/9-10/81/contents

19. World Health Organization. (2023). *Global health expenditure database*. https://apps.who.int/nha/database

20. Commonwealth Fund. (2023). *Mirror, mirror 2023: Reflecting poorly on U.S. health care*. https://www.commonwealthfund.

org/publications/fund-reports/2023/jun/mirror-mirror-2023

REFERENCES - CHAPTER V

1. Congressional Budget Office. (2024). *The budget and economic outlook: 2024 to 2034*. https://www.cbo.gov/publication/59710

2. Social Security Administration. (2024). *Annual statistical supplement to the Social Security Bulletin, 2024*. https://www.ssa.gov/policy/docs/statcomps/supplement/

3. Centers for Medicare & Medicaid Services. (2024). *2024 Medicare trustees report*. https://www.cms.gov/oact/tr/2024

4. Congressional Research Service. (2024). *Defense spending and the budget*. https://crsreports.congress.gov/product/pdf/R/R46929

5. Committee for a Responsible Federal Budget. (2024). *Federal deficit trends and projections*. https://www.crfb.org/papers/deficit-tracker

6. Emergency Medical Treatment and Labor Act. (1986). *42 U.S.C. § 1395dd*. https://www.cms.gov/Regulations-and-Guidance/Legislation/EMTALA

7. American Diabetes Association. (2023). *Economic costs of diabetes in the U.S. in 2022. Diabetes Care*, 46(Supplement 1), S141-S157. https://diabetesjournals.org/care/article/46/Supplement_1/S141/148057

8. Urban Institute. (2023). *What would happen if the ACA were repealed?* https://www.urban.org/research/publication/what-would-happen-if-aca-were-repealed

9. American Journal of Public Health. (2019). *Medical bankruptcy in the United States, 2007: Results of a national study.* https://ajph.aphapublications.org/doi/10.2105/AJPH.2018.304901

10. Consumer Financial Protection Bureau. (2022). *Medical debt burden in the United States.* https://www.consumerfinance.gov/about-us/newsroom/cfpb-estimates-88-billion-in-medical-bills-on-credit-reports/

11. Himmelstein, D.U., Lawless, R.M., Thorne, D., Foohey, P., & Woolhandler, S. (2019). Medical bankruptcy: Still common despite the Affordable Care Act. *American Journal of Public Health,* 109(3), 431-433. https://ajph.aphapublications.org/doi/10.2105/AJPH.2018.304901

12. Health Affairs. (2020). *Medicaid expansion reduced medical debt and increased financial security.* https://www.healthaffairs.org/doi/10.1377/hlthaff.2020.00547

13. Federal Reserve Board. (2022). *Medical debt and homeownership.* https://www.federalreserve.gov/econres/feds/medical-debt-and-economic-security.htm

14. Kauffman Foundation. (2021). *Healthcare costs and entrepreneurship.* https://www.kauffman.org/entrepreneurship/reports/healthcare-costs-entrepreneurship/

15. National Bureau of Economic Research. (2022). *The long-term effects of health insurance on education and earnings.* https://www.nber.org/papers/w29447

16. Centers for Medicare & Medicaid Services. (2024). *National health expenditure accounts: Historical.* https://www.cms.gov/

data-research/statistics-trends-and-reports/national-health-expenditure-data/historical

17. Journal of Occupational and Environmental Medicine. (2023). *Health insurance and worker productivity*. https://journals.lww.com/joem/

18. RAND Corporation. (2021). *Health insurance and labor supply*. https://www.rand.org/pubs/research_reports/RRA308-2.html

19. Social Security Administration. (2023). *Annual report of the Supplemental Security Income program*. https://www.ssa.gov/oact/ssir/SSI23/

20. Kaiser Family Foundation. (2024). *Medicaid spending per enrollee*. https://www.kff.org/medicaid/state-indicator/medicaid-spending-per-enrollee/

21. Health Affairs. (2023). *Administrative costs in the ACA marketplaces versus employer-sponsored insurance*. https://www.healthaffairs.org/doi/10.1377/hlthaff.2022.01255

22. American Journal of Public Health. (2009). *Health insurance and mortality in US adults*. https://ajph.aphapublications.org/doi/10.2105/AJPH.2008.157685

REFERENCES - CHAPTER VI

1. Sherman Antitrust Act. (1890). *15 U.S.C. §§ 1–7*. https://www.law.cornell.edu/uscode/text/15/chapter-1

2. U.S. Department of Justice. (2023). *Sherman Antitrust Act*. Antitrust Division. https://www.justice.gov/atr/antitrust-laws-and-you

3. Kovacic, W.E., & Shapiro, C. (2000). Antitrust policy: A century of economic and legal thinking. *Journal of Economic Perspectives*, 14(1), 43-60. https://www.aeaweb.org/articles?id=10.1257/jep.14.1.43

4. Yergin, D. (1991). *The prize: The epic quest for oil, money, and power*. Simon & Schuster. https://www.simonandschuster.com/books/The-Prize/Daniel-Yergin/9781439110126

5. McGee, J.S. (1958). Predatory price cutting: The Standard Oil (N.J.) case. *Journal of Law and Economics*, 1, 137-169. https://www.journals.uchicago.edu/doi/10.1086/466547

6. Standard Oil Co. v. United States. (1911). *221 U.S. 1*. https://supreme.justia.com/cases/federal/us/221/1/

7. Granitz, E., & Klein, B. (1996). Monopolization by "raising rivals' costs": The Standard Oil case. *Journal of Law and Economics*, 39(1), 1-47. https://www.journals.uchicago.edu/doi/10.1086/467342

8. Temin, P. (1987). *The fall of the Bell system*. Cambridge University Press. https://www.cambridge.org/core/books/fall-of-the-bell-system/

9. Noll, R.G., & Owen, B.M. (1989). The anticompetitive uses of regulation: United States v. AT&T. In J.E. Kwoka & L.J. White (Eds.), *The antitrust revolution* (pp. 290-337). Scott, Foresman. https://www.brookings.edu/articles/the-anticompetitive-uses-of-regulation/

10. United States v. AT&T. (1982). *552 F. Supp. 131 (D.D.C.)*. https://law.justia.com/cases/federal/district-courts/FSupp/552/131/1883520/

11. Crandall, R.W., & Waverman, L. (2000). *Who pays for universal service? When telephone subsidies become transparent*. Brookings Institution Press. https://www.brookings.edu/books/who-pays-for-universal-service/

12. Evans, D.S., Nichols, A.L., & Schmalensee, R. (2000). *United States v. Microsoft: Did consumers win?* National Bureau of Economic Research. https://www.nber.org/papers/w27505

13. United States v. Microsoft Corp. (2001). *253 F.3d 34 (D.C. Cir.)*. https://caselaw.findlaw.com/court/us-dc-circuit/1060915.html

14. Gilbert, R.J., & Katz, M.L. (2001). An economist's guide to U.S. v. Microsoft. *Journal of Economic Perspectives*, 15(2), 25-44. https://www.aeaweb.org/articles?id=10.1257/jep.15.2.25

15. Bresnahan, T., & Greenstein, S. (2014). Mobile computing: The next platform rivalry. *American Economic Review*, 104(5), 475-480. https://www.aeaweb.org/articles?id=10.1257/aer.104.5.475

16. Mathews, A.W. (2024). UnitedHealth's doctor empire: How it controls physician practices. *Wall Street Journal*. https://www.wsj.com/health/healthcare/unitedhealth-optum-doctors-hospitals-medical-care-

17. Baker, J.B. (2019). *The antitrust paradigm: Restoring a competitive economy*. Harvard University Press. https://www.hup.harvard.edu/catalog.php?isbn=9780674984356

18. United States v. Google LLC. (2023). *Civil Action No. 1:20-cv-03010 (D.D.C.)*. https://www.justice.gov/atr/case/us-v-google-llc

19. U.S. Department of Justice. (2023). *Justice Department wins landmark antitrust case against Google*. https://www.justice.gov/opa/pr/justice-department-wins-landmark-antitrust-case-against-google

20. U.S. Department of Justice. (2024). *Justice Department sues Apple for monopolizing smartphone markets*. https://www.justice.gov/opa/pr/justice-department-sues-apple-monopolizing-smartphone-markets

21. Federal Trade Commission. (2023). *FTC sues Amazon for illegally maintaining monopoly power*. https://www.ftc.gov/news-events/news/press-releases/2023/09/ftc-sues-amazon-illegally-maintaining-monopoly-power

22. Federal Trade Commission. (2020). *FTC sues Facebook for illegal monopolization*. https://www.ftc.gov/news-events/news/press-releases/2020/12/ftc-sues-facebook-illegal-monopolization

23. American Hospital Association. (2024). *Fast facts on U.S. hospitals, 2024*. https://www.aha.org/statistics/fast-facts-us-hospitals

24. Cooper, Z., Craig, S.V., Gaynor, M., & Van Reenen, J. (2019). The price ain't right? Hospital prices and health spending on the privately insured. *Quarterly Journal of Economics*, 134(1), 51-107. https://academic.oup.com/qje/article/134/1/51/5090426

25. Prager, E., & Schmitt, M. (2021). Employer consolidation and wages: Evidence from hospitals. *American Economic Review*, 111(2), 397-427. https://www.aeaweb.org/articles?id=10.1257/aer.20190690

26. Fein, A.J. (2023). *The 2023-24 economic report on pharmaceutical wholesalers and specialty distributors*. Drug Channels Institute. https://www.drugchannels.net/2023/08/the-2023-24-economic-report-on.html

REFERENCES - CHAPTER VII

1. U.S. Department of Justice. (2010). *Horizontal merger guidelines*. U.S. Department of Justice and Federal Trade Commission. https://www.justice.gov/atr/horizontal-merger-guidelines-08192010

2. Gaynor, M., Mostashari, F., & Ginsburg, P.B. (2017). *Making health care markets work: Competition policy for health care*. Brookings Institution. https://www.brookings.edu/research/making-health-care-markets-work-competition-policy-for-health-care/

3. Fulton, B.D. (2017). Health care market concentration trends in the United States: Evidence and policy responses. *Health Affairs*, 36(9), 1530-1538. https://www.healthaffairs.org/doi/10.1377/hlthaff.2017.0556

4. Berenson, R.A., Ginsburg, P.B., & Christianson, J.B. (2012). *The growing power of some providers to win steep payment increases from insurers suggests policy remedies may be needed*. Health Affairs, 31(5), 973-981. https://www.healthaffairs.org/doi/10.1377/hlthaff.2011.0920

5. Dafny, L. (2014). Hospital industry consolidation—still more to come? *New England Journal of Medicine*, 370(3), 198-199. https://www.nejm.org/doi/full/10.1056/NEJMp1313948

6. Sood, N., Shih, T., Van Nuys, K., & Goldman, D. (2017). *The flow of money through the pharmaceutical distribution system*. USC Schaeffer Center for Health Policy &

Economics. https://healthpolicy.usc.edu/research/the-flow-of-money-through-the-pharmaceutical-distribution-system/

7. Kaiser Family Foundation. (2024). *2024 Employer health benefits survey*. https://www.kff.org/health-costs/report/2024-employer-health-benefits-survey/

REFERENCES - CHAPTER VIII

1. U.S. Department of Veterans Affairs. (2024). *VA budget highlights and performance metrics: Fiscal year 2024*. https://www.va.gov/budget/products.asp

2. Government Accountability Office. (2015). *Veterans Health Administration: Actions needed to improve wait time data*. https://www.gao.gov/products/GAO-15-202

3. U.S. Department of Veterans Affairs Office of Inspector General. (2014). *Veterans Health Administration: Interim report on systemic issues affecting access to care*. https://www.va.gov/oig/pubs/VAOIG-14-01844-178.pdf

4. U.S. Department of Veterans Affairs Office of Inspector General. (2014). *Veterans Health Administration: Audit of the Phoenix VA Health Care System*. https://www.va.gov/oig/pubs/VAOIG-14-02603-267.pdf

5. U.S. Department of Veterans Affairs Office of Inspector General. (2015). *Review of alleged patient deaths, patient wait times, and scheduling practices at the Phoenix VA Health Care System*. https://www.va.gov/oig/pubs/VAOIG-14-02603-267.pdf

6. Casalino, L.P., Nicholson, S., Gans, D.N., et al. (2009). What does it cost physician practices to interact with health

insurance plans? *Health Affairs*, 28(4), w533-w543. https://www.healthaffairs.org/doi/10.1377/hlthaff.28.4.w533

7. Kaiser Family Foundation. (2019). *Medicare Advantage prior authorization and coverage rules*. https://www.kff.org/medicare/report/medicare-advantage-prior-authorization-and-coverage-rules/

8. Commonwealth Fund. (2024). *2024 health care affordability survey: Prior authorization impacts*. https://www.commonwealthfund.org/publications/surveys/2024/health-care-affordability-survey

9. Schwartz, L.M., & Woloshin, S. (2019). Medical marketing in the United States, 1997-2016. *JAMA*, 321(1), 80-96. https://jamanetwork.com/journals/jama/fullarticle/2720029

10. Jain, S.H., Lucey, C., & Crosson, F.J. (2022). The revolving door between health policymakers and industry. *JAMA*, 327(13), 1234-1235. https://jamanetwork.com/journals/jama/fullarticle/2790412

11. Lurie, P., Almeida, C.M., Stine, N., Stine, A.R., & Wolfe, S.M. (2006). Financial conflict of interest disclosure and voting patterns at Food and Drug Administration Drug Advisory Committee meetings. *JAMA*, 295(16), 1921-1928. https://jamanetwork.com/journals/jama/fullarticle/202726

12. Kerr, E.A., Gerzoff, R.B., Krein, S.L., et al. (2004). Diabetes care quality in the Veterans Affairs Health Care System and commercial managed care: The TRIAD study. *Annals of Internal Medicine*, 141(4), 272-281. https://www.acpjournals.org/doi/10.7326/0003-4819-141-4-200408170-00007

13. Crowley, M.J., Edelman, D., McAndrew, A.T., et al. (2013). Practical telemedicine for veterans with persistently poor

diabetes control: A randomized pilot trial. *Telemedicine and e-Health*, 19(5), 1-7. https://www.liebertpub.com/doi/10.1089/tmj.2012.0242

14. Stevens, C.D., Schriger, D.L., Raffetto, B., Davis, A.C., Zingmond, D., & Roby, D.H. (2004). Diabetes quality measures in VA versus academic settings. *Diabetes Care*, 27(7), 1570-1575. https://diabetesjournals.org/care/article/27/7/1570/23989

15. Hyre, A.D., Krousel-Wood, M.A., Muntner, P., Kawasaki, L., & DeSalvo, K.B. (2007). Prevalence and predictors of poor antihypertensive medication adherence in an urban health clinic setting. *Journal of Clinical Hypertension*, 9(3), 179-186. https://onlinelibrary.wiley.com/doi/10.1111/j.1524-6175.2007.06372.x

16. Carey, R.M., Calhoun, D.A., Bakris, G.L., et al. (2018). Resistant hypertension: Detection, evaluation, and management: A scientific statement from the American Heart Association. *Hypertension*, 72(5), e53-e90. https://www.ahajournals.org/doi/10.1161/HYP.0000000000000084

17. Weiner, M.G., Embi, P.J., Shapiro, J.S., Payne, P.R., & Speedie, S. (2012). Translational research informatics and data resources: Current successes and future prospects. *Applied Clinical Informatics*, 3(2), 112-125. https://www.thieme-connect.com/products/ejournals/html/10.4338/ACI-2011-12-IE-0077

18. Haggstrom, D.A., & Schapira, M.M. (2006). Practical approaches to shared decision making in oncology. *Journal of Oncology Practice*, 2(6), 288-292. https://ascopubs.org/doi/10.1200/JOP.2006.2.6.288

19. Resick, P.A., Wachen, J.S., Dondanville, K.A., et al. (2015). Effect of group vs individual cognitive processing therapy in active-duty military seeking treatment for posttraumatic stress disorder: A randomized clinical trial. *JAMA Psychiatry*, 74(1), 28-36. https://jamanetwork.com/journals/jamapsychiatry/fullarticle/2593557

20. Steenkamp, M.M., Litz, B.T., Hoge, C.W., & Marmar, C.R. (2015). Psychotherapy for military-related PTSD: A review of randomized clinical trials. *JAMA*, 314(5), 489-500. https://jamanetwork.com/journals/jama/fullarticle/2427861

21. Pogach, L.M., Rajan, M., Maney, M., et al. (2010). Patient-aligned care team and diabetes outcomes in Veterans Affairs primary care clinics. *The Joint Commission Journal on Quality and Patient Safety*, 36(11), 481-489. https://www.sciencedirect.com/science/article/abs/pii/S1553725010360670

22. Resick, P.A., & Schnicke, M.K. (1992). Cognitive processing therapy for sexual assault victims. *Journal of Consulting and Clinical Psychology*, 60(5), 748-756. https://psycnet.apa.org/record/1993-07615-001

23. Resick, P.A., & Schnicke, M.K. (1993). *Cognitive processing therapy for rape victims: A treatment manual*. Sage Publications. https://us.sagepub.com/en-us/nam/cognitive-processing-therapy-for-rape-victims/book3896

24. Monson, C.M., Schnurr, P.P., Resick, P.A., Friedman, M.J., Young-Xu, Y., & Stevens, S.P. (2006). Cognitive processing therapy for veterans with military-related posttraumatic stress disorder. *Journal of Consulting and Clinical Psychology*, 74(5), 898-907. https://psycnet.apa.org/record/2006-20172-011

25. U.S. Department of Veterans Affairs & U.S. Department of Defense. (2023). *VA/DoD clinical practice guideline for the management of posttraumatic stress disorder and acute stress disorder*. https://www.healthquality.va.gov/guidelines/MH/ptsd/

26. Foa, E.B., Rothbaum, B.O., Riggs, D.S., & Murdock, T.B. (1991). Treatment of posttraumatic stress disorder in rape victims: A comparison between cognitive-behavioral procedures and counseling. *Journal of Consulting and Clinical Psychology*, 59(5), 715-723. https://psycnet.apa.org/record/1991-32779-001

27. Foa, E.B., Hembree, E.A., Cahill, S.P., et al. (2005). Randomized trial of prolonged exposure for posttraumatic stress disorder with and without cognitive restructuring: Outcome at academic and community clinics. *Journal of Consulting and Clinical Psychology*, 73(5), 953-964. https://psycnet.apa.org/record/2005-13254-020

28. U.S. Department of Veterans Affairs & U.S. Department of Defense. (2004). *VA/DoD clinical practice guideline for the management of post-traumatic stress*. https://www.healthquality.va.gov/guidelines/MH/ptsd/

29. Powers, M.B., Halpern, J.M., Ferenschak, M.P., Gillihan, S.J., & Foa, E.B. (2010). A meta-analytic review of prolonged exposure for posttraumatic stress disorder. *Clinical Psychology Review*, 30(6), 635-641. https://www.sciencedirect.com/science/article/abs/pii/S0272735810000656

30. Cusack, K., Jonas, D.E., Forneris, C.A., et al. (2016). Psychological treatments for adults with posttraumatic stress disorder: A systematic review and meta-analysis. *Clinical*

Psychology Review, 43, 128-141. https://www.sciencedirect.com/science/article/abs/pii/S0272735815001579

31. Hagberg, K., Branemark, R., Gunterberg, B., & Rydevik, B. (2008). Osseointegrated trans-femoral amputation prostheses: Prospective results of general and condition-specific quality of life in 18 patients at 2-year follow-up. *Prosthetics and Orthotics International*, 32(1), 29-41. https://journals.sagepub.com/doi/10.1080/03093640701553922

32. Resnik, L., Klinger, S.L., & Etter, K. (2014). The DEKA Arm: Its features, functionality, and evolution during the Veterans Affairs Study to optimize the DEKA Arm. *Prosthetics and Orthotics International*, 38(6), 492-504. https://journals.sagepub.com/doi/10.1177/0309364613506913

33. Defense Advanced Research Projects Agency. (2018). *Revolutionizing Prosthetics: Final report*. https://www.darpa.mil/program/revolutionizing-prosthetics

34. Perry, B.N., Moran, C.W., Armiger, R.S., et al. (2018). Initial clinical evaluation of the modular prosthetic limb. *Frontiers in Neurology*, 9, 153. https://www.frontiersin.org/articles/10.3389/fneur.2018.00153/full

35. U.S. Food and Drug Administration. (2014). *FDA approves DEKA Arm prosthetic limb*. https://www.fda.gov/news-events/press-announcements/fda-approves-complex-innovative-prosthetic-device

36. Brown, S.H., Lincoln, M.J., Groen, P.J., & Kolodner, R.M. (2003). VistA—U.S. Department of Veterans Affairs national-scale HIS. *International Journal of Medical Informatics*, 69(2-3), 135-156. https://www.sciencedirect.com/science/article/abs/pii/S1386505602001314

37. Kizer, K.W. (1999). The "new VA": A national laboratory for health care quality management. *American Journal of Medical Quality*, 14(1), 3-20. https://journals.sagepub.com/doi/10.1177/106286069901400102

38. Evans, R.S., Pestotnik, S.L., Classen, D.C., et al. (1998). A computer-assisted management program for antibiotics and other antiinfective agents. *New England Journal of Medicine*, 338(4), 232-238. https://www.nejm.org/doi/full/10.1056/NEJM199801223380406

39. Ash Center for Democratic Governance and Innovation. (2006). *Innovations in American Government Award: VistA*. https://ash.harvard.edu/innovation-government

40. Kolodner, R.M., Cohn, S.P., & Friedman, C.P. (2008). Health information technology: Strategic initiatives, real progress. *Health Affairs*, 27(5), w391-w395. https://www.healthaffairs.org/doi/10.1377/hlthaff.27.5.w391

41. U.S. Department of Veterans Affairs. (2016). *Office of Patient Centered Care and Cultural Transformation: Whole Health System origins*. https://www.va.gov/PATIENTCENTEREDCARE/about.asp

42. U.S. Department of Veterans Affairs. (2017). *VHA Directive 1137: Provision of complementary and integrative health*. https://www.va.gov/vhapublications/ViewPublication.asp?pub_ID=5401

43. Kligler, B., Hyde, J., Gantt, C., & Bokhour, B. (2022). The Whole Health System of Care: Development, implementation, and evaluation. *Medical Care*, 60(Suppl 2), S105-S112. https://journals.lww.com/lww-medicalcare/Abstract/2022/04001/The_Whole_Health_System_of_Care__Development,.2.aspx

44. Taylor, S.L., Reiber, G.E., Crain, A.L., et al. (2021). Complementary and integrative health therapy use in patients with chronic musculoskeletal pain at Veterans Health Administration Whole Health demonstration sites. *Pain Medicine*, 22(11), 2548-2558. https://academic.oup.com/painmedicine/article/22/11/2548/6307894

45. Darkins, A., Ryan, P., Kobb, R., et al. (2008). Care Coordination/Home Telehealth: The systematic implementation of health informatics, home telehealth, and disease management to support the care of veteran patients with chronic conditions. *Telemedicine and e-Health*, 14(10), 1118-1126. https://www.liebertpub.com/doi/10.1089/tmj.2008.0021

46. Heyworth, L., Kirsh, S., Zulman, D., Ferguson, J.M., & Kizer, K.W. (2020). Expanding access through virtual care: The VA's early experience with Covid-19. *NEJM Catalyst Innovations in Care Delivery*, 1(4). https://catalyst.nejm.org/doi/full/10.1056/CAT.20.0327

47. Ferguson, J.M., Jacobs, J., Yefimova, M., Greene, L., Heyworth, L., & Zulman, D.M. (2021). Virtual care expansion in the Veterans Health Administration during the COVID-19 pandemic: Clinical services and patient characteristics associated with utilization. *Journal of the American Medical Informatics Association*, 28(3), 453-462. https://academic.oup.com/jamia/article/28/3/453/5943839

48. Bestsennyy, O., Gilbert, G., Harris, A., & Rost, J. (2020). *Telehealth: A quarter-trillion-dollar post-COVID-19 reality?* McKinsey & Company. https://www.mckinsey.com/industries/healthcare-systems-and-services/our-insights/telehealth-a-quarter-trillion-dollar-post-covid-19-reality

49. U.S. Office of Personnel Management. (2024). *Federal workforce statistics: September 2024*. https://www.opm.gov/policy-data-oversight/data-analysis-documentation/federal-employment-reports/

50. Darkins, A., Cruise, C., Armstrong, M., Peters, J., Finn, M., & McMullen, P. (2019). Expanding telehealth across the continuum of care: Lessons from the Department of Veterans Affairs. *Federal Practitioner*, 36(Suppl 4), S14-S18. https://www.fedprac.com/article/expanding-telehealth-across-continuum-care

REFERENCES - CHAPTER IX

1. Government Accountability Office. (2015). Veterans Health Administration: Actions needed to improve wait time data. https://www.gao.gov/products/GAO-15-202

2. U.S. Office of Personnel Management. (2024). Federal workforce statistics: September 2024. https://www.opm.gov/policy-data-oversight/data-analysis-documentation/federal-employment-reports/

3. U.S. Department of Veterans Affairs. (2024). VA budget highlights and performance metrics: Fiscal year 2024. https://www.va.gov/budget/products.asp

4. Kaiser Family Foundation. (2019). Medicare Advantage prior authorization and coverage rules. https://www.kff.org/medicare/report/medicare-advantage-prior-authorization-and-coverage-rules/

5. Commonwealth Fund. (2024). 2024 health care affordability survey: Prior authorization impacts. https://www.commonwealthfund.org/publications/surveys/2024/health-care-affordability-survey

6. Casalino, L.P., Nicholson, S., Gans, D.N., et al. (2009). What does it cost physician practices to interact with health insurance plans? Health Affairs, 28(4), w533-w543. https://www.healthaffairs.org/doi/10.1377/hlthaff.28.4.w533

7. Schwartz, L.M., & Woloshin, S. (2019). Medical marketing in the United States, 1997-2016. JAMA, 321(1), 80-96. https://jamanetwork.com/journals/jama/fullarticle/2720029

8. Jain, S.H., Lucey, C., & Crosson, F.J. (2022). The revolving door between health policymakers and industry. JAMA, 327(13), 1234-1235. https://jamanetwork.com/journals/jama/fullarticle/2790412

9. Lurie, P., Almeida, C.M., Stine, N., Stine, A.R., & Wolfe, S.M. (2006). Financial conflict of interest disclosure and voting patterns at Food and Drug Administration Drug Advisory Committee meetings. JAMA, 295(16), 1921-1928. https://jamanetwork.com/journals/jama/fullarticle/202726

10. Cooper, Z., Craig, S.V., Gaynor, M., & Van Reenen, J. (2019). The price ain't right? Hospital prices and health spending on the privately insured. Quarterly Journal of Economics, 134(1), 51-107. https://academic.oup.com/qje/article/134/1/51/5090426

11. Prager, E., & Schmitt, M. (2021). Employer consolidation and wages: Evidence from hospitals. American Economic Review, 111(2), 397-427. https://www.aeaweb.org/articles?id=10.1257/aer.20190690

12. U.S. Department of Justice. (2010). Horizontal merger guidelines. U.S. Department of Justice and Federal Trade Commission. https://www.justice.gov/atr/horizontal-merger-guidelines-08192010

13. Gaynor, M., Mostashari, F., & Ginsburg, P.B. (2017). Making health care markets work: Competition policy for health care. Brookings Institution. https://www.brookings.edu/research/making-health-care-markets-work-competition-policy-for-health-care/

14. Fulton, B.D. (2017). Health care market concentration trends in the United States: Evidence and policy responses. Health Affairs, 36(9), 1530-1538. https://www.healthaffairs.org/doi/10.1377/hlthaff.2017.0556

15. Berenson, R.A., Ginsburg, P.B., & Christianson, J.B. (2012). The growing power of some providers to win steep payment increases from insurers suggests policy remedies may be needed. Health Affairs, 31(5), 973-981. https://www.healthaffairs.org/doi/10.1377/hlthaff.2011.0920

REFERENCES - CHAPTER X

1. U.S. Department of Defense. (2020). Qualified military available: A look at American youth eligibility for military service. https://www.defense.gov/News/News-Stories/Article/Article/2094251/

2. Centers for Disease Control and Prevention. (2024). Obesity prevalence among military-age population. https://www.cdc.gov/obesity/data/adult.html

3. World Health Organization. (2023). Life expectancy and healthy life expectancy: Data by country. https://www.who.int/data/gho/data/themes/mortality-and-global-health-estimates/ghe-life-expectancy-and-healthy-life-expectancy

4. Centers for Disease Control and Prevention. (2024). Infant mortality rates by country. National Center for Health

Statistics. https://www.cdc.gov/nchs/data/databriefs/db485.pdf

5. Congressional Budget Office. (2024). The budget and economic outlook: 2024 to 2034. https://www.cbo.gov/publication/59710

6. Congressional Research Service. (2024). Defense primer: Military health system. https://crsreports.congress.gov/product/pdf/IF/IF10530

7. U.S. Department of Defense. (2024). Defense manpower data center: Active duty military personnel strengths by service. https://dwp.dmdc.osd.mil/dwp/app/dod-data-reports/workforce-reports

8. Watson Institute for International and Public Affairs. (2023). Costs of the post-9/11 wars. Brown University. https://watson.brown.edu/costsofwar/

9. U.S. Department of Defense. (2023). Casualty status as of: Iraq and Afghanistan conflicts. https://www.defense.gov/casualty.pdf

10. Centers for Disease Control and Prevention. (2024). Leading causes of death. National Center for Health Statistics. https://www.cdc.gov/nchs/fastats/leading-causes-of-death.htm

11. Kaiser Family Foundation. (2022). Americans' challenges with healthcare costs. https://www.kff.org/health-costs/issue-brief/americans-challenges-with-health-care-costs/

12. U.S. Army. (2023). Army recruiting: Fiscal year 2023 results. https://www.army.mil/recruiting

13. Government Accountability Office. (2022). Military recruiting: Army and Marine Corps need better data to improve recruiting. https://www.gao.gov/products/GAO-22-104554

14. Federal Ministry of Family Affairs, Senior Citizens, Women and Youth. (2023). Voluntary services in Germany. https://www.bmfsfj.de/bmfsfj/service/publikationen/voluntary-services-in-germany

15. Israel Defense Forces. (2024). National service in Israel. https://www.idf.il/en/minisites/national-service/

16. Swiss Federal Department of Defence. (2024). Civil service in Switzerland. https://www.zivi.admin.ch/en

REFERENCES - CHAPTER XI

1. World Health Organization. (2023). Health systems financing: Germany. https://www.who.int/countries/deu/

2. Wharam, J.F., Zhang, F., Wallace, J., et al. (2023). Vulnerable and less vulnerable women in high-deductible health plans experienced delayed breast cancer care. Health Affairs, 42(5), 644-652. https://www.healthaffairs.org/doi/10.1377/hlthaff.2022.01434

3. Cleary, E.G., Beierlein, J.M., Khanuja, N.S., et al. (2018). Contribution of NIH funding to new drug approvals 2010-2016. Proceedings of the National Academy of Sciences, 115(10), 2329-2334. https://www.pnas.org/content/115/10/2329

4. Prasad, V., & Mailankody, S. (2017). Research and development spending to bring a single cancer drug to market and revenues after approval. JAMA Internal

Medicine, 177(11), 1569-1575. https://jamanetwork.com/journals/jamainternalmedicine/fullarticle/2653012

5. Azoulay, P., Graff Zivin, J.S., Li, D., & Sampat, B.N. (2019). Public R&D investments and private-sector patenting: Evidence from NIH funding rules. Review of Economic Studies, 86(1), 117-152. https://academic.oup.com/restud/article/86/1/117/5090178

6. Paris, V., & Belloni, A. (2014). Value in pharmaceutical pricing. OECD Health Working Papers, No. 63. https://www.oecd-ilibrary.org/social-issues-migration-health/value-in-pharmaceutical-pricing_5jz0j63kjqf8-en

7. Congressional Research Service. (2024). Defense primer: Military health system. https://crsreports.congress.gov/product/pdf/IF/IF10530

8. Centers for Medicare & Medicaid Services. (2024). 2024 Medicare trustees report. https://www.cms.gov/oact/tr/2024

9. U.S. Department of Veterans Affairs. (2024). VA budget highlights and performance metrics: Fiscal year 2024. https://www.va.gov/budget/products.asp

10. Kaiser Permanente. (2024). Fast facts about Kaiser Permanente. https://about.kaiserpermanente.org/who-we-are/fast-facts

11. UnitedHealth Group. (2024). Annual report 2024. https://www.unitedhealthgroup.com/investors/annual-reports.html

12. Kaiser Family Foundation. (2024). Medicare enrollment.

https://www.kff.org/medicare/issue-brief/medicare-enrollment/

13. U.S. Department of Defense. (2024). Military health system overview. https://health.mil/About-MHS

14. Kaiser Family Foundation. (2024). Health insurance coverage of the total population. https://www.kff.org/other/state-indicator/total-population/

15. Centers for Medicare & Medicaid Services. (2024). National health expenditure accounts: Historical. https://www.cms.gov/data-research/statistics-trends-and-reports/national-health-expenditure-data/historical

16. World Health Organization. (2023). Life expectancy and healthy life expectancy: Data by country. https://www.who.int/data/gho/data/themes/mortality-and-global-health-estimates/ghe-life-expectancy-and-healthy-life-expectancy

17. Centers for Disease Control and Prevention. (2024). Infant mortality rates by country. National Center for Health Statistics. https://www.cdc.gov/nchs/data/databriefs/db485.pdf

18. World Health Organization. (2023). Maternal mortality ratio (per 100,000 live births). https://www.who.int/data/gho/indicator-metadata-registry/imr-details/26

19. Fein, A.J. (2023). The 2023-24 economic report on pharmaceutical wholesalers and specialty distributors. Drug Channels Institute. https://www.drugchannels.net/2023/08/the-2023-24-economic-report-on.html

20. AARP. (2022). Rx Price Watch Report: Trends in retail prices of brand name prescription drugs widely used by older

Americans, 2006-2021. https://www.aarp.org/ppi/info-2022/trends-in-retail-prices-of-drugs.html

REFERENCES - CHAPTER XII

1. OpenSecrets. (2024). Pharmaceuticals/health products: Lobbying spending 2024. Center for Responsive Politics. https://www.opensecrets.org/federal-lobbying/industries/summary?id=H04

2. OpenSecrets. (2024). American Hospital Association: Lobbying profile 2024. Center for Responsive Politics. https://www.opensecrets.org/orgs/american-hospital-assn/summary?id=D000000116

3. OpenSecrets. (2024). Pharmaceutical Research and Manufacturers of America: Lobbying by quarter 2024. Center for Responsive Politics. https://www.opensecrets.org/federal-lobbying/clients/summary?id=D000000504

4. OpenSecrets. (2024). Pharmaceutical Care Management Association: Lobbying spending trends. Center for Responsive Politics. https://www.opensecrets.org/federal-lobbying/clients/summary?id=D000022165

5. STAT News. (2019). Scott Gottlieb joins Pfizer board. https://www.statnews.com/pharmalot/2019/06/27/pfizer-gottlieb-fda-board/

6. McCrain, J. (2018). Revolving door lobbyists and the value of congressional staff connections. Journal of Politics, 80(4), 1369-1383. https://www.journals.uchicago.edu/doi/10.1086/698889

7. OpenSecrets. (2024). Pharmaceuticals/health products: Top recipients 2023-2024. Center for Responsive Politics. https://

www.opensecrets.org/industries/recips.php?ind=H04&cycle=2024

REFERENCES - CHAPTER XIII

1. Cornell Law School. (2024). 15 U.S.C. § 2 - Monopolizing trade a felony; penalty. Legal Information Institute. https://www.law.cornell.edu/uscode/text/15/2

2. U.S. Department of Justice. (2024). Sherman Act violations. Antitrust Division. https://www.justice.gov/atr/sherman-act-violations

3. Wisconsin Office of the Commissioner of Insurance. (2024). Health insurance market share report. https://oci.wi.gov/Pages/Consumers/HealthInsuranceMarketShare.aspx

4. Cornell Law School. (2024). 15 U.S.C. § 18 - Acquisition by one corporation of stock of another. Legal Information Institute. https://www.law.cornell.edu/uscode/text/15/18

5. U.S. Sentencing Commission. (2024). Guidelines manual: Antitrust offenses. https://www.ussc.gov/guidelines/2024-guidelines-manual/annotated-2024-chapter-2-r

6. Congressional Research Service. (2023). Comparison of prescription drug prices across federal programs. https://crsreports.congress.gov/product/pdf/R/R47202

7. Congressional Budget Office. (2023). Options for a carbon tax. https://www.cbo.gov/publication/58861

8. Congressional Budget Office. (2023). Options for a financial transaction tax. https://www.cbo.gov/budget-options/58803

9. Cornell Law School. (2024). 38 U.S.C. § 1701 - Scope of care. Legal Information Institute. https://www.law.cornell.edu/uscode/text/38/1701

10. Cornell Law School. (2024). 38 U.S.C. § 8110 - Purchase, lease, or transfer of land. Legal Information Institute. https://www.law.cornell.edu/uscode/text/38/8110

11. U.S. Senate. (2024). Budget reconciliation process. Committee on the Budget. https://www.budget.senate.gov/imo/media/doc/reconciliation_guide.pdf

Made in the USA
Coppell, TX
17 March 2026

73725992R00164